The Art of the Actor-Manager

Wilson Barrett and the
Victorian Theatre

Theater and Dramatic Studies, No. 15

Bernard Beckerman, Series Editor

Brander Matthews Professor of Dramatic Literature
Columbia University in the City of New York

Other Titles in This Series

The Art of the Actor-Manager
Wilson Barrett and the
Victorian Theatre

by
James Thomas

UMI RESEARCH PRESS

Ann Arbor, Michigan

Copyright © 1984
James Thomas
All rights reserved

Produced and distributed by
UMI Research Press
an imprint of
University Microfilms International
Ann Arbor, Michigan 48106

Library of Congress Cataloging in Publication Data

Thomas, James.
    The art of the actor-manager.

    (Theater and dramatic studies ; no. 15)
    "Based on the author's thesis, University of Texas at
Austin, 1975"—T.p. verso.
    Bibliography: p.
    Includes index.
    1. Barrett, Wilson, 1848-1904. 2. Actors—Great
Britain—Biography. 3. Theatrical producers and
directors—Great Britain—Biography. I. Title.
II. Series.

PN2598.B427T48 1984   792'.028'0924 [B]   83-17864
ISBN 0-8357-1492-6

For Fran Hodge, Jack Brokaw,
Bob Hedley, and Jim Willaert

1. Wilson Barrett as Hamlet. Painting by Frank Holl.

Contents

List of Illustrations

Acknowledgments

I wish to thank Mr. Frank Wilson Barrett, Mrs. Elizabeth Lynch, and the directors of the University of Texas Humanities Research Center for providing access to the material that served as the basis for most of this book. Further thanks go to Francis Hodge, John Brokaw, Joseph Donohue, and James Ellis for their advice and encouragement. I am also grateful for support in the form of grants from Mount Holyoke College.

Finally, a special acknowledgment is due Margaret and Jessica for their patience over the long haul.

Introduction

Wilson Barrett's character and adventures form a biography of singular interest for the student of theatre and popular entertainments. Barrett is a perplexing theatrical phenomenon since he gives contradictory signals about what kind of person he was. Certainly he was a purveyor of sensational popular melodramas. There were plenty of those spectacular, excessively emotional, action-filled, and sometimes silly effects in his productions that we count on finding in traditional stage melodramas. On the other hand, from his career also arise actions of such high artistic quality and of such striking imagination that we are led to treat him as a genuine artistic force. Everywhere in his work there are the signs of painstaking effort, aesthetic integrity, and attention to detail which mark the career of the significant artist.

But the fact is that Wilson Barrett is not yet a thoroughly respected individual; his name for years has been a byword for hissing among sophisticated playgoers because of his attraction to melodrama. The opinion of American dramatic critic John Rankin Towse typifies the most extremely negative attitude. Barrett, he said, was no more than "a shrewd and clever showman [who] made a great splurge and much money. . . . He depended chiefly upon sensationalism, spectacle, sentimentalism, and advertisement."[1] In thorough agreement with Towse were many of the Victorian theatre's new school adherents led by the modernist critic William Archer. Others perhaps were not so violently opposed to Barrett; instead, theirs was a case of damning with faint praise for the narrow field of melodrama, "the side-line goods of theatrical entertainment," as George Arthur said.[2] William Winter, for example, thought he put Barrett in his place once and for all when he wrote, "He seemed an outcome of the revolt against asceticism and excessive intellectuality in art, and as such congenial to the multitude."[3] Nevertheless, there were certain cultivated observers who disagreed. George Bernard Shaw admitted that despite his disagreement with some of Barrett's populist policies, he held him "in high esteem as a stage manager and actor."[4] Critic Clement Scott believed that Barrett's management was "only second in importance to that of Henry Irving."[5] Moreover, Austin Brereton, Irving's biographer, wrote of Barrett, "There are few who have done so much for the good of the stage and who are so well deserving of praise from all true lovers of the drama."[6]

Part of the paradox arising from these contradictory views may be traced to excessive modernist rhetoric. It seems that certain new school critics and historians, having deduced or observed deficiencies in Barrett's aesthetic philosophy, were determined that not a particle of craftsmanship should be attributed to him. George Bernard Shaw accused William Archer of harboring "a violent prejudice against Wilson Barrett."[7] Modernist rhetoric was exacerbated by class snobbery. "It was the fashion among highbrows . . . to jeer at poor Wilson Barrett," J.B. Booth wrote;[8] "In spite of his immense following, few stage favourites have suffered so much from the disdainful attitude of critics."[9] The author H. "Chance" Newton added, "It is doubtful . . . whether any modern great favourite of the stage has suffered quite so much from a pooh-poohful attitude as Wilson Barrett."[10] For complex reasons Barrett's opponents were incapable of impartiality toward him.

It is the point of view of this book that Wilson Barrett was an actor-manager of the first rank, flawed here and there as any artist must be, but the real thing nonetheless. What his flaws were will be readily apparent. Barrett was a matinee idol with many of the vain habits of the popular entertainer. He was also overendowed with the many sensibilities of his age, which means that his theatrical productions, and even his personal actions or pronouncements, were often soft with too much sentiment or insufficient consistency. But to dwell on his flaws in the first chronicle of his life would be a critical error. Many of Barrett's shortcomings are removed from his shoulders and from the reader's discrimination when Barrett's populism and staunch Victorianism are simply accepted. The result is that Barrett's actions may then be recognized for their intrinsic worth instead of continually being judged against an irrelevant ideal. More to the point in this introduction, then, is a short overview of the theatrical and social context in which Barrett appears and some brief comments on the purpose of this book and on the reasons why his biography has been so late in arriving on the scene.

Wilson Barrett lived during a period of radical change in the life of the English theatre, but despite his active involvement with certain of these changes, Barrett himself was actually closely allied with the traditions and ideals of the previous theatrical generation. Many of the conventions and techniques being discarded by the modernists were being self-consciously maintained by Barrett in hopes of restoring a sense of aesthetic balance to the theatre. He was not alone in these attempts. Strong opposition to change existed both in and out of the profession and created a paradoxical life for the theatre exemplified by a personality such as Barrett.

No more evident transformation occurred than the new taste for the theatre shown by the middle class. The genteel Shakespearean revivals of Charles Kean and Samuel Phelps in the 1850s and 1860s prepared the way for a large-scale infusion of middle-class audiences into the theatre beginning in the 1870s. Managers, sensing a reliable new source of box office revenue, made concessions to these audiences which, though subtle, were to alter fundamentally the structure of the theatre from that time forward. Managerial deference to the middle-class routine of daily life was typified by the change of curtain time from 6:30 P.M. through the 1860s to a standard of 8:00 P.M. by the late 1870s. The earlier time had been established by tradition for over a century and had certain advantages, notably the potential for a long evening of theatre, a variety of fare, a kind of vivacious and rough-hewn quality to the productions and, most important, a suitability to the daily routine of the idle rich and the itinerant who made up most of the audience. Barrett was trained in this kind of theatre, as were Henry Irving, John Hare, J.L. Toole and others of this generation. But the schedule of the middle class was not so relaxed. Their lives were governed by their mercantile responsibilities, and they required time for an evening meal before their theatrical entertainment. The 8:00 P.M. curtain allowed for this and more: it shortened the evening; it diminished the number of plays presented; and it allowed for a gentlemanly departure time, so important in sprawling and often dangerous industrial London. Since the bill was reduced to one or at most two major plays, rehearsal time was thereby increased and plays tended to become more polished as a result. In this way the simple decision to alter curtain times to suit the middle class was actually the harbinger of the more complete transformation beginning to take place in the theatre. The administrative superstructure of the profession had been altered to prepare for the creation of a genteel, conventional, and highly safe theatrical evening.

By the late 1870s the Church's traditional antipathy for the stage and its artists had also begun to change. It was becoming increasingly popular for prominent clergymen to speak out and ally themselves with the drama, seeing its great potential for good. On many occasions Henry Irving, for example, supported Church involvement with the theatre, and in one speech on the moral state of the theatre Wilson Barrett cited several influential churchmen whose ideas on the association of Church and stage were even more strongly liberal than his own. This emphasis on the moral responsibilities of the drama, however, was also the immediate cause of misconceptions which occasionally shrouded the artistic *raison d'etre* of the theatre.

Public opinion of theatre artists changed in line with the middle class' new attraction for the stage and with the Church's growing support. In the past stage artists were often publicly vilified, but the period beginning in 1880 was to see the rise of a phenomenon which we know so well today: popular adulation of actors. This new attitude eventually resulted in the knighthood of many of the English stage's finest artists; by the turn of the century it was common practice for leading English actors and managers to be so honored. Henry Irving accepted his knighthood in 1895, and at least six other notable actors followed within fifteen years. Not only had theatre become a safe commodity, but its practitioners had come to assume the dignified cloak of authority.

The influx of new audiences and attitudes was to have an additional effect that few could have envisioned. Middle-class audiences were, among other things, more educated than their predecessors, and it was not long after their renewed introduction to the theatre that many of their most advanced thinkers began to see the theatre in more humanistic terms than before. The critic William Archer thought that an entirely new drama was called for which dealt with the problems of life. But to his dismay this rallying cry did not have the unifying effect that it might have had because to him and his associates "problems" meant all those socially taboo subjects that for years had been withheld from the stage by common consent. He called for a new drama of ironic overtones and serious criticism of the quality of life in Victorian England, but the majority of playgoers were satisfied with their lives and declined to be criticized on the stage when they had come to expect no more than an evening of superficial entertainment. The result was the separation of the audience into two distinct claques: one attached to conservative dramatic tradition and favoring a theatre of optimism, the other attached to more radical aesthetics and favoring a theatre of cynicism. The latter was a small group composed of artists and free-thinkers; while they were outnumbered by their conservative counterparts, they did have the ability and power to articulate their ideals through the press.

Before 1870 emphasis in the theatre had been on acting in the virtuoso old school style, but the twenty years through 1890 witnesed a gradual change towards new school acting methods. The passing of English old school stage tradition began seriously with the efforts of Charles Kean at the Princess's during the 1850s. Kean, however, limited his innovations mostly to his "gentlemanly melodramas." His Shakespearean productions remained quite firmly rooted in the old patterns. E.B. Watson points out that Charles Kean's major contribution was in predisposing middle-class audiences in behalf of new school methods. Charles Fechter carried on new school reforms with his *Hamlet* in 1861 and with other plays during his tenure at the Lyceum through 1867. Fechter's challenge, the challenge of the new school, consisted of a confident disregard for traditional interpretations of Shakespearean roles and a conscious attempt to include the histrionic effects of melodrama within the Shakespearean repertoire. Fechter introduced, for example, vivid facial and bodily adjustments, extensive detailed stage business, and frequent climactic pictorial tableaux where previous actors on the English stage had been content for the most part with static statuesque repose and rhetorical intonations. Moreover, Fechter's productions were fully developed "interpretations" (albeit occasionally misconceived) that were staged with extraordinary attention to the dramatic effect of the whole play. The acting "points" and flights of turgid rhetoric which were the stock-in-trade of the previous generation of English classical actors were done away with in one motion. Later on, during the 1870s, Tomasso Salvini also used the new school approach, emphasizing to an even greater degree the reforms successfully carried out by Fechter.

It might be helpful to point out here that regardless of the complex technicalities of new school reforms, among Victorian audiences new school acting consisted mainly of two elements. First, new school actors began to adapt the behavioral mannerisms of everyday life to their roles in place of the accepted stage patterns of courtly manners. In practice, this turned out to be a lowering of the socioeconomic decorum of the characters. Second, new school speech was quiet speech, a marked contrast to traditional "received" stage speech with its conventionalized pronunciations and rhythms and its often excessive volume.

The Bancrofts were the first English actor-managers to adopt new school methods. They called for an end to what they perceived as the falseness of old school style. They did this by championing at the Prince of Wales theatre the new realistic plays of Tom Robertson, whose characters were seldom moved by the high emotions which denoted the old school. The Bancrofts' example caught on, and the results were radical. Unlike their predecessors, new school actors could not be trained in the full range of their craft. They were experimenters with no tradition to support them except their own enthusiasm; they had cut loose from the past. Consequently, fewer young actors could portray the heroic characters from the traditional repertory because fewer actors had the capacity to speak well, move with authority, wear historic costume, or play strong emotions. This emphatic shift transformed stage acting of this period into a confused mixture of two styles. Old school actors maintained the preservation of power, elocution, majesty, gusto, and personal electricity. Wilson Barrett was a member of this tradition, as was, in part, Henry Irving. New school actors rejected these conventions in favor of reservation, elegance, subtle miming and facial expressions, and a belief in the ensemble of the acting company as opposed to the star system.

The significant aspect of this struggle for a new style was the one between the actor and the dramatist for supremacy in the theatre. Old school actors had little respect for the integrity of the script and took liberties with it to enhance their own effectiveness. The younger breed of educated play-wrights were appalled by this practice. They demanded respect for their work and favored the new school actor with his devotion to the script.

Consequently, two opposing schools of playwriting emerged which coincided with their counterparts in acting. The old school dramatists, many of them drawn from the ranks of novelists and poets, tended to create plays of idealism, strong melodramatic convention, and vivid action for the proper display of old school acting. The writers of the old school saw the problems of society in those of individual characters. Barrett's authors were members of this informal group. The newer playwrights turned their attention in the direction of Ibsen, realism, and unconventionality. They wrote directly about the problems of their society. George Bernard Shaw, Arthur Wing Pinero, and Henry Arthur Jones were among the most important advocates of this new school, though Jones and others in fact served their apprenticeships under the old system and therefore maintained a strong, traditionally melodramatic strain in many of their plays.

At the center of all this controversy was the actor-manager, whose role was created in the complexities of this period. Before the 1870s organized confusion reigned over theatrical production, with tradition or the whims of the star actor claiming ultimate authority. This practice began to change as early as the 1850s with the work of Charles Kean, whose Shakespearean revivals were masterpieces of organization and preparation. Dion Boucicault contributed his share to the growth of the manager's power by his elaborate attention to stage effects, lighting, and the placement of actors on the stage. The Bancrofts and Robertson carried this new work forward with their introduction of detailed pantomimic dramatization into acting and with their increased attention to minor roles as well as major ones. William S. Gilbert carried the role of manager to its limits with his autocratic control of the Savoy operettas. The manager's role was formalized during the 1880s, and by 1887 the London stage could count Henry Irving, Wilson Barrett, John Hare, Charles Wyndham, Herbert Beerbohm Tree, George Alexander, and Henry Neville among its finest actors as well as its greatest managers. Because actor-managers held so much power in the theatre, they came under increasing attack, especially from new playwrights. It was alleged that actor-managers chose plays only for their starring roles, and then mainly from authors whose popularity had been previously tested. New writers saw little hope for success in this situation. Actors, too, had little sympathy for actor-managers, for it was believed that even they could not receive their just merits in this authoritarian arrangement. Moreover, less successful managers attacked successful ones for their extravagant expenditures on decorations, allegedly resulting in the debasing of public tastes.

Two other important changes occurred during this period which led to significant improvements in the conditions of theatre business. First, the increased efficiency of trains created the opportunity for vastly improved touring arrangements around the world and, consequently, for more profits. While touring itself had begun as far back as the 1840s, it was not until the late 1870s and 1880s that whole companies of English and American actors traveled between and across continents. Both Barrett and Irving were a part of this. They trouped their companies as many as ten or twelve times out of England and across the United States, Canada, Australia, New Zealand, and South Africa. Second, the rights of playwrights to participate in the monetary rewards gained from productions of plays mounted in strength. Boucicault initiated the practice when in 1860 he demanded a percentage of the receipts for all the productions of *The Colleen Bawn.* By the 1880s the practice of royalties was common, while the signing of the international copyright law and the American copyright agreement in the late 1880s and early 1890s formalized the new position of the playwright.

Another notable sign of this period was the almost universal taste for visual realism in the presentation of drama. The movement gathered momentum early in the century with Charles Kean's archeologically correct productions of Shakespeare and with the spectacular technical feats of Boucicault. Visual realism became still more popular after the visits of the Saxe-Meiningen company to London in 1881, the Rotterdam Company in 1880, and Augustin Daly's company beginning in 1884. All these organizations, especially the Meininger, placed great emphasis on the visual trappings of realism, the settings, and the effective arrangement of crowds, none of which had been seen to much advantage in London playhouses. The effect on London managers was immediate: Irving, Barrett, Hare, and others capitalized on the popular sentiment for realism by incorporating it more and more into their own productions. Actually, much of the desire for visual reality was no more than the traditional craving for scenic spectacle, and it took little time for astute managers to recognize that impressive productions could be achieved by the increased use of spectacularly realistic scenic effects. The 1880s saw a tremendous growth in the use of built-up settings, pivoting scenes, sliding scenes, platforms, lighting effects, and so on. It was the beginning of the complete exploitation of the scenic potential of the proscenium stage.

Respect for the role of the dramatic critic grew hand in hand with the popular revival of interest in the theatre. During the Victorian period an unusually large number of newspapers and journals that included dramatic criticism began life and flourished. In 1892 fifteen practicing dramatic critics were writing in London for more than a dozen periodicals. Ideas about the theatre and other arts were subjects of frequent discussion, with writers and readers alike contributing their thoughts on criticism, censorship, dramatic academies, and a national theatre, among other topics.

Dramatic criticism was informally divided into two opposing schools, labelled the "ancients" and the "moderns." The leader of the former group, Clement Scott, had influence which no single critic before him had held, and his writings for *The Daily Telegraph* and *The Theatre* were decidedly conservative. William Archer, leader of the "moderns," had less influence, but he made up for this in the quality of his criticism. Substituting a coldly analytical approach for Scott's highly emotional one, Archer typified the change in the target of dramatic criticism away from acting and toward the playscript. The virtue of this activity in dramatic criticism was that it exposed many of the failings of the emotionally slanted critics and thereby increased the appreciation of all drama.

Yet despite the enormous number of changes taking place in the world of the theatre, traditional melodrama remained the major attraction. Melodrama was in fact the Victorians' distinctive entertainment. Unfortunately, the term melodrama has suffered from a legacy of mistrust and derision and is now often taken to be a synonym for "excessively emotional," referring to the form's self-conscious power to induce strong feelings of pathos in its audience. Melodrama as Barrett understood it, and as most Victorians who were not modernists took it, was not a perjorative adjective, but the description of a legitimate form of dramatic composition intended for a popular audience. Melodrama is conventional—always moral, always hopeful, and, most important, always humanitarian in its viewpoint. In melodrama vice is punished so vehemently that a distinct partiality for goodness is strongly shown. Yet it must be remembered that crime and vice are viewed differently now than in the past. To the Victorians virtue was necessary; it was its own defense—a viewpoint modernists have lost since Ibsen demonstrated that "virtue is its own reward." The larger world of aesthetic experience was also viewed differently in the past, when art was not considered to be a closed world subservient to its own laws and applicable to a few initiates. Drama was considered to be the recorder of right sentiments, and in following this ideal melodramatists such as Barrett were no different in their form than Tennyson, Longfellow, Macauley, Hugo, and Dickens were in literature or Millais, Leighton, and Watts in art.

Barrett was a melodramatist, a species of artist that appeared in the midnineteenth century and flourished until the advent of the motion picture, which usurped its status. The roots of the melodramatic sensibility in the theatre may be traced to the dramatic apprenticeship of actors, a rigid traditional theatre education based on the antiquated provincial stock system. Since it was an apprenticeship shared at the time by virtually everyone in the profession and one, moreover, which reinforced melodramatic techniques and tastes, it might be helpful to summarize its important elements. The system functioned something like this: Over a period of years in a given provincial city, one enterprising person usually managed to make his name synonymous with theatre there, as John Coleman did around this time at Leeds and Hull. In the major cities, like Halifax, Leeds, or Nottingham, the manager was often fortunate enough to have a theatre; elsewhere managers used concert halls or other similar arrangements. Nowhere in the provinces were there first-class theatrical premises such as might be found in London at the Princess's, for example. Most provincial managers worked in miserable conditions. But however dingy the conditions were, the theatrical activity was constant, with daily changes of bill delivering four or five hours of continuous entertainment in which one major play was produced with variety acts, dances, and acrobatics. Provincial companies were connected in a circuit defined by a given geographical area of Britain. The Portsmouth circuit included the southern counties, the Norwich circuit the eastern counties, and the York circuit—the best of the three—the northern counties. Actors tended to associate themselves with one circuit and in doing so they appeared regularly in that circuit's theatres. There were also strolling players, called "loners," who moved loosely over the countryside, often following the assizes, respecting no circuit guidelines and playing whenever and wherever they could.

Provincial theatres encouraged deplorable work habits. Good native playwrights were never to be found, much less supported, because provincial playbills emulated so many London successes. Productions were often cheap, and rehearsals, when there were any, were cursory. The stock system, moreover, generated the practice wherein leading actors held onto parts long after they were capable of playing them. Free expression was at a premium since tradition alone dictated the acting and staging of the plays. Barrett later condemned the bad effects of this system, confessing that it was not even possible to learn lines accurately under such conditions, but he and his colleagues did learn the habit of rehearsing and preserving the dramatic situation of a scene. Crude popular melodramas encouraged this approach because of their strong emphasis on action and their cursory attention to literary finish. Audiences, in turn, learned to disregard the words and watch for the effects. The action told the story more than the words, and though the results were usually stilted and stagey, the overall impression could often be powerful. This melodramatic manner of playwriting and acting made such an impression on Barrett and his colleagues during their apprenticeships that it became the guiding principle for much of their work later on.

Melodrama, however, was not strictly a dramatic phenomenon, but a social and intellectual one as well. The Victorians' was a melodramatic sensibility. Moral ideas of all kinds and of every extreme were the subjects of frequent and often passionate debate. The rush towards a money-centered society had created a financial depression which fueled the belief that times were unstable and insecure, and there were complicated problems with liberalism, socialism, and imperialism together with much disagreement as to how to correct them. This restlessness appeared to be almost neurotic. Some advanced thinkers gleefully recognized in the confusion the signs of the end of an exhausted era and the beginning of a more humanitarian future. Conservatives, on the other hand, feared the total collapse of English culture and their collective reaction was an obstructionist, neotraditionalist morality that exalted the conventional beliefs and manners of the previous generation. Extremes of nationalism, tight domestic discipline, and preoccupation with morality were the motivating forces behind both Victorianism and melodrama, creating an organic bond between the two.

In conclusion, the era 1870–1900 witnessed the complete transformation of the European stage from its neoclassical heritage into what can now be recognized as modernism. As an actor-manager, Wilson Barrett was among those most responsible for this remarkable theatrical revival, for, as E.J. West has pointed out,[11] it was mainly the collective managerial skill of the actor-managers and not (as is commonly supposed) the quality of native drama, acting, or business improvements that provided the motive force behind the theatre of the period. Moreover, Barrett was perhaps the perfect paradigm of the complete actor-manager, combining as no other could all the skills of actor, director, producer, critic, author, and thinker and using this combination as a powerful tool for progress in theatrical reform.

There have been five previous attempts to tell Barrett's story. In the later years of his career Barrett signed a contract with author Richard LeGallienne to write a biography, but LeGallienne gave up after writing only a few chapters and taking all of his fee. Another aborted attempt followed, this time by journalist Elwyn Barron, coauthor with Barrett of several plays. Following Barrett's death in 1904, his daughter Dorothy tried to forestall any further biographies. She was so adamant in this that she even refused permission to Reverend Frank Heath, Barrett's brother-in-law and financial advisor, on the grounds that her father's life was too sacred to be tampered with. Worse still, just before she died she set fire to her collection of Barrett's papers in the hope that historical curiosity about her father would be prevented once and for all. A short time later, W. MacQueen-Pope began to gather information for a fourth bid, but he stopped because he could not locate enough data to suit his needs. In the interim, Frank Wilson Barrett, the grandson who was also a successful actor-manager, salvaged enough from the fire to write a biography of his own. Unfortunately, he relied too much on family recollections and neglected to mine the collection as completely as he might have. Wilson Barrett's papers were subsequently sold to the University of Texas Humanities Research Center. The study that follows was developed from examination and evaluation of the entire collection of materials, and corroborated by extensive cross-referencing with published information.

1

The Provinces (1846–1878)

Preparation for a Career

Wilson (born William Henry) Barrett was born on 18 February 1846 at Manor House Farm near the city of Chelmsford in Essex. His mother, the former Charlotte Mary Wood, raised a family of four children that included Barrett's older sister Mary (Polly) Brunell, and two younger brothers, George Edward and Robert Reville. George Barrett senior, of Hertfordshire descent, was a gentleman farmer who cultivated a small parcel of his own land. He was a freeholder of the class of Englishmen immediately below that of the gentry, and his family lived in modest prosperity. There are paintings of Mr. and Mrs. Barrett dressed in fashionable attire showing that William inherited his father's dramatic profile and his mother's keen dark eyes. Barrett was deeply affected by his early years in rural Essex.

> My first recollections are of [mother's] beautiful face with tender, loving eyes, bending over me after some childish ailment, when I must have been about three years of age; and of being carried from a room into the sunshine of an old-fashioned garden, and nursed in my mother's arms with the tenderness she showed me the whole of her life. Of a plantation of firs at the back of my father's house, at the end of which there was a windmill. Of waving cornfields, of boys with their wooden clappers frightening away the crows.[1]

Any sort of education a boy might have had in Essex at this time must have been severely restricted. As a member of a devout churchgoing family, William heard many sermons, and, if typical practice is a guide, he probably read aloud many more at home. The slight learning received from this and a little Sunday school could have been improved only somewhat by attendance at a country grammar school whenever farm chores did not interfere. One and a half or two years of such a school was all most children received, and since most of the work there was focused on character building, literary education was not of high quality. Students generally maintained the literary tastes of their parents and their pastor. This practice was particulary harmful to Barrett, who enjoyed reading, but who never managed to raise his literary taste beyond the fundamental level.

Barrett's first theatre experience is said to have occurred in 1853 when he attended the annual Chalk Farm fair in northwest London, where he witnessed a traveling booth production of *Uncle Tom's Cabin*. Significantly, this popular melodrama left an indelible mark on Barrett's memory. "I can still see in my imagination," he later wrote, "Eliza, with the child in her arms, staggering aross the stage of bare planks, yelling that the ice was giving way under her feet, and that the bloodhounds were on her track."[2]

In 1857 Barrett's family was forced to give up their farm. The specific circumstances behind this action are not known, though Barrett said that his father's life in those early years was plagued by "disaster after disaster," and that the actual cause may have been "a series of ill-advised ventures" on his father's part.[3] But whether it was his father's risky investments or just gambling, the result was bankruptcy. The family had to move to London, settling in the borough of St. Pancras, where George Barrett took up a new trade and where young Barrett supplemented the family's small income by working as a laborer at a nearby corn exchange.[4] Most of Barrett's concern was for his mother, a beautiful and sensitive woman whose life, it seemed to her son, was being ruined. George Barrett's volatile temperament and the vicissitudes of the family's life together (including the death of an infant son soon after arrival in London) was for her "an unmitigated horror."[5] "It saddened my childhood," Barrett confessed, "and left an impression on my mind that can never be erased."[6] His job offered him at least one positive dimension, however. Though small in stature, he always had been a strong boy, and now he began to attain a muscular physique that eventually played an important part in his success as an actor. Barrett's only genuine pleasure at this time seems to have been his position as choirboy at St. Peter's Anglican Church.

One evening, as Barrett was walking in the neighborhood of Tottenham Court Road, he was met by a boy who offered him a ticket to the Queen's Theatre. The Queen's, renamed the Prince of Wales in 1865, later became one of London's most influential playhouses. In the first half of the 1860s, however, the Queen's had an unsavory reputation and was known through-out the city as the "Dust Hole." The drama Barrett subsequently saw there was *Oliver Twist*, and its actors seemed to the impressionable boy part of a special world. He knew then, he said, that he wanted to be an actor and to exercise over others the fascination he felt himself.[7]

Barrett returned frequently to the "Dust Hole," and the plays stirred in him a renewed interest in his education. There were few books at home be-sides the Bible, and his father was opposed to education beyond the minimum, but Barrett luckily met a schoolmaster who was willing to tutor him twice a week for 2d. per lesson. Barrett's employer agreed to keep quiet with the understanding that the schooling would not interfere with work, but later he angrily withdrew his permission altogether, forcing Barrett to give up his education.[8] Barrett reported that his lunch hours now became more important than ever to him for they were the only times he could read. It was around this time that Barrett began to develop his fine memory, a handy talent for a would-be actor.

There were about twenty major playhouses in London at the time; by 1899 there would be forty-one more. According to Clement Scott, theatre was beginning to grow rapidly as a popular form of entertainment,[9] yet for a while Barrett's allegiance to the Queen's was so strong that he would visit no other playhouse. After a time, however, he discovered Charles Kean's Princess's Theatre among the newer successful playhouses. Kean's Shakespearean productions were noted for their polish and expensive mountings. Barrett was impressed by the "shining armour, the measured periods of the grand verse," and the "earnestness" of the princes and nobles he saw before him at the Princess's.[10] This was far from the tawdry melodrama of the "Dust Hole." One play he saw there was Shakespeare's *Henry V*, and Barrett remembered leaving the theatre with the pictures of the battle of Harfleur before his eyes and the rhythm of the verse still in his ears. "I would not rest content," he said, "until I had made a name for myself as the chief actor and manager at that very Princess's Theatre."[11] There was something else in store for Barrett in connection with the Princess's. Kean's productions were not only famous for their scenic splendor, but also for their beautiful women.[12] Twelve-year-old Barrett could hardly have paid much attention to this, yet it was nevertheless true that he must have seen his future wife, actress Caroline Heath, in dozens of plays there.

After his introduction to the Princess's Barrett widened his theatrical tastes. The Queen's remained an important place for him, but now he took every opportunity to attend the Princess's and elsewhere. His passionate interest in playgoing even led to pneumonia one time after a trip across the city to see one of his favorite actors.[13]

Barrett's next job was with Perkins, Bacon, and Company, a firm of printers and engravers located in Fleet Street. The company was large and well established, having the Scottish government's contract for printing pound notes and postage stamps. Barrett was responsbile for counting. He had a room reserved to himself expressly for the purpose, and there he could often be found at lunchtime, he said, reading Shakespeare while lying on stacks of pound notes. His employer was a keen businessman, and for the next five years Barrett stayed with the firm receiving an education in sound business practices which were to be so important to his future work.

Meanwhile Barrett began his formal theatrical training with dancing lessons. Within a short time he and his brother George developed a variety act that led to Barrett's first recorded theatrical appearance, at the Grecian Theatre, City Road. The Grecian had been taken over in 1851 by the variety artist George Conquest, who, with his wife and daughters, offered evenings of family entertaiment. With the aid of some professionals and many amateurs, the Conquests produced variety shows, melodramas, and occasionally Shakespeare. Erroll Sherson relates that the Grecian was a veritable nursery for the theatrical and musical profession at the time. George Conquest provided practical, if unsophisticated experience in acting fundamentals, while his wife trained aspirants in dancing and acrobatics. Barrett's debut at the Grecian occurred in 1861 when he and his brother sang and danced as part of John Manning's benefit.[14] Manning eventually took Barrett under his wing and treated him very well. (Manning's son Ambrose was later a member of Barrett's company.) After a time Barrett was promoted to the role of Harlequin in the pantomimes at a salary of £1 per week. He later performed at the Eclectic Theatre in Soho and at the Highbury Barn in Islington, theatres with policies similar to those of the Grecian.

Sometime during this period Barrett's handsome looks and fine voice were noticed by a wealthy authoress who was going blind. She hired Barrett to read poetry and to recite sermons by the preacher J.M. Bellew, a popular orator who had published several volumes of sermons. Barrett remembered that his benefactress was not a beautiful woman and that she did not possess the kind of soft voice his mother did. She was sharp mannered and seldom spoke a kind word to him, but the extra half crown enabled him to live a little more comfortably and to contribute more to his family's income.[15]

Not long after Barrett's debut at the Grecian, an opportunity arose for him to display the writing and management skills he had been developing, when he produced his own adaptations of *Robin Hood* and other plays with several young friends. A crudely rigged arrangement of boards, calico, and oil lamps served as their "playhouse" behind a shop on the corner of Goodge Street and Tottenham Court Road.

By 1864 Barrett had accumulated nearly seven years' amateur training. He had witnessed scores of plays performed by England's best actors and variety performers. Moreover he had been tutored in comedy, singing, and dancing, and he had also accumulated a great deal of experience fending for himself. He felt that he was ready to strike out on his own as a professional actor. Earlier, John Manning had introduced Barrett to Edwin Danvers, a versatile old comic who often played at the Highbury Barn. Danvers is usually remembered for his comic portrayal in *Black-Eyed Susan* at the Royalty, but his importance to Barrett lay in the fact that he occasionally secured jobs for young actors with various provincial stock companies. Barrett had discovered this advertisement: "Wanted, a young actor with good stage presence. Must provide own props and dress like a gentleman both on and off the stage. Salary one Guinea weekly."[16] After Danvers agreed to secure Barrett the engagement, Barrett was not anxious to confront his employer with the news of his plans. Barrett recorded the following short conversation.

Employer: "What do you want?"
Barrett: "I am going to leave you."
Employer: "What for?"
Barrett: "I am going on the stage."
Employer: "Go away, you beast."

The conversation with his father was equally abrupt: Barrett could expect no help from home if he chose this "sinful career."[17]

Barrett's letter of recommendation from Danvers was successful, and in 1864 he undertook his first professional engagement at the Theatre Royal, Halifax, under the management of Messrs. Mutton, Rawlings, and Graydon, playing "general utility" and dancing between the acts for £1 1s. per week. He walked from London to Halifax, a distance of about 160 miles, for railways were not yet universal and fares often amounted to more than a week's salary for an apprentice. Barrett's first speaking role at Halifax was that of Hyland Creagh in Boucicault's play *The Colleen Bawn*; his only words were "Take me." Enthusiasm and an ability to learn lines quickly enabled him to move up to more responsible parts, and in six weeks he held the position of "juvenile lead" at a salary of £1 7s. 6d. The Irish actor George Owen was also helpful. Owen and his wife were making the rounds with their production of the Irish play *Thackeen Dhu*. At Halifax Owen's juvenile lead became sick, and Owen offered Barrett the part on the condition it could be learned in one night. Barrett acted with the Owens for several weeks.

After eleven weeks, two more than his original contract, Barrett's work at Halifax came to an end. Still not a very marketable commodity, he offered as a temporary measure to appear in a friend's booth at a local fair similar to the one Barrett had seen at Chalk Farm years before. His friend advised him not to do it, for such a job would adversely affect his budding acting career; Barrett was to be an actor, the friend pointed out, not a variety performer. Eventually Barrett assumed the responsibilities of "heavy business" with Mrs. E. Faucit Saville's company at Nottingham, where he began in-auspiciously by fainting dead away on the stage. It was later discovered that he had again walked to his new job, this time being without food for several days. Despite this precarious beginning, Barrett later recalled his work at Nottingham with some joy. Mrs. Saville was the sister-in-law of the famous actress Helen Faucit, formerly actor William Charles Macready's leading lady, who later became one of Barrett's closest friends. The Nottingham company operated more efficiently than most provincial troupes and was responsible for the beginnings of many famous stars, including Mrs. Kendal (later Dame Madge Kendal). No work could have been better for a young actor in Barrett's place. Barrett later wrote:

In spite of the work, which often made it necessary for me to sit up all night studying, Mrs. Saville and her daughters were kindness itself, the practice was good and continuous and the audience warm hearted and enthusiastic and looked upon the company as dear personal friends.[18]

Barrett became especially good friends with Mrs. Saville's daughter Kate.

The "good and continuous" practice that Barrett spoke about was actually the essence of what made a provincial apprenticeship so valuable for an actor, and so problematic. On the negative side, some provincial theatres encouraged deplorable work habits, and free expression was at a premium since tradition alone dictated the acting and staging of the plays. Barrett later condemned the bad effects of this part of the provincial system. "Blind adherence to tradition stifles originality and destroys individuality," he complained in 1887.

To what an extent adherence to tradition was carried in the stock companies few people can imagine. When I was a youth and a member of a stock company in England, actors were engaged for a "line of business"—and were expected to be ready at a moment's notice to play, with or without rehearsal, any character in the line of business for which he was engaged. He was expected to know, if he played Horatio, exactly where his Hamlet would be standing, and what he would be doing in any scene in which he was concerned. To such an extent was this adherence to tradition carried that a dozen Hamlets might come to a theatre during the course of one season and not one of them call for or expect a full rehearsal. . . . Just think how mechanical, how utterly devoid of originality of thought or conception performances given under such circumstances must have been. And yet the conditions of the stage of that period rendered any other system utterly impossible. . . . Careful rehearsals under such circumstances would be out of the question.[19]

Such excesses did not prevent beneficial experiences, however, for there were also worthwhile elements in the stock system. The most obvious of these was the thorough training in acting fostered by comprehensive experience. In some instances managers, such as Mrs. Saville, carefully developed their companies, engaging actors for a longer time than usual and taking great care with artistic concerns. Under these conditions a special rapport, occasionally even a mutual repsect, arose between the audience and actors. And if provincial audience tastes were uneducated, they nevertheless had the advantage of being indigenous. The manager had his finger on the pulse of the community, and the theatre was in important ways rooted in the life of the community.

In 1884 Barrett still retained vivid memories of the routine at Mrs. Saville's.[20] The actors usually had only one worn copy of the play to share, and the time alloted to each player for copying his lines was marked on a slip of paper. Barrett's good memory must have helped during his first week at Nottingham when he was assigned to play Brabantio in *Othello* and a farce on Monday, Barados in *Richelieu* and "something else" on Tuesday, Stukely in *The Gamester* on Wednesday, Coitier in *Louis XI* and Jupiter in a burlesque on Thursday, Edmund in *King Lear* and the father in *The Little Treasure* on Friday, and Francis in *The Robbers* together with Major Galbraith in *Rob Roy* on Saturday. He also danced between pieces and played harlequin in the seasonal pantomime. He began at 25s. a week at Nottingham, then advanced to £1 12s., and finally to over £3, making him at that time the highest paid member of the permanent company.[21]

After Nottingham and a subsequent engagement with George Owen at the Princess's Theatre in Leeds, Barrett proceeded to Liverpool in 1865, where he joined W.S. Bronson's company at the Adelphi. Here, three months after his debut in Halifax, he played his first leading role, Hardress Creegan in Boucicault's *The Colleen Bawn*. At the end of this engagement, however, Barrett was brought temporarily to a standstill. He had no new position to look forward to and he was broke. Until now Barrett had steadfastly refused to ask for any aid from his father. But in Liverpool he was despondent and finally asked his father for money. He drew a sketch of a sad boy walking the streets of Liverpool carrying a shovel on which was written, "Starving in the streets of Liverpool," and sent it to his father in London. A few days later came the reply: "Starving in the streets of Liverpool, are you? Well can't you appreciate the artistic fitness of things: You ought to be able to. Where do you want to starve—in Buckingham Palace?"[22] Appealing now to George Owen for help, Barrett received a recommendation to the Theatre Royal in Blackpool, a better class of theatre than the one in Liverpool. Here appeared some of the first evidence of the nature of Barrett's acting, for after his success as Sir Philip Blandford, a leading role in *Speed the Plough*, one of the senior actors clapped him on the back and cried, "Bravo, my young Kean!"[23] Barrett was probably modeling himself after provincial favorite Charles Kean, whose methods Mrs. Saville and George Owen strongly favored.[24]

After Blackpool, Barrett embarked on his first adventures in theatre management. Failing even to secure a usable hall in Blackburn, his first choice, he moved on to Burnley, where he had only a little more luck: a hall was found, but only one patron appeared for the performance, which was summarily cancelled. A more successful attempt was made at Chorley, where Barrett and a companion finally succeeded in completing a full evening's worth of mixed musical and dramatic entertainment for a real audience. Box office receipts amounted to 9d.

Miss Heath

After Chorley, Barrett secured an engagement at Preston for a few weeks and after that for a longer time he was a member of John Mosley's company at the Theatre Royal in Douglas, Isle of Man. From there he proceeded to

Dublin where, oddly enough, his first appearance in Ireland was applauded with surprising warmth, leading him to believe that his reputation had preceeded him across the Irish Sea. Actually, it was only that a local patriot named Barrett had recently been hanged, and the audience thought the actor was a relation of his. Barrett made his way back to Bradford in the autumn of 1865; there he played in *Macbeth, Jane Shore,* and *The Lady of Lyons* under Charles Rice. Despite a drop in salary to 9s. per week, Barrett arranged to have his first play, *Twilight,* produced there. An engagement with J.H. Seater's company in Durham followed Bradford.

Late in 1865 Barrett found himself for the first time in Scotland working briefly at Glasgow, then afterwards in A.D. MacNeil's troupe at the Marischal Street Theatre in Aberdeen. MacNeil was a genial man, talented, and an excellent manager and good citizen. Along with George Owen and Mrs. Saville, he was evidence of what provincial theatre could be at its best. He took a personal interest in Barrett's training, though John Coleman recalled that at this time Barrett seemed to "give little or no indication of either the ability or the ambition which lay within him."[25]

At Aberdeen Barrett met one of the more attractive and talented actresses he had seen at the Princess's in London, Caroline Heath. Born in 1837, Miss Heath was the illegitimate daughter of Andrew Watson, a Scottish barrister, and Caroline Marrow. She had been schooled in opera at a private theatre in London operated for amateur actresses by Miss Fanny Kelly. After Miss Kelly's school, however, she found immediate success as a dramatic actress. Miss Heath made her debut in 1852, at the age of fifteen, playing Stella in Boucicault's play *The Prima Donna,* and in 1854 she was the first Maude Nutbrown in Douglas Jerrold's play *A Heart of Gold.* A short time later she was discovered by Boucicault himself, who thought she was the perfect incarnation of the "sweet sixteen" heroines of his plays. He recommended her to Charles Kean, and she remained with Kean's company for several years. At the Princess's she played, among other roles, Anne Boleyn in *Henry VIII,* Ophelia in *Hamlet,* Cordelia in *King Lear,* and Florizel in *The Winters Tale.* Then Miss Heath had a stroke of good luck: when Mrs. Kean became ill and could not participate in the regular Windsor theatrical entertainments, Miss Heath took her place. The queen was so taken with the actress that she requested her to return often to perform dramatic readings for the royal family, later bestowing on Miss Heath the official title of Reader to the Queen.

Miss Heath left the Princess's in 1860 to join Samuel Phelps at Sadler's Wells, where she played Fiorella in *The Fool's Revenge* by Tom Taylor, among other parts. She returned to the Princess's in 1860 in support of Charles Fechter during his season, playing the Queen in *Ruy Blas* and Ophelia in *Hamlet,* a play which Henry Irving recorded as his first theatre experience. In 1861 Miss Heath began a three-year engagement at Drury Lane, acting in *Manfred* and playing Olympia in Edmund Falconer's drama *Night and Man*. During this time she acted again with Phelps, both at Drury Lane and at Windsor, this last in *Richelieu*. After one year at the Haymarket under the management of Walter Montgomery, she began a series of tours in the provinces, where she was extremely popular.

Miss Heath's specialty was the portrayal of characters with gentle, sweet, and refined natures, but with elegant and prepossessing appearances. She occasionally showed traces of study, but this was balanced by her considerable stage charm, in which she was helped by her tall, slender figure, her well modulated voice, her beautiful face, and her long blond hair. She also had fine taste in her wardrobe. In short, she was a beautiful and talented woman who rightly used all the professional artifices at her command to keep her looking much younger than her years. She was twenty-eight in 1865; Barrett was nineteen.

Actually, Barrett met Miss Heath first in Glasgow, where he had arrived the week after the Drury Lane company had completed their engagement. Barrett subsequently became a close friend of hers, escorting her in Glasgow and once taking her on a day trip to nearby Loch Lomond. At the end of the week Miss Heath continued with the Drury Lane troupe to Manchester where her company disbanded. At this point John Coleman, a leading manager in the Yorkshire Circuit, stepped in. Actress Avonia Jones had opened with an adaptation of Mrs. John Wood's *East Lynne* in one of Coleman's circuit theatres a few weeks earlier. Originally intended for a short run, the new play soon proved immensely successful. Coleman decided that Miss Heath should take over the play after Miss Jones returned to America. Miss Heath then led the play on a tour of the provinces, eventually reaching Aberdeen, where she renewed her friendship with Barrett.

Barrett was a reluctant suitor at Aberdeen. He felt that Miss Heath was a star and that there was an immeasurable gulf between them. This feeling even extended into his work onstage with her. He could face Miss Heath when he played the Captain to her Pauline in *The Lady of Lyons*, but he was embarassed to be seen playing lowly Harlequin in the accompanying farce.[26] At the close of the run Miss Heath decided to rest for a few days at Arbroath, while Coleman visited London to arrange new engagements for her. The company was upset with Barrett because he did not see her off at the station; they thought he lacked the courage to say goodbye. Actually, he was waiting to meet Miss Heath in Arbroath, where they were married on 21 July 1866. The wedding was kept a secret from Miss Heath's family. She informed her clergyman brother that she wished him to perform the ceremony, but that she also wished to avoid family displeasure over her marriage to a man nine years her junior.

2. Caroline Heath in an unknown role (c. 1873).

After the wedding, the Barretts were immediately engaged at Aberdeen again, where Barrett began by complimenting the management and discussing his future plans:

> When I first engaged for Aberdeen I learned that I was coming to stern dramatic schoolmasters. I must own I rather liked your teaching—liked it so well indeed that I determined to return; and that I might better profit in my education, I brought, as you know, a school mistress with me—one whose instructions you approve—out of whose stage book I mean to take many lessons.[27]

MacNeil engaged the couple at a handsome contract of fifty percent over the first £60 each night and one-half clear benefit on Fridays. Barrett and Miss Heath stayed in Aberdeen three weeks, and though *East Lynne* was the favorite play, Barrett managed to make a mark as Hamlet, his first major leading role. The team received £10 profit the first week, £32 the second, and £50 the third.[28]

Barrett and Miss Heath then chose to work the Yorkshire Circuit under Coleman, touring Hull, Leeds, York, Huddersfield, Lincoln, and other circuit towns throughout the spring season of 1867. Coleman arranged for Barrett to become company acting manager when they played in the larger cities, and in this way Barrett's experience in the responsibilities of management grew under expert guidance. Coleman further recorded that Barrett adored his wife and that he showed respect for her talents. After the end of the Yorkshire tour, Miss Heath used her influence to secure a summer booking for herself and Barrett at the Surrey Theatre in London, where she was to star in *East Lynne* the third week in June. The Surrey, a "transpontine" theatre, specialized in intense melodramas. Charles Reade's realistic prison yarn, *It's Never Too Late to Mend*, was making a hit there with actor Richard Shepherd in the leading role of Tom Robinson. Upon arriving at the theatre, Barrett and Miss Heath learned that their engagement for the next week's play might be cancelled because Shepherd was ill, and William Creswick, the manager, feared to put any other actor in his place. Shepherd himself challenged Barrett to come up with a solution. Barrett memorized the role of Robinson in an afternoon and made his professional London debut that night, 26 June 1867. A critic reported,

> Mr. Barrett, . . . who is new to the London stage, acts with uncommon intelligence and ease. His style is good and free from mannerisms of all kind, and he has quiet dignity and modesty such as we are glad to hail in a new actor. He will yet, if we mistake not, be heard of in his profession.[29]

In fact, Barrett was so successful in the role that he continued to act it through the end of the play's scheduled run, after which he and Miss Heath began their official engagement in *East Lynne*.

During the summer and autumn seasons of 1867 Barrett and Miss Heath returned to the provinces. This time, however, they did not tour the circuit in weekly engagements, but instead remained at individual theatres for extended periods of time while Barrett undertook stage management responsibilities. It was highly unusual for someone of Barrett's age to be stage managing at major provincial houses, and during this time an incident occurred which shows something of why he was so exceptional in this regard, specifically in his foresight and cool demeanor under pressure. He was managing and acting his London success, *It's Never Too Late to Mend*, in Manchester when, during the last act of one performance, a fire broke out in the gallery due to a patron knocking out his pipe dottle on the floor. It was a small fire, and Barrett did not discover the news until moments before he was to go on stage for his scene. He knew that a fire alarm would panic the audience so he quickly gave orders, then arranged with the cast to rush through the forty-minute act in less than ten minutes while his assistant assembled the staff and made the necessary safety arrangements. Everyone escaped safely and the fire was extinguished with little damage to the theatre.

More evidence of practical thinking occurred with respect to Barrett's acting at the time. In November he and Miss Heath found themselves at Belfast playing several weeks at the Theatre Royal. It had only been a year since Barrett had begun working with Miss Heath, but already there seemed to be in him more than a hint of special ability. A local reviewer, for example, commented about Barrett's Claude Melnotte:

> There is material in this gentleman which, if developed properly, may soon constitute him one of our most favorite tragedians. He speaks very distinctly, is cool and gentlemanly in his movements, and guards himself against the ranting style.[30]

In Belfast Barrett signed a contract with F.B. Chatterton, the well-known manager of Drury Lane, who made a trip to Ireland to engage the couple, whom he had seen at the Surrey in *East Lynne*. A London engagement at this prestigious theatre was a rapid advance so soon after the Surrey, especially since Barrett and Miss Heath were to act there in support of the popular actors Charles Dillon and Samuel Phelps. Chatterton agreed to hire the couple for one season beginning Easter 1868; they would be paid £12 a week plus first-class train fares both ways from their home in the provinces. Barrett would undertake "juvenile and responsible business," and Miss Heath would assume "leading juvenile business." Meanwhile, Barrett was assigned to stage manage at the playhouse at York and then at another at Leeds for the winter of 1867-1868. Thus, at age twenty-two, four years after his professional debut, Barrett was managing at several of the provinces' most prestigious playhouses.

The year at Drury Lane proved to be an intense period of learning for

Barrett. While his wife played major roles in Shakespeare and other classics, he played supporting roles in the same casts. The manner of his billings suggests the rapid progress of his work. Early in the season it was "Mr. W.H. Barrett," while a few weeks later it became for the first time "Wilson Barrett."[31] In the interim he gained experience as Malcolm in *Macbeth*, Laertes in *Hamlet*, Cassio in *Othello*, and Thomas Percy in *Henry VI*. Barrett also played in lighter plays, including *Peep o'Day* and *Man of Two Lives*. The critic H. "Chance" Newton remembered first seeing Barrett at this time "learning his business with Phelps."[32]

Afterwards, Barrett and Miss Heath, now billed "of the Theatre Royal, Drury Lane," returned to Scotland, where they played in Edinburgh through April 1869. A.D. MacNeil by this time had expanded his operations and was manager of the plush Royal Princess's there. One year under masterful training in London performed wonders on Barrett's quick perceptions. He and his wife opened ambitiously with *Romeo and Juliet*, and audience members who had seen Barrett before immediately recognized a change. "He plays with marvelous spirit," said one reporter; "His acting throughout was unexceptionable, being energetic without rant and pathetic without whining."[33] Barrett had incorporated what he learned from Miss Heath, Phelps, Dillon, and others and was beginning to develop a style that successfully undercut common melodramatic ranting. He and Miss Heath closed their Edinburgh engagement with a production of MacNeil's play *Wandering Steenie*, then returned yet again to Aberdeen, where they began in a spectacular production of *Faust* with Barrett as Mephistopheles and Miss Heath as Marguerite. This play was followed in November by *The Merry Wives of Windsor*, in which Barrett played Master Ford. Barrett's first benefit in Edinburgh was as Triplet in *Masks or Faces* with Miss Heath in the leading role of Peg Woffington. This play later became one of the staples of Barrett's provincial touring company.

The Barretts had been married now for nearly three years and there were children. Anna Ellen was born in 1867, Katherine in August 1868, Frank in 1869, and during 1870 and 1871 two more children would arrive. John Coleman recognized that Barrett was probably seeking a more settled life and offered to the young actor the operation of the Theatre Royal, Halifax, but there was a drawback. Halifax was not a good theatre town. An old actor's saying went, "From Hull, Hell, and Halifax, Good Lord deliver us!" Coleman reported that he never once turned a profit there in all of his years as manager. Perhaps sensing a challenge, Barrett took Halifax seriously, raising the artistic standards of production there far beyond what the city had been used to and gaining the lasting respect of the community. Furthermore, Coleman recorded Barrett as the first manager to make Halifax pay.[34] Barrett's Halifax experience proved to be an example in microcosm of his future successes in London.

The Wilson Barrett Company

By the time his contract at Halifax expired in the spring of 1870, Barrett had accumulated management experience at almost every provincial playhouse on the Yorkshire circuit. But the sad fact was that the more competent Barrett became, the wider the gap between his high aspirations and the commonplace realities of the circuit. He was finding it increasingly difficult to get his plays properly produced. Consequently he determined that he should form his own company instead of depending on local support. It was with this in mind that Barrett formed his first combination touring company in the summer of 1870. This action, coming at age twenty-four, only six years after his professional debut, marked the end of his apprenticeship.

Like Barrett, Henry Irving, age thirty-two, was also about to enter the journeyman phase of his career. In 1871 he would make his debut under Bateman at London's Lyceum playing Jingle in *The Pickwick Papers*. His very next role, as Mathias in *The Bells*, elevated him into stardom.

Forming a touring company was a radical decision, but there were signs that it might be successful. Despite the benevolent despotism of provincial administrators like John Coleman and A.D. MacNeil, the internal management of the circuits in 1870 was insecure. No playhouse was consistently profitable because managers were failing to keep up with changing theatrical conditions. There was growing evidence of a lack of organization, an increase of irregular scheduling, and too many dark nights. At the same time, provincial Britain was wealthier than at any time in history: seaside resorts flourished, hotels and boarding houses appeared virtually overnight, and escorted holidays became increasingly popular. (Thomas Cook's tour service began at this time.) New wealth was especially evident in and near the Yorkshire circuit towns where coal and iron were mined and processed and where textiles were manufactured. The railroads, backbone of the English economy, were also improving, and the increase in the efficiency of transportation that this allowed encouraged extensive theatrical touring. Railways had the potential to add economic cohesion to British trade and, increasingly, to the British theatrical profession. England—and soon the world—could open up to the theatrical touring company.

The genesis of the idea of provincial touring is vague. The stock company system at the end of the eighteenth century initiated the practice by sending to certain major provincial towns London stars with two or three leading actors in support, the rest of the mounting and cast supplied by the local playhouse. There were even a few times as early as 1830 in which entire companies from London were engaged in the provinces. Historians generally agree, however, that 1867 was the first time a London company was sent out specifically to tour. The play was *Caste* by Tom Robertson. Yet in an important way this was not a touring company as Barrett and later managers conceived of one. *Caste* was a fit-up company; that is, a troupe of actors assembled exclusively for one play. A true touring company functioned under a combination system like Barrett's that allowed for a wide repertory of plays. Barrett recognized he was a pioneer, saying that he "was among the first, if not the first to establish the . . . combination system, and the first to make it a permanent thing."[35]

Barrett's first company consisted of actors he knew from Edinburgh, along with his brother George and Miss Heath. The tour commenced on 11 July 1870 and progressed through assorted Yorkshire towns in one-week stands for thirteen weeks through 24 October. Their repertory, which gives a good indication of the meagre tastes of the day, included eighteen unexceptional plays, about half of which were comedies. The main attraction was *East Lynne*, but others were *London Assurance*, *The Marble Heart*, and Wilkie Collins's *Woman in White*. Some indications of the ripeness of the touring scheme may be seen in the company's accounts, which show a profit in each town where they played. Average production expenses including salaries in each town were £86, and averaged receipts were £110, leaving £300 profit at the end of the season. A typical company member received £1 to £2 per week, roughly equal to what their salaries would have been in a good stock company.[36] During the following winter season Barrett once more managed Coleman's Halifax theatre while Barrett's own actors found other work, relieving the company of the expensive necessity of traveling during the winter months.

The 1871 company tour, which included Barrett's younger brother and sister, Robert and Mary, began in March, concluded in December, and was divided into three separate seasons of about thirteen weeks. The profits from the previous tour and from Halifax enabled Barrett to be more generous this time with expenses for scenery, while salaries for most of the actors went up by about half a pound per week as the season progressed. Barrett's increased expenditures on scenery, the variety of the offerings in his twenty-five play repertory, and the longer tour schedule together generated profits of £1,500.[37] Among the new plays this year were Schiller's *Mary Stuart*, an adaptation of Sardou's *Fernande*, and *Twilight*. At the end of the tour Barrett, Miss Heath, and a few company members returned to Halifax.

The Wilson Barrett company continued this pattern of activities for the next four years, each winter engaged at Halifax at the end of the tour. Barrett's generosity also continued. By 1875 there were twenty-five actors in the company playing a repertoire of about twenty plays on a fixed schedule of sixteen to twenty provincial towns. Increasing amounts were spent on productions, and though income increased correspondingly, profits after 1871 were a smaller percentage of gross receipts. Advances in other directions placed Barrett's profit picture in perspective. He was becoming well known. During his winters as manager at Halifax, for example, he gained a reputation as a skilled producer of sensational Christmas pantomimes. From a loss of £70 there for the winter season in 1873, Barrett managed to raise pantomime profits by 1875 to nearly £400, even though spending more each year for spectacle.[38] People began to come from nearby towns to see the celebrated Halifax pantomimes, and this gave a considerable boost to the image of the city. Moreover, the polish, spectacle, and competent acting of Barrett's tour productions served to reinforce the reputation he was gaining for his work in other provincial towns. In short, by 1875, one year after Henry Irving's smash hit as Hamlet in London, Barrett had become a provincial success. His company had been touring profitably for four years, and he had proven that his idea of a combination touring company could compete successfully with the stock system. Wilson Barrett was an ambitious man, however, so it was unlikely that he would have remained for long in one situation. And as is always the case in the theatre, he probably realized that the key to real achievement was a successful new play.

Ever since Nicholas Rowe's drama in 1714, the story of the pathetic treatment received by Edward IV's mistress, Jane Shore, at the hands of Richard III had been a popular vehicle for the right actress. Anne Oldfield and Sarah Siddons, for example, made the role of Jane, the estranged wife of a commoner, one of the highlights of their repertoires. Rowe's play incorporated a legend that a baker, in defiance of the Lord Protector's orders, gave Jane bread to eat. Actually, the historical Jane Shore lived comfortably to be quite old, but rumors about the baker persisted and the role in the play was always a popular one. The character was treated as a low comedy part, but in 1866 the actor John Ryder got the idea of making the baker into a serious role more important to the plot. He asked William Gorman Wills, the vagabond poet and playmaker, to write the script. Wills rewrote, but Ryder's actress refused the part because she felt it was too degrading. So Wills was left with his script, only one of scores he wrote that were never produced.

Barrett first met Wills at the Surrey during the spring of 1867 when Miss Heath was doing so well with her tear-compelling power as Lady Isabel. At dinner in Wills's tumble-down artist's flat, Barrett was introduced to the play Wills had recently finished for Ryder. Barrett was not satisfied with it. The part of Master Shore was too small for him, and the original happy ending was not right for Miss Heath. Consequently, *East Lynne* remained the staple item on Barrett's tours. During the eight years that had elapsed since he first read Wills's play, however, Barrett's management and critic's skills had improved to a point where Wills's play no longer seemed quite as dramaturgically problematic. In 1875 Barrett wrote to Wills asking for *Jane Shore* and purchased it for £100. There would never be much in the way of an acting role for Barrett in the play, but Barrett recognized that its ending—

the famous penance scene—had potential for his wife. He altered the scene, adding lots of snow and a bitter conclusion to make it more pathetic, and he exploited even further the serious benevolence of the baker. Realistic touches were added to the penance scene. For example, Jane was to seize a loaf of bread and indecorously devour it after she was reconciled with her husband. Miss Heath's sense of costume design also came into play in the scene. Traditionally, Jane Shore wore a common pauper's dress. Miss Heath astutely recognized the value of the stage floor to a costume and designed instead a low cut black dress with a long train that trailed dramatically behind her when she crawled.

Jane Shore opened at the Leeds Amphitheatre on 8 March 1875. The press reception was mixed, but the favorable audience response encouraged Barrett to continue working with the play on tour. At the end of the 1875 season in September, he arranged to lease the Amphitheatre in Leeds in order to present the revised version of the play along with other plays from his company's repertoire. *Jane Shore* was received this time "with rapture," chiefly due to Miss Heath.[39] Throughout all the deeply emotional scenes in the play she managed to raise the character to heights which few actresses of her time could equal. Playgoers were impressed by the new finale, by the ravenous manner with which she devoured the bread, and by her heart-rending cry of gratitude as her husband forgave her.[40] Those critics who were repulsed by the realism of these actions were unaware that the core of the play's popular appeal lay in such intense scenes.

The Amphitheatre was not a good playhouse. It was run down and attracted criminals and young delinquents. Nevertheless, Barrett thrived on challenges, and in the first few months he significantly raised the level of production at the theatre, just as he had done at Halifax. Barrett also took over the Christmas pantomime at the Amphitheatre. The result was that in the eyes of Leeds townsmen, Barrett was fast becoming the major theatrical force in Leeds. His one-third share of the profits at the Amphitheatre was not high, but profits were less important at this time than reputation.

In late February 1876 a fire destroyed the Amphitheatre and its contents. No one was injured, but Barrett's theatrical activities were brought to a complete standstill. All his scenery and costumes, the accumulation of over five years of work, were lost. "The theatre is a heap of charcoal," he wrote,

> the [adjoining] concert hall is saved. . . . Carry's personal dresses are saved. So are Polly's and mine—everything else is lost—scenery, wardrobe, properties, in fact the whole stock in trade. The poor company have lost everything.

He continued,

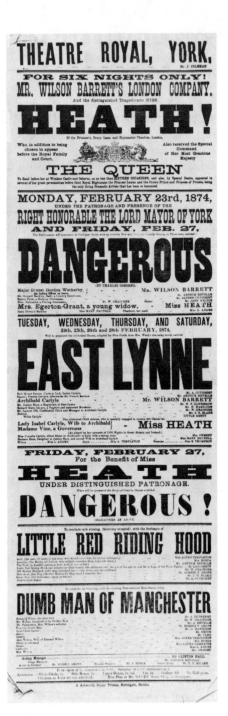

3. Playbill. The Wilson Barrett Company,
    Theatre Royal, Hull, 1874.

I have insurance in the "Commercial Union." Hobson [the owner of the playhouse] insured for about £5000 only. This for the place he refused to take £20,000 for three months ago [Barrett's offer]—what a mercy he *did* refuse. Except for a few bruises, no one injured.

Excuse haste—up all night in the fire, water, and smoke. . . . Do not worry about us—I open in Wakefield with the company on Saturday—*somehow*.[41]

Barrett was characteristically hopeful. His competitor, Coleman, whose own playhouse had suffered the same fate only a few months before, had since left Leeds for good. What's more, since Barrett had made a fine impression on the Leeds public, his request to be granted the lease to the town's new playhouse was granted.

There followed a period of several months during which Barrett and Miss Heath took stock of themselves and their work, and made plans for the future. This comparative inactivity did not last long, though, for in November they began another engagement with F.B. Chatterton at Drury Lane, where they were to play *Jane Shore* for six weeks. The Drury Lane contract states that Barrett and Miss Heath were to receive fifty percent over the first £600 each week through the first four weeks, ascending to the same percentage over £450 during the last week of the original term.[42] Originally scheduled as a filler between major productions, *Jane Shore* became an overnight success. Joseph Knight, the theatrical critic, observed that "a favourable verdict was loudly accorded" at the theatre.[43]

At Drury Lane, Barrett also showed that his character had grown as much as his abilities, suggested by the way he paid authors. He had already purchased *Jane Shore* outright from Wills, but he felt that the Drury Lane production was so successful that Wills deserved some of the rewards. He voluntarily paid Wills £400 more, four times the initial fee. Furthermore, he promised Wills five percent of all profits from the play from that time onward.[44]

After the Drury Lane success, *Jane Shore* seemed to be constantly in demand in the provinces, and with the profits from London Barrett had little trouble assembling a company to support him and Miss Heath on a new tour. From June 1877 through early September 1877 the company of twenty-five actors toured the Yorkshire Circuit with a repertory of nearly twenty plays, though *Jane Shore*'s popularity made few other plays necessary for them. Profits for this brief tour amounted to £1,000.[45]

In September Barrett learned that the Theatre Royal, Hull, was available, and he signed a lease in October for seven years at a rent of £1,000 down and £25 per week with an option to renew.[46] He inherited the complete stock of fixtures, properties, costumes, and scenery with the agreement, a welcome addition since the destruction of inventory in Leeds. The company subsequently played in Hull most of the time from October through May 1878. When they left the playhouse to tour, Barrett hired a manager and staff and kept the theatre going with other touring combination troupes, by now a common practice in the provinces. As might be expected, Barrett's tenancy at Hull began a complete transformation of the policy there. Local affiliations, so much a part of the old stock system, gradually disappeared as newer and better plays produced by combination touring companies occupied more of the bills each succeeding season.[47] By 1880 Barrett's keen business sense and increasing attention to respectability had elevated lowly Hull to the status of a first-class theatre town. Pantomimes played an important part in this, and within a few years Hull pantomimes attracted playgoers from all over Britain. Special trains from London became a regular practice during the pantomime season.

In June 1878 Barrett and the company began another London run, this time under Walter Gooch at the Princess's. In Leeds and on tour Barrett had played the role of Jane Shore's husband, Henry; at the Princess's, with more money to be made, Barrett relinquished the part to the popular actor Charles Warner and contented himself with managing. Besides *Jane Shore*, the company's bill included *Uncle Tom's Cabin* and *It's Never Too Late to Mend*, along with several comedies. The engagement concluded in May 1879.

Miss Heath had been energetically touring now for twelve years. She was forty-one in 1878; Barrett was only thirty-two. In the meantime, with the artistic weight of an entire company on her shoulders, she had managed to raise a family of five children and create a substantial hit besides. Moreover, whether because of the circumstances of her birth or because of some natural infection which she sustained on tour, she also bore the seeds of the disease that eventually ruined her health. The first tangible evidence of this occurred when she had a mild nervous breakdown on tour in 1877. More problems occurred during the Princess's engagement. She had always shown a touch of self-conscious technique in her acting; now it began to color her performances too much. Critics noticed that she was aging rapidly and that she failed to hide this in roles which needed youth, though she still brought considerable talent to her work. The critic Dutton Cook saw her in *Jane Shore* at this time. Her acting was cultivated, he observed, but "unconcealed." She possessed "a studied picturesqueness of mien, and an elaborate series of postures and gestures, sinuous swimming movements, woven paces, and waving hands; but regard for nature is omitted from her histrionic method." "Dreadfully artificial," he concluded.[48] Cook could not have known that the real source of her trouble was not artistic but psychophysiological, possibly exacerbated by drugs.

Meanwhile, the new theatre in Leeds was nearing completion. Leeds's new wealth had created a kind of affluence in the city. Town leaders sensed this and wanted a tradition of civic good works to go along with their prosperity. They threw their support behind the new playhouse, promising it would be the best in the provinces. Barrett's professional achievements in Leeds were just what the city wanted, and from the beginning city leaders called on him for advice gained from years of acquaintance with theatres all over Britain. Naturally, there was concern over the fire precautions to be taken in the new building. The various departments of the new theatre—auditorium, stagehouse, dressing rooms, shop—were designed in architecturally independent fireproof blocks. All the passages from one department to another were also fireproof. Furthermore, the number of gas jets in the theatre was increased to 400, and a system was installed whereby water could be instantly forced through the jets, creating a network of fire extinguishers. Audience comfort was increased by expanding the seating to 2,600, 3,200 with standing room. Decoratively, four fluted vaults supported a domed ceiling, and bas-relief gilt plasterwork covered every convenient surface. Technically, the auditorium, with its two dress circles, gallery, stalls, and boxes, was a masterpiece. Perfect sightlines—rare in British theatres—guaranteed that every spectator would soon enjoy plays in splendid surroundings.

Backstage was as efficient for production as the auditorium was comfortable. Dressing rooms were steam heated, and separate green rooms were constructed for leading actors and for the inevitably large numbers of supers hired during pantomime season. Adjacent to the stage a large shop was built containing four full paint frames. Speaking tubes connected every important crew position. Finally, the stage house was equipped with the latest in machinery, the entire stage floor being trapped and bridged in the manner of Covent Garden. The new theatre, rightly called the Grand, eventually cost £65,000 and was a model for the provinces. In fact, the playhouse was so well designed and constructed that it is still in use today, serving touring troupes and providing a permanent home in the north for the English National Opera.

The first lease for the theatre stipulated a rent of £1,700 per year with an increase of £100 each year, payable quarterly, and with an option to renew given to Barrett at the end of three years. The lease holders provided £800 worth of scenery and the use of a superintendent; Barrett promised to provide a carpenter and at least £100 per year to maintain the stock.[49] Barrett was to receive fifty percent of gross receipts. Barrett had many friends who warned him about Leeds because they felt it was too expensive to operate there. Leeds was a good theatre town, but audiences balked at stall prices higher than 3s. By careful supervision learned through years of experience, Barrett eventually made it possible to play as many as seven or eight plays per week at 4s. to 6s., the common provincial fee for stalls.

The Grand opened on 16 November 1878 with a gala performance of *Much Ado About Nothing*, in which Barrett played Benedick. At the dinner after the performance the Bishop of Truro exhorted Barrett "to endeavor to give Leeds people something to elevate them, something to take away which will help to make them better men and better women."[50] The original lease was to last five years; Barrett eventually managed there for sixteen, leading the historian Erroll Sherson to observe that Leeds's Grand was "one of the handsomest and best managed of all provincial playhouses."[51] By 1879 Barrett had proved himself a successful provincial actor-manager. The journeyman phase of his work was complete. He was ready to advance to London, where Henry Irving had just inaugurated his management of the Lyceum with a revival of his famous *Hamlet*, an interpretation critics hailed as "the Hamlet of our age."

2

London Management (1879–1882)

The Royal Court Theatre
and Helena Modjeska

While his company was engaged under Walter Gooch at the Princess's, Barrett learned that John Hare, manager of the Royal Court, was about to retire. The Royal Court had been constructed from the framework of an old chapel in 1870 and had passed through the hands of three managers, three different names, and at least one renovation before Hare took over in 1875. It was located on Sloane Square in Lower George Street, Chelsea, and separated from the western boundary of the theatre district by Knightsbridge and Hyde Park. The theatre was small, seating 728 patrons; two tall playgoers could practically touch hands across the sides of the dress circle. The size and location, and unimportance, of the Royal Court seemed to remove it from the interest of the Lord Chamberlain, who permitted it to operate without his formal approval using only a magistrate's license.

The Royal Court was certainly not the kind of playhouse Barrett originally had in mind for a major London operation. In an otherwise hopeful letter written to his sister (now married to Reverend Frank Heath, Miss Heath's brother) after the lease was arranged, he added a trace of misgiving. "Dear Polly," he wrote, "Just a word to say they have accepted my proposal for the Court Theatre. . . . Carry is delighted and I think it was wise and the right thing to do. We shall see."[1] Barrett leased the Royal Court from owner D.L. Claremont for six and one-half years beginning 1 March 1880. Rent was £2,100 per year for the playhouse plus £200 per year for adjoining land and buildings used for storage and shop facilities.[2] John Hare was anxious to leave, however, so Barrett arranged to take over in September 1879 at an additional cost of £1,000.

Barrett's lease of the Royal Court threw him headlong into London managerial activities, but with this difference: he had a solid financial footing with his operations in Leeds and Hull, and his company was making money at the Princess's as well. This was insurance against immediate and drastic failure. Equally important, Barrett was highly regarded by metropolitan critics even before his arrival. Competition for audiences was strong in London. Henry Irving would produce *The Lady of Lyons* and *The Merchant of Venice* this year at the Lyceum. He was rapidly advancing to the head of the profession. Besides Irving, there were Charles Wyndham, Squire Bancroft at the Prince of Wales, and comedian J.L. Toole, who was about to open his own playhouse after ten successful years at the Gaiety. In this kind of company, the high opinion of influential drama critics was essential for any newcomer to get started on the right foot. Fortunately, this was the case for Barrett, about whom the critic for *The Figaro* observed,

> By this accession to its strength, our list of London managers is increased by the acquisition of a scholar and a gentleman. Nor does Mr. Wilson Barrett come to London without the knowledge necessary to make a successsful metropolitan theatre manager. Mr. Wilson Barrett has had large practical theatrical experience in both town and country; he is not only an actor of acknowledged ability, but has for some time past directed the Grand Theatre, Leeds and the Theatre Royal, Hull with genuine success.[3]

Even with all the planning, however, Barrett did not have time to find and mount a new play for his opening on 10 October. Consequently, he left most of his company at the Princess's to play a repertoire of their past touring successes, while he and Miss Heath went with the remainder of the troupe to open *Fernande* at the new theatre. This was the same adaptation of Sardou's play that had been in their bills for years but it needed only a small cast, had a good part for Miss Heath, and was already expensively mounted.

Fernande was reasonably well received when it was first presented in London with Mrs. John Wood in 1870 and had been successful for Barrett in the provinces, but London critics found faults in the production that Mrs. Wood's performance had covered up. They called the adapter to task for not updating the language and they condemned the story as dull and redundant. Miss Heath, who was growing more ill each week, seems to have badly wanted her husband to make a success at the Royal Court. She forced her way through the lead role of Clotilde with such determination that her artificiality, until now controlled by good taste in her best roles, showed itself to be as dated as it really was. She had lost the light touch that she used to be noted for, and the result was a humorless and an inappropriate characterization in which no one saw much good. Barrett must have known that the day was approaching when Miss Heath would no longer be able to support the company.

Other considerations in the performance were of interest because of what they revealed about Barrett's own development. His acting in the role of Pomerol was well received. Critics were surprised at the restraint, intelligence and vigor of this newcomer, and Clement Scott, seeing Barrett for the first time, was especially struck by the earnestness of Barrett's characterization, a trait that was an important element of Barrett's style.[4]

The mounting of the play also merited notice because expense and detail were evident. One critic complained of overelaboration in this regard, but another noticed that Barrett was successfully using the innovative box-set style introduced only a few years earlier at the Prince of Wales. Stage illusion was better maintained when walls came down to the proscenium lines and hid prompters, scene shifters, and actors waiting for their cues.[5]

On tour *Fernande* was accompanied by a farce, and Barrett thought a similar companion piece might prove useful in picking up attendance now. He had in hand a short play which had been approved by the Lord Chamberlain only a few weeks before and which was written by an untested English author. Henry Arthur Jones's playlet *A Clerical Error* was subsequently placed on the bill with *Fernande* on 13 October, adding some necessary humor to Sardou's dreary romance. Barrett first met Jones at Leeds in August where Barrett produced Jones's play *It's Only Round the Corner, or Harmony Restored*, unsuccessfully produced by another manager at Exton the year before. Jones was new to playwriting and thought Barrett's production came off very well, but Barrett wrote to him that the piece was nevertheless "a little amateurish, wanting in finish and strength of dialogue."[6] Meanwhile, Barrett continued to help Jones with comments about play craftsmanship, and in May he wrote asking Jones to undertake a new play which would be used for the opening of the Royal Court. Miss Heath's part, Barrett said, "must not be a young girl nor an old woman, as she will play neither." What was wanted was a light play with good parts all around, but with "enough pathos to hold the story together and sufficient comedy to be thoroughly amusing."[7]

Barrett did not receive that play, but he did receive *A Clerical Error*, a short romantic comedy about a pastor who charitably gives up the woman he loves to a younger man whom he believes better able to take care of her. This was the first play written to display Barrett's particular talent for drawing utmost sympathy from characters who make generous self-sacrifices unknown to those they benefited. It was a hit.[8] *Fernande* held the stage for only two weeks, but Jones's play was carried over into the next bill. Barrett was patient with Jones, generously giving him £20 in advance of fees for this little play and paying £2 2s. per week during the run until a total of £50 was reached. This was unusual benevolence to an author as untrained as Jones. Barrett recognized talent in him, and immediately after the success of the play he wrote to Jones in an effort to maintain their professional relationship. It was common knowledge that the key to successful management was a hit play, but unlike his peers Barrett was willing to take the necessary time to work with a new author. Barrett wrote in a letter regarding the play,

My Dear Sir,

Please send me the detailed acceptance of my offer for *A Clerical Error* and that will stand until there is time to draw up a more legal, though not less binding, agreement.

Then, as a warning, Barrett added,

> You had better keep the other copies of the piece by you, call in those out, if possible.

Finally, he encouraged Jones,

> The author who can do in three acts what you have done in one in *A Clerical Error* will take as strong a stand now as Tom Robertson took years ago.[9]

The association between Jones and Barrett was to be a fruitful one because of Barrett's willingness to encourage like this.

Trying to get a firmer foothold at the Royal Court, Barrett next revived H.J. Byron's comedy *Courtship* beginning 16 October. Unlike Jones, Byron was not new to the stage, for he was noted for dozens of hit comedies and burlesques, one of which, *Our Boys*, was then playing at the Criterion and would eventually run for over 1,000 performances. *Courtship* deals with a wealthy heiress who assumes a false poverty to test her suitor's sincerity. Critics saw too much of Byron's sloppy writing habits in the play, but the jokes were good and audiences were content if they were made to laugh. Barrett was a hit as DeCourcey, giving some indication of apprentice training that enabled him to play comedy as well as he did pathos. The play ran until 14 December. Before *Courtship* opened Miss Heath had become weak and was sent home to recuperate for what she believed would be only a few weeks; Amy Roselle, a member of the company for several years, assumed the role which Miss Heath had rehearsed. The short rest proved to be longer than planned, however, because Miss Heath's health did not improve. She remained at home in reasonable comfort for the next few months, but she never again returned to the stage. The company had lost its star.

Amy Roselle performed well in place of Miss Heath, but her limits would show as soon as more difficult plays were produced at the Royal Court. Barrett bought time by quickly putting together a new adaptation of Bronson Howard's play *The Banker's Daughter* entitled *The Old Love and the New*. Under this disguise Howard's play kept the company on its feet for a while longer. In fact, for the first time since he leased the theatre Barrett had a major hit on his hands. Howard's domestic comedy about a young suitor cynically discarded for an older and wealthier one was received, according to Dutton Cook, "with exceptional favour."[10] One fault of construction, however, drew criticism from patriots in the audience. It seems that when Florence jokingly speculated about an early widowhood after her marriage to a wealthy man of seventy, the conservative critic of *The Theatre* indignantly reported that "English girls are not familiar with those sentiments."[11] The vivacious humor of the actress Emmeline Ormsby obviated for most playgoers the superficial heartlessness of the girl, however, and helped to make the play popular through the end of the season. Nevertheless, the company had been without a well-known leading actress now for six months, and Barrett could not expect to come across comedies like Byron's or Howard's with much luck any longer.

As early as 1878 Edwin Sargent had visited London seeking bookings for his client, the Polish actress Helena Modjeska. Until now, and ever since Charles Fechter's Shakespeare successes in 1861, there had been a prejudice against foreign actors playing the legitimate English repertory, notwithstanding foreign companies successfully playing foreign plays. Augustin Daly and Sarah Bernhardt challenged this, but it took all the efforts of their very influential organizations to do so. Modjeska was a loner who spoke with a thick accent; many thought she should not act in plays made famous in London by English actors. Barrett, however was desperate. When he was approached by Modjeska's husband, Polish Count Chlapowski, he agreed to engage her. It was risky. Not only was Modjeska a foreigner and an unknown in London, but she also would be acting at the same time as Sarah Bernhardt in her Comédie Française productions and the American actress Genevieve Ward in her own immensely popular play *Forget Me Not*. Moreover, Miss Beermans was also making a great hit in London with the visiting Dutch company from Rotterdam. Modjeska would have considerable female competition. To his credit, Barrett did not allow his eagerness for success to cloud his managerial judgment. He knew Modjeska would be difficult to introduce no matter how good she was. He proposed that she play two weeks of afternoon matinees at the Royal Court while Bronson Howard's play continued at night. Matinees were less well attended than evening performances, and Barrett could introduce her without the pressure that a formal debut might impose. A one-year contract was arranged whereby Modjeska would receive one-half of the receipts after expenses, which at the Royal Court were about £425 per week.

In the meantime, the actress made necessary preparations. Barrett hired Augustus Harris of Drury Lane to help him adapt Modjeska's own scripts for a London audience. She was so nervous that at first she wanted to rush in with all of her major roles. On Barrett's advice, however, she began spending several hours each day improving her English. Above all, she labored to eliminate the "Yankee twang" (Barrett's phrase) she had unconsciously picked up during her American tours; even her Polish accent, Barrett said, would be better than that. Barrett was planning to present Modjeska first in *Camille*, a play in her repertoire but not often done in London due to the censor's disapproval. He arranged with James Mortimer, the original translator, to make a new adaptation which played down some of the more objectionable incidents; after all, there had been a riot when the play premiered at the Princess's in 1875. Barrett and Mortimer changed the title to *Heartsease*, and Camille's profession was slightly altered, while Dumas Fils's name did not appear on the program. A minor conflict occurred when Charles Coughlan, Barrett's leading man, balked at having his name placed beneath Modjeska's in the playbills, but this was quickly resolved after Barrett simply replaced Coughlan with another actor from the company, Arthur Dacre. Barrett had offered himself for the role, but Modjeska declined. During the next several weeks she plagued Barrett with letters about arrangements for her engagement. She apologized for distracting him so much, but pleaded that her attentions would at least show him "how much I take to heart our tour and how I try to do my best to satisfy the audience."[12] Modjeska was impressed with Barrett's efficient organization and operation, and pleased that he promised to mount her productions as lavishly as the small Royal Court stage would allow.[13]

Heartsease opened on the afternoon of 1 May 1880. Modjeska's reception was cold and no one in the audience even acknowledged her first entrance, but the force of her acting eventually won them over. By the final curtain she was received with acclaim. Critics were sorry that she was a little older than they had hoped; nevertheless, her acting was thought un-surpassed. Like Eleonora Duse, she was adept at dramatic stage business, and this quality struck critics the most in her debut. Her characterization, they said, was like a mosaic "built up of an infinite number of little bits of bye-play ... that one cannot forebear comparing her art with Balzac's literary work."[14] Reporters looked forward to the time when she would be seen in better roles. Barrett's risky undertaking was a success. After two weeks of matinees, *The Old Love and the New* was removed from the boards and replaced by *Heartsease*, which played to full houses through August.

Much of Modjeska's success in London was due to her wide acceptance by "society," presided over at Marlborough House by Albert Edward and Alexandra. Appropriately enough, when the royal couple were seen attending Modjeska's first evening performance, waving to her during the call, and then visiting her in the dressing room afterwards, these actions were taken as a signal to welcome the foreign actress with all the attention "society" could muster. The result was that throughout Modjeska's entire engagement Barrett found himself swept up in an endless succession of parties, "charities," and "five o'clocks." And there was even a rumor that a certain Lady Jeune, wife of a prominent barrister, offered to become Barrett's "guardian angel," like Baroness Burdett was doing for Henry Irving.

The success of *Heartsease* still did not convince Barrett that Modjeska would be easily accepted in the traditional English repertoire. He decided to revive *The Old Love and the New* for a short time in September while he took Modjeska and some of the company to the Alexandra Theatre in Liverpool to try out *Adrienne Lecouvreur*, *Romeo and Juliet*, and a few other plays on a provincial audience. The verdict was positive, and the company returned to London in mid-September fully committed to presenting the Polish actress in her complete repertoire.

Barrett opened the second phase of her engagement with Schiller's *Mary Stuart*, well-known enough but not often done in London despite its theme. This was one of the actress' favorite roles, and she showed substantial interest in arranging a proper text for her debut in it. Her version—an adaptation by Lewis Wingfield—shortened Schiller's by omitting the Leicester scene in the last act. This particular amendment, however, was not appreciated by Johnston Forbes-Robertson, who was originally contracted to play Leicester. Forbes-Robertson was fresh from success as the original Sir Horace Welby in *Forget Me Not* with Miss Genevieve Ward and thought he deserved better treatment. He resigned from *Mary Stuart* and was replaced by John Clayton. *Mary Stuart* opened on 9 October, but Schiller's politics did not go well with English tastes. The actress was praised, the play attacked. London critics remained anxious for Modjeska to undertake Shakespeare because they wished to compare her to English actresses. They had to wait because Barrett now seemed to be exploiting what he perceived to be a growing popular interest in the actress by forestalling anticipated roles as long as possible. *Mary Stuart* played until 10 December and was followed by *Adrienne Lecouvreur*, the first production in which Forbes-Robertson acted with Modjeska. He played Maurice, the role taken by Arthur Dacre at the Alexandra. The new play proved to be the actress' biggest success to date, and she was compared favorably to Bernhardt, who played the role earlier in the season.[15] Modjeska was praised for her ability to make Adrienne's love for Maurice seem heroic, not just passionate. *Adrienne Lecouvreur* ran until 25 March.

All the while Modjeska was engaged Barrett contented himself for the most part with management because Modjeska's London debut involved careful planning and organization. Barrett was also learning about publicity. Playbills were the form of outdoor advertising used most often by managers at that time; Barrett, on the other hand, put his money into large posters, relatively new devices for English theatrical publicity. For Modjeska's debut he caught the attention of the London public by papering the city with large posters bearing the single word MODJESKA. No one knew what it meant. Posters were often used in other business enterprises, and it was thought by some that the name might be a new brand of tooth powder, a medicine, or even a cure for rheumatism. This had the effect of making people curious about the name, and the results were so successful that Barrett hereafter relied heavily on poster advertising, perhaps more than any other London manager.

Other managerial activities also continued. During the 1879–1880 season Barrett arranged for three fit-up companies to tour the provinces playing *Proof*, *The Old Love and the New*, and *For Life*, plays originally staged for his company's 1878–1879 engagement at the Princess's. These road companies played one-week stands, and Barrett received one-half the gross receipts for their efforts. This was the beginning of Barrett's practice of touring his own companies in his own hits. The traditional practice was to sell the rights for hits to other managers; Barrett did not abandon this but combined it with his own tours, knowing that there was more money to be made from tours of good productions well rehearsed by himself than from shoddy productions quickly thrown together by others. This practice of combining tours with purchased rights was first undertaken by Dion Boucicault in the 1860s with his production of *The Colleen Bawn*, and since then many managers had failed trying to emulate his success. Barrett succeeded because he possessed an ability to organize and manage road companies that later became unsurpassed, even by Boucicault himself.

In the meantime, Barrett's provincial theatres were also active. During the pantomime season at Hull, for example, the theatre was averaging nearly £70 profit per week, while Leeds often surpassed £250.[16] Again, this was done exclusively through the agency of Barrett's supervisory talent, for despite the attention required by Modjeska's engagement and three fit-up companies, he also made frequent trips to Hull and Leeds to keep an eye on operations there. Nothing escaped his notice. At Leeds in 1880 he even found time to criticize the jewelry worn by the actresses in the pantomime. They insisted on wearing their own, he complained, and that was out of place with the tone of the ensemble. He also watched over the actors, making sure that each one was playing up to his capabilities. Moreover, when actor-families in the company grew, he became the benevolent overseer, rearranging roles to insure their security while maintaining proper balance to the company. He once wrote to his acting manager at Leeds:

> Mrs. Grainger was playing Diana and evidently will again become a mother in a week or so. There was such a want of a "sense of fitness of things" in this that it was a shock to me, which is not lessened by the fact that Vesta and the principal dancer were in the same condition. I do not think I will engage married couples for pantomime. If I do it will be as well to cast them [as] married ladies ... then if the theatre is turned into a lying-in hospital it will not matter so much.[17]

Barrett's managerial mind was now running well-tuned and would continue to do so as more outlets for his energy were added in the years to come. There was a sense of satisfaction and confidence implicit in his actions and explicit in the flair with which he was now beginning to arrange all his activities. But though this complex and harried life suited him, his wife's health continued to be poor. Moreover, living in Leeds at the family home the past two years she could see Barrett only occasionally. Since she wished to be nearer to him and to her brother, who was living in Brighton, Barrett made plans to settle in London. He arranged with the critic George Henry Lewes and his companion George Eliot to purchase their home, The Priory, for £2,500.[18] Then, writing to inform his sister of the new home, he mentioned Caroline's wish to be with her brother and warned of her increasingly distressful mental condition, even hinting that her presence in the house with the children was beginning to cause trouble:

> All the kids seem very well, but Carry has been unwell. She is, I am thankful to say, much better. She wants to be with you, and you must take her out on long drives and keep her out as much as possible.[19]

These personal matters in hand, and with Modjeska's most demanding successes behind him, Barrett finally agreed to present the actress in *Romeo and Juliet*. In Liverpool, during the tryout a few weeks before, he had played Romeo, but at the Royal Court the role was given to Forbes-Robertson; Barrett followed the examples of John Philip Kemble and Samuel Phelps by playing Mercutio. With leading actors of this caliber, *Romeo and Juliet* may be said to have been Barrett's first major London play. The production opened on 26 March 1881 and met with the same kind of mixed praise that had accompanied Modjeska's other pays. Some critics were a little upset by her emphasis on Juliet's coyness, a trait patriots felt to be out of place in a young English girl (though Juliet is of course, Italian); nevertheless, Modjeska showed evidence of the same careful effort, the same imagination, and the same degree of talent as her other roles. Forbes-Robertson's zealous lover was also praised, as were the scenery, costumes, and staging.

Paradoxically, it was neither Modjeska nor Forbes-Robertson but Barrett whom many critics claimed to be the most original and effective element in the production. He had not been seen in a major role for some time, and his reintroduction to playgoers at this time suggested that management was not the only area in which he was improving. Barrett's Mercutio was a bold stroke of unconventional acting, revealing traits in the part that had been hidden from many actors in the past. He was brave, reckless, cheerful, and friendly, "a glittering splendor of vitality."[20] Most important, his portrayal showed a thorough grasp of the part as it related to the whole; a high order of stage intelligence was displayed. Mercutio's death was especially remarkable. "In its detail, its thought, and its thorough unconventionality," declared Clement Scott, it was

> a sincere contribution to art. It was not the death of a stage Mercutio, with repetition of old tricks and theatrical devices, but the death of such a man as Shakespeare depicted, with a sense of grim humour in his extreme agony and an honest smile upon his lips.[21]

Here was evidence of the actor Barrett would shortly become. Until now he was a supporting actor, but after Mercutio he would be a star. No doubt

Modjeska's example had something to do with this, and, in fact, throughout his career Barrett was sensitive to the influence of good actresses to no ordinary degree.

Barrett next produced for Modjeska a new play by William Gorman Wills entitled *Juana*, a sombre affair probably originally intended for Miss Heath. Wills had first worked with Barrett on the gloomy *Jane Shore*, and as time went on he was to work with Barrett on other plays as well. Educated at Trinity College in Dublin, Wills was the son of a poet and a biographer. His first artistic efforts were in painting, and he was especially adept at children's portraits, at which task he made something of a living for himself. Later on he took up playwriting and play adapting and became house dramatist at the Lyceum, where he wrote *Charles I* for Henry Irving. Wills was a strange character, a curious blend of the aristocrat and the Bohemian. Oliver Goldsmith was his idol, and he emulated Goldsmith's shiftless habits of work. He wrote his plays while in bed, for example, where he would scribble notes and toss them on the floor in heaps. Later his butler would assemble them and piece together the scenes. This was how *Jane Shore* was written and is also evidence of why Wills's plays were not well constructed. From this can also be deduced how important Barrett's structural work was in the eventual success of *Jane Shore*.

Juana is the passionate story of a young princess who is saved from criminal disgrace by the quiet heroism of a friar who was once her suitor. Barrett tried a slightly different version, *The Ordeal*, at Liverpool in late October of the previous year, and since then Juana's role had been considerably enlarged. But despite the full-blown emotions ready-made for Modjeska's touch, the new version did not succeed. One reason was that Barrett had arranged with E.W. Godwin, an academically inclined architect and scene designer who was a close friend of Wills, to perform the "archeology" of the play, and the results were simply too unusual for London audiences. Barrett's association with Godwin was evidence of a serious interest in the detailed realistic scenic conventions of the period. Nevertheless, picturesque processions of monks and strange religious rituals set within careful reproductions of Spanish cloisters and castles proved too strange when led by a woman speaking pretentious English verse in a Polish accent. Barrett played well, this time with excellent articulation and quiet imposing restraint; Forbes-Robertson as Don Carlos also received good notices. But the sombre tone of the play and its loose construction— combined with a sudden new development in Barrett's career—forced the play to close by the end of the month.

Modjeska blamed the failure of this particular play on Barrett's acting; Barrett blamed it on bad luck, for along with the increase in his powers as manager and actor had come an acute case of stage superstition. The day after the opening Modjeska found Barrett in his dressing room surrounded by all the newspaper reviews and looking so pale that he was unable to smile. This was highly uncharacteristic of his usually sanguine personality. "I knew the play would prove a failure," he groaned, "because just as I was leaving my house, a funeral appeared at the corner of the street, and being in a great hurry, I was obliged to cross it, and there it is!"[22]

Financially, the Royal Court project did well for Barrett. His production costs were high by the standards of that house (*Adrienne Lecouvreur*, for example, cost nearly £1,000 to prepare), but weekly operating expenses were low enough and average receipts high enough to leave a reasonable profit.[23] Moreover, Leeds and Hull were doing well and the three fit-up companies were also running at a profit. Barrett could have continued at the Royal Court if he wanted to, but he chose instead to leave for a new adventure. He learned that the Princess's was available, and now that he had capital and experience, he was ready to fulfill his boyhood ambitions.

The Princess's Theatre and the Gospel of Rags

Princess's manager Walter Gooch was a frankly commercial manager. Originally connected with the Metropolitan Music Hall, his association with Barrett started in 1875, then continued in 1878 when Barrett's company began their second engagement at the Princess's. Gooch made money with Barrett, and he made still more money the next season with Charles Reade's popular prohibitionist melodrama *Drink*, in which Charles Warner's realistic depiction of an alcoholic in the throes of delerium tremens drew so much attention. Gooch decided to use the profits from Barrett and Reade on a season-long return engagement of Edwin Booth beginning in the fall of 1879, though he had neither the money nor the expertise to promote Booth properly in London. Furthermore, Booth himself was terribly depressed by personal problems at the same time. The result was a series of disastrous productions at the Princess's that ended in a bad season for manager and star alike. In the spring of 1881 Gooch simply disappeared, leaving the financial affairs of the theatre in complete disarray. Years later it was discovered that he fled to New York where he died under an assumed name.

When he abandoned the Princess's, the affairs of the playhouse were taken over by the lawyer James Crowdy, who spent weeks unraveling the finances and legal difficulties that had accumulated while Gooch was manager. Barrett found out about all this from Gooch's stage manager, Harry Jackson, who told him that Crowdy was seeking to lease the theatre as soon as possible in order to eliminate some of the debts and get matters back on an even keel there. Actually, Barrett may have been close to leasing the theatre even before Gooch's departure. In the fall of 1879, prior to Booth's engagement, Gooch decided to renovate the playhouse. Gooch's redecorating ideas, however, were not consistently pleasing to Barrett, whose personal interest in the theatre led him to complain. Whether Barrett and Gooch had an informal agreement about the Princess's at the time or whether Barrett's unusual interest in the renovations was purely personal, the fact remains that when he heard the news from Jackson, Barrett immediately leased the playhouse.

The Princess's has an importance to English theatre perhaps rivaled only by the Drury Lane or the Haymarket. The revival of the English stage in the nineteenth century began there. Erroll Sherson recalls that its stage witnessed the transition from the old style to the new, from Macready's stately heroism all the way "to the more natural school of Fechter, Boucicault, and Barrett,"[24] with Barrett's mentor, Charles Kean, forming a connecting link between the two. Built in 1836 at the cost of £47,000, the theatre first had musical affiliations. There in 1845 two Americans, Charlotte Cushman and Edwin Forrest, acted together in *Romeo and Juliet* and *Macbeth*. In 1850 Charles Kean began his long tenure, playing one successful Shakespearean revival after another and elevating the art of melodrama closer to middle-class respectability. Fechter was at the Princess's in 1860, and in 1863 James Vining began there in a series of Boucicault's most popular plays, including *The Streets of London* (1864) and *Arrah na Pogue* (1865). Fechter returned in 1867 for a year, followed by Benjamin Webster in 1869, F.B. Chatterton in 1874, then by a series of turns to Walter Gooch in 1876.

The theatre was located at 73 Oxford Street in the district of St. Marylebone and had undergone three complete renovations, including Gooch's, since it was first built. The newest included seating for 1,750, of which 550 were in the pit (later reduced by 54 new stall seats), 207 in the dress circle, 269 in the upper circle, 511 in the gallery, and 92 in the boxes. Across Oxford Street opposite the theatre was the Pantheon, and on one side of the Princess's was the liquor store owned by Mr. Gilbey. On the other side of the theatre was the famous theatrical hotel and restaurant, Inman's, where stage celebrities liked to gather in an assembly room behind the bar. The Princess's in 1881 was one of the most sumptuous and well equipped playhouses in London, yet despite its large capacity the feeling inside was intimate, perhaps because the proscenium was only thirty-two feet wide. Backstage was a marvel of efficiency precisely suited to present the elaborate spectacles Victorian audiences loved to see with their Shakespeare and other plays. There were forty-two feet of depth beyond the proscenium and sixteen feet of wing space on either side of the stage. A spacious scene dock opened through sliding doors and into the stage left wings, and there was more than enough dressing room and shop space to suit the size of the theatre.

Yet even with all its physical beauty, the Princess's was not the great playhouse it had been in Charles Kean's days, for it had lost its greatest asset, its audience. Recognizing that the quality of his achievements as manager at the Princess's depended greatly upon the quality of the audience there, Barrett added to his original boyhood resolve a desire to restore the playhouse to the public prominence it formerly held. This meant he had to have a definite and original policy, and for this he returned to Charles Kean for inspiration. Taking up Kean's banner, Barrett pushed the policy even further than Kean himself, who resolved "to banish from the stage . . . adaptations and translations from foreign sources and to produce instead the works of Englishmen."[25] Influential critics had been complaining for years now of the poor quality of English theatre. "The theatre," it was often argued, "no longer holds an attraction for lovers of poetry, of refined art, and of intellectual work."[26] Barrett felt that the commitment to foreign dramatic adaptations was the main cause. Such plays, after all, were inexpensive to produce and resulted in more profits. If only English authors were given the opportunity to write, he believed, good drama could once again return to the stage. For the rest of his career, Barrett made it his personal artistic goal to produce English plays on English themes by English authors. He was the only London manager to do so in 1881 and was still the only one at the time of his death in 1904.

But play choice alone would not resurrect the Princess's to its previous position of eminence. Kean was not only dedicated for the most part to English drama (at least Shakespeare), but more important, to quality productions, "to a concept and programme of dramatic art without regard to commercial success."[27] By 1880 Kean's ideals had grown dim in the eyes of the majority of London managers, and theatres had fallen too often into the hands of people like Gooch. "These men," Dion Boucicault bitterly complained in 1878,

> have obtained possession of first-class theatres and assume to exercise the artistic and literary functions required to select the actors, to read and determine the merit of dramatic works, and preside generally over the highest and noblest efforts of the human mind.[28]

The lowest public taste was consistently catered to at houses such as the Britannia, the Effingham, the Pavilion, the Standard, the Grecian, the Marylebone, the Queen's, and lately at Sadler's Wells and the Princess's. In order to counteract this trend, Barrett resolved never to put on a play or assume a part without doing his fullest to assure that it would deserve, if not achieve, artistic success.[29] Here Kean had run into problems, for though he had a calculated and astute business policy to support his artistic aims, he was not financially talented enough to succeed. Barrett, on the other hand, was a financial wizard. He hoped that with luck the business skill he had gained during his previous ten years would enable him to succeed where Kean had not.

Barrett's plans for the Princess's did not come to him in a single flash of inspiration, however, but were instead the result of his practices, failures, and successes during his first few years as manager there. In 1881 his immediate difficulty was the adjustment involved in moving from the intimate Royal Court to the spacious Princess's and the successful completion of Modjeska's engagement. When Barrett had decided to lease the Princess's, he had leased the Royal Court to Marie Litton, a member of his company. *Juana* closed there at the end of May, then Barrett opened with Modjeska at the Princess's in *Frou Frou* by Comyns Carr on 4 June. Bernhardt was seen in the same play at the Gaiety Theatre in May 1880; it was difficult for critics to avoid comparisons, and in this instance Modjeska came out second best, for the role of Gilbrette was the kind of girlish charmer that Bernhardt took to naturally. Modjeska had turned a play intended to be full of lively human interest into a display of tragic emotions. Barrett's acting of Henri de Sartorys did not suffer the same kind of criticism. "This clever artist," wrote one reporter, "follows up success with success."[30]

Frou Frou was the last of Modjeska's plays under the terms of the contract and the last for Forbes-Robertson as her leading man. With characteristic flair Barrett arranged a gala farewell benefit for Modjeska that was held at the Princess's on 28 June. The evening began with the actress in scenes from her most popular plays done at the Royal Court. Along with these were included a dramatic recital by Henry Irving and the performance of Ophelia's mad scene by Ellen Terry. Also attending were Sarah Bernhardt, Mr. and Mrs. Kendal, J.L. Toole, and a host of other London theatrical luminaries. "So remarkable a gathering has seldom been found even in these days of brilliant surprises," declared Clement Scott.[31]

Frou Frou closed on 2 July, a few days after the benefit. Unlike earlier Modjeska plays, it did not make any money for Barrett, and he lost nearly £100 during the play's short one-month run. This was to be expected, for the Princess's was, after all, a larger theatre and cost proportionately more to operate than the Royal Court. Barrett did learn, however, that he would have to increase his efforts in every direction if he was to succeed in the new playhouse. An undertaking of this kind needed a premiere in the grand manner. While this was in preparation, Barrett kept the Princess's active by reviving Bronson Howard's comedy yet again.

One of the most colorful characters of the London literary and dramatic world at this time was George R. Sims, whom Barrett first met at Leeds during the pantomime season in the late winter of 1881 at the meeting arranged by Charles Reade, a mutual friend. Sims had in hand a play that he had been unsuccessfully peddling to various London managers for months. Barrett asked if the play was a big melodrama, which was what he wanted to open with, having already taken an option on Boucicault's plays *The Streets of London* and *After Dark*.[32] Seeing that Sims's play fulfilled this requirement, he immediately offered to produce it. Sims was broke and timidly requested only £500, but Barrett offered to pay him by results and drew up a contract which suited Sims far better. The terms were that Sims would receive two guineas per performance in London up to £600 in weekly receipts (£600 was approximately the operating cost of the Princess's when Barrett took over). If the receipts were between £600 and £700, Sims would receive five percent; if between £700 and £800, seven and one-half percent; and if over £800, ten percent. Barrett also agreed to pay Sims five to ten percent of the provincial receipts.[33]

Sims's journalistic, socially committed literary background furnished the key to Barrett's new policy of English spirit and was the major reason why Barrett joined forces with Sims so quickly. The new play, called *Lights o' London*, was a spectacular melodrama. It is the story of a prodigal son wrongfully imprisoned and deprived of his inheritance. The play's novelty arose from the fact that it used English rather than foreign sources, that its characters were drawn from the rank and file of the London streets, and that its settings were the well-known habitations of the London poor. Barrett was embarking on a new phase of his career with this play. The scenery alone would cost more than any full production he had done before; more important, he decided to undertake the heavy responsibilities of the leading role himself. There would be no more distress over finding an actress of Miss Heath's caliber to hang his fortunes on. His future was now entirely in his own hands.

Barrett intended at that time to spend the rest of his career at the Princess's, so it was logical that he would take great care in selecting a company to support him. Many were members of his original company now playing at the Royal Court. His brother, George, who was developing into a fine character comedian, was one of these along with the familiar names of Ormsby, Clitheroe, Cooke, and Wright—supporting actors with wide ranges. But Barrett needed to add other actors who were capable of making a strong impact in melodrama in the important roles of female lead, antagonist, and rival-to-the-hero. In the young actress Mary Eastlake Barrett found all the qualities necessary for a melodramatic heroine; she was a beautiful blond whose appearance of vulnerability cloaked just the faintest hint of sexuality. In fact, Barrett first saw her playing in the racy comedy *Where's the Cat?* at the Criterion Theatre with Charles Wyndham in November 1880 and came back later to see her in two similar comedies, *The Great Divorce Case* and *Pink Dominoes*. She began at the Princess's with the role of Lillian in the July revival of *The Old Love and the New*. The position of rival-to-the-hero was a common one in melodramas, and Barrett engaged another young actor, Walter Speakman, to assume this responsibility with the new company. Speakman began his acting career in the provinces and had managed to gain a reputation playing at some of the lesser known theatres in London. He was well built and possessed a striking stage presence and a voice of considerable power and flexibility. Barrett had first seen Speakman's work in 1875 when he was engaged to play in one of the early provincial productions of *Jane Shore*. A provincial discovery, actor E.S. Willard, was hired to fulfill the antagonist's responsibilities. Barrett was taking a decided risk hiring relatively unknown actors to play such important parts in his new play, but this practice, too, proved to be a major point of his style as his career developed.

Lights o' London opened on 10 September 1881. Not since *East Lynne* had a play struck the sympathies of the English public so much. Spectators seemed to be entranced as settings and characters revealing their native London passed before their eyes. Of course it was no small help that the play also contained escapes, fights, crowd scenes, trials, and a great deal of pathos. There were special elements, however, which made the new Princess's play the hit that it was, the first being its writing. The critic Dutton Cook recognized it immediately. "Mr. Sims does not simply address himself to the eyes of the public," Cook wrote, "he compels them to listen, he interests them deeply, he is now humorous, now pathetic, he persuades them to laugh and to weep alternately."[34] This observer's comments reveal an element of style which was to become one of the hallmarks of Barrett's future work. *Lights o' London* was not just spectacle, but also drama; its incidents were presented with proper attention to motivation, and its dialogue was carefully crafted—traits which earlier melodramas generally ignored. Melodrama had historically been a slapdash affair in which characters and dialogue were merely skeletons on which to hang lots of stage activity. Barrett, on the other hand, took the form seriously and demonstrated this by helping a great deal in the careful dramatic shaping of this play. He tightened the structure, clarified the motives and characters, and made alterations and suggestions throughout the preparation period. Barrett applied to melodrama the craft of the French "well-made play." Barrett's practice of putting his hand actively into the work of his dramatist was not in itself unusual among managers; what was unusual was that he did it with skill, tact, and deep concern for the wishes of the author. For *Lights o' London* the result was, the critics said, a play "full of passion and humanity," that is, psychological truth and consistent characterization. *Lights o' London* was "far removed," said the reporter for *The Theatre*, "from the so-called 'sensational' or panorama play."[35] *Punch* agreed that the new play at the Princess's had "thrown all recent productions of the same class into the shade."[36] The dialogue was "rarely on stilts, never flat, and generally easy, epigramatic, and . . . perfectly natural," concluded the same critic.[37]

Further indication of good writing in the play could be seen in the scope given to the acting of all the roles and the praise accorded the acting by the press. Mary Eastlake, more used to light comedies, had some difficulty sustaining the effort needed for the entire melodrama of this sort, but her looks and her potential were noticed. George Barrett as Jarvis made an impression as an excellent comedian and began to build a reputation as the company's strong character comic. Walter Speakman made a hit as the mysterious rival to Barrett, Seth Preene. One of the most conspicuous acting successes in the play was that of E.S. Willard as the antagonist. His surprising interpretation of "Spider," the "cool, white livered, and coldly satirical villain, took everyone by surprise by its thorough unconventionality," said one observer. "This was no traditional stage villian, but a wholly new contribution to character."[38] Willard's "Spider" became a prototype for the sophisticated antagonists who take a positive fascination in their crimes.

Perhaps the most surprising acting was that of Barrett himself, whose portrayal of the hero Harold Armytage was singled out as exceptional. He exhibited an amount of intensity, said *The Athenaeum*, "of which he hardly seemed capable, bearing the entire weight of the melodrama entirely on his shoulders" as a true star actor.[39] *Lights o' London* was an arduous undertaking, but Barrett did not rely exclusively on muscle for his accomplishments; he brought to bear on his role all he had learned from Miss Heath about sympathy and detail, with the result that Harold became a character, not just a melodramatic cipher. Barrett's acting was "from the heart, but never noisy." He "quickly appreciated all the fine touches" in Sims's writing and helped to give the play the note of tenderness and human interest that made it so popular.[40] "Of such acting as this," observed one critic later, "it was what Goldsmith wrote of Garrick that he was 'natural, simple, affecting' . . . it displays a 'thorough knowledge of the human heart.'"[41]

All this is not to say that *Lights o' London* was merely good conventional spectacle with the addition of some good acting; there was more. The play was designed and cast with a skill seldom seen in a London manager. There was one small staging difficulty, but it was immediately put right. In his haste to get the new play on the boards, Barrett's designer had neglected to remove the border introduced to diminish the size of the proscenium for the smaller settings of the first two plays Barrett presented at the Princess's. On opening night the upstage portion of the larger *Lights o' London* setting could not be seen from the gallery because of this border. After a few moments of yelling from the patrons, Barrett's stage manager quickly raised the border, and the action progressed smoothly from then on. Now the entire audience could see that Barrett had added detailed setting, costumes, and properties to Sims's detailed character-drawing, using real items wherever possible. In itself this practice was not new; Tom Robertson and the Bancrofts had done the same years before at the Prince of Wales.

William Archer had complained that the public taste for such practices was increasing to the point where what was wanted from dramatists was observation, not playwriting. Nevertheless, audiences still thrilled at the sight and use of real objects and locales on the stage. Barrett took the process one step further by introducing the actual costermongers and other inhabitants of the London alleys. Barrett hired these people with their own barrows and items that they were unable to sell during their time on the streets the day of the performance. The supers, furthermore, were not actors, but actual inhabitants of the London slums. "If anything," said one critic,

> it is all too real, too painful, too smeared with the dirt and degradation of London life, where drunkenness, debauchery, and depravity are all shown in their naked hideousness.[42]

All this led Augustin Filon, the French historian of the Victorian stage, to joke that *Lights o' London* was "the only play of the period in which you can really smell the East End."[43] "Zola at Aldgate pump," declared Errol Sherson.[44] A popular label stuck with the play and others like it which followed, the Gospel of Rags, a label both for this kind of play and the superrealistic philosophy of art it espoused.[45]

Barrett staged all this with great technique. The Meiningen troupe from Germany had played in London only a few months before, and their stage work, particularly their crowd scenes, was new to English playgoers. Critics praised their efforts while at the same time lamenting the fact that such directing was absent in London. The lesson of the Meiningen troupe was not lost on Barrett, who imitated their techniques with great facility. The last scene but one, located outside the borough police station, was especially noteworthy in this regard. The substance of the scene was a long fight between Harold and Seth which was witnessed by the entire company onstage. The fight began in a second floor garret (reminiscent of the French melodrama *Two Orphans*), then moved onto the roof of a nearby tenement. As both combatants leaped to the stage floor, the struggle continued with the accompaniment of the crowd until the fight finished with an exhuberant celebration and Seth's capture by the police. "We do not believe, said a reporter, "that anything more effective has been seen in modern times." The play "distances all yet attempted in the manipulation of stage crowds."[46] *Lights o' London* ran for 226 performances.

Barrett had made the move from the Royal Court to the Princess's in a big way. His total expenditures for *Lights o' London* (and for two curtain-raisers that alternately accompanied it, *Turn Him Out* and *A Photographic Fright*) were £32,000, an average of £800 per week for each of the thirty-seven weeks of the run.[47] This was twice the expense of the Royal Court and fully one-third more than the cost of any other London playhouse. Receipts for the play, however, offset expenses by more than £200 per week, leaving a profit for the show of nearly £6,000. Sims received £1,400 for the first London run of his play; eventually he would receive over £14,000 during the thirty-five year record of the play.[48] Everywhere in the production there was evidence of ingenuity, painstaking effort, and liberal and unselfish treatment of actors. Barrett had discovered the style of theatre needed to make the Princess's and his policy there a success. All that remained was refinement, and in an opening night speech, Barrett promised that this would come in the form of increasing attention to the literary quality of his future scripts. Barrett concluded the premiere festivities with a banquet on stage in the manner of Henry Irving's at the Lyceum.

In December 1881, amid the success of his first major Princess's play, Barrett moved his family to their first permanent London home, which *Lights o' London* enabled him to pay off. The Priory was a lovely example of Victorian domestic design. Located at 21 North Bank, St. John's Wood, near Regents Park, it was bordered in the back by the Regents Park Canal— then a charming waterway weaving through scenes reminiscent more of the country than the city. The house was built in the American style, spread out, not with one room on top of the other like most London homes, and was surrounded and isolated by a rose garden. The interior of the home was designed by Owen Jones in the style of William Morris so popular at the time.[49] There was a large studio upstairs where Barrett, who loved to paint, often showed his work to friends, though it is doubtful whether he was ever any more than a gifted amateur. An interesting anecdote occurred in connection with the redecoration of the home which Barrett undertook before moving in. He thought the workmen were doing a wonderful job executing his wishes and generously gave them each a free pass to attend his hit play at the Princess's. They were grateful, but at the end of the redecorating Barrett received their bill . . . with four hours overtime added for seeing the play. Barrett enjoyed the joke and paid the bill.

Meanwhile, Barrett's provincial touring companies were still at work. Number One was out with Henry Arthur Jones's *No Escape*, and Number Two with *The Old Love and the New*. At Leeds this year's special attraction was Henry Neville in *Proof*, while Hull was enjoying William Sydney's company in *The O'Dowd*. As time progressed this simple One and Two arrangement, with no substantial difference between them except their bills, would develop into a more sophisticated practice in which companies were specifically adjusted to different kinds of towns and audiences. Charles Frohman was using this method in the United States; it was only a matter of time before Barrett would recognize its greater efficiency.

Barrett and George R. Sims worked together on the next Princess's play, *The Romany Rye*, a title first used by George Bonow in his 1857 novel. The title is gypsy (Romany) slang for "gypsy gentleman," and the play

4. Architectural drawing of the Princess's Theatre by C. Powers.

capitalized once more on working class themes derived from Sims's journalistic writing, this time with a new appeal. The plot centers around the gypsy Jack Herne, born an English gentleman but wrongfully deprived of his birthright. This structure gave Sims the opportunity to display his keen knowledge of gypsy culture and gave playgoers a unique insight into this mysterious world. And Sims added to it every tawdry detail he couldn't find room for in *Lights o' London*. *The Romany Rye* was written and staged with the same flair as its predecessor, and the dialogue, motivation, and character were far better crafted than traditional melodramas. This time, moreover, Sims included the kind of social criticism he was inclined to add in his journalism. *The Romany Rye* also contained more of the Gospel of Rags elements that had characterized its predecessor. One reporter wrote:

> Take the convict business out of *Great Expectations*, Orlick and the other scoundrels; take Bill Sykes and his companions from *Oliver Twist*; mix them up with a suggestion of the grim trade of Rogue Riderhood, and the Dickensy passages that deal with the River Thames in particular and dead bodies in general; pour into the salad the cream of the famous chapter on beggars in Victor Hugo's *Notre Dame de Paris* and a sufficiency of the oil of Eugene Sue; pepper it with the smart situation of Hawkshaw, the detective, out of *The Ticket-of-Leave Man* and add to it the salt of the old nag, Frochard, in *The Two Orphans*, and even then you will not get an idea of this successful dramatic panorama.[50]

The Romany Rye was such a nightmare of crime, poverty, and violence that it actually frightened the more tender hearts in the audience. "It *is* reality!" wrote Clement Scott.[51]

The Romany Rye opened on 10 June 1882. To those observers who expected the immediate literary advances which they heard Barrett promise, the new play was a "sad dissappointment."[52] Nevertheless, despite the thin plot and the rather bald treatment of crime, there were such demands for higher priced stalls and boxes that neither the theatre nor the libraries could supply them. One reason for this was that Barrett produced the play with the same kind of artistic finish that had been so roundly applauded in the first play. The mechanical effects and scene changes were declared to be "far finer than anything the stage has probably ever seen."[53] In the first act, for example, there were two complete "set scenes" (full stage scenes); there were eight in the entire play. Twenty years before, this kind of managerial extravagance would have been unheard of; even in 1882 it was unusual, especially as a continuous practice. Barrett's acting was praised, proving that his success in the earlier play was not an accident. His leading lady, Miss Eastlake, found herself more up to the effort and managed to portray the gentle and long-suffering Gertie with equal effectiveness from beginning to end, and George Barrett and Walter Speakman were once again praised for their work. E.S. Willard, who had done so well with "Spider," was continuing to be a surprise. His Phillip Roysten was another cold and sophisticated villain and was favorably compared with Henry Irving's portrayal in *The Bells*.[54]

The Romany Rye ran for 138 performances. Operating expenses of nearly £900 per week were evidence of Barrett's generosity with this play, but the results were losses on the order of £1,000. This was easily offset, however, by profits from the touring companies of this play and from *Lights o' London*, which Barrett sent out almost immediately after the opening. Now he was using the more sophisticated A and B touring system; this practice, combined with his customary care in casting and staging, resulted in a healthy financial picture overall. Receipts for the production of *Lights o' London* then on tour in the United States were a record high.[55]

Barrett's provincial playhouses continued to flourish. At Hull Barrett hit upon the idea of a Christmas pantomime on the theme of Robinson Crusoe, who purportedly set sail from the port of Hull. At Leeds Barrett pantomimes were becoming legendary. The 1882 Leeds's pantomime of *Robin Hood* by J. Wilton Jones had a company of fifty actors and sixty supers and dancers. This extravaganza included fifteen scenes by scenic artists William Beverly, Walter Telbin, Walter Hann, Stafford Hall, and others—the best scene painters in London. Barrett was coming into his maturity as a producer and took all this activity in stride. The writers he was collaborating with, however, were afraid that such a large dose of heavy work might affect his health and their financial well-being. Henry Arthur Jones took the occasion to warn Barrett, "Please don't try your health too much," he pleaded jokingly, "for the sake of all the throng of aspiring young dramatists whom you are lifting to fame and fortune."[56]

After *The Romany Rye* the Gospel of Rags had no more artistic appeal for Barrett. He had perfected a particular style of play and in doing so had claimed a place for himself among the best managers and producers in London, but he was not satisfied to rest on present accomplishments. In the past, after each success, he had found a new challenge with fresh risks and hopes. His next step, into a higher level of acting achievement, was to be no exception to this practice.

3

London Management (1882–1886)

Henry Arthur Jones and *The Silver King*

Barrett had two friends at this time who were to become strong influences in the development of his populist melodrama policies. The first was Henry Arthur Jones, whom Barrett had worked with at Leeds and the Royal Court. Jones was a farmer's son with little formal education; his first professional efforts were in business as a salesman, but in 1869 he turned to playwriting. This began a thirty-year literary career during which Jones was to work with many of the leading managers of his day and become a pioneer in the turn of English drama toward social realism. In 1882, however, Jones was virtually unknown except to Barrett and the second person referred to above, Henry Herman. Augustus Moore, Barrett's Royal Court literary advisor, discovered Herman sleeping on a bench in Hyde Park at the time of Modjeska's engagement at the Royal Court. Herman, whose real name was Henri d'Arco, was an eccentric character of Anglo-German royal descent. Moore was fascinated by him and introduced him to Barrett, who hired him when it was discovered that Herman was an inventive man with a flair for theatrical composition, especially for spectacular scenes of cataclysm and catastrophe.

Barrett had remained in close touch with Jones since 1879 in hopes of inducing him to write another play. In the summer of 1881, for example, Barrett had asked Jones to translate a German melodrama for use by one of his road companies. What Barrett was really seeking, however, was a new play that would crystallize all his ideas about the Princess's new dramatic policy. The first two Princess's plays were a good beginning. They were English through and through but still retained too much of the baggage of transpontine melodrama, and their literary merit, though far better than most, was still below what Barrett was wishing for. In a letter which shows his distaste for the Gospel of Rags, Barrett wrote to Jones regarding his hopes for the new play.

The public are pining for a pure English comedy, with a pure story, in which the characters shall be English, with English ideas, and English feelings, honest true men, and tender, loving women, from which plague, pestilence, adultery, fornication, battle, murder, and sudden death shall be banished.

Barrett went on to define how this new melodrama should differ from its predecessors.

The characters must not preach virtue, let them act it, not spout self-denial, but show it. The public taste is depraved no doubt, the more depraved the greater certainty of success for the man who will raise it. This seems paradoxical, but do not the most abandoned women *in their hearts* admire virtue most, the greatest cowards worship bravery?[1]

Jones had been working on this particular dramatic paradox for some time without much success. Though he could write dialogue well, he had little ability for play construction at this time. Barrett then hit upon the idea of Jones collaborating with Henry Herman. Jones had reservations about this, but since Barrett was the only manager who would look at his work at the time, he consented.

Even so, the Jones-Herman partnership was not immediately successful, and Barrett rejected the first two scenarios they presented to him. What he wanted, he told them, was a play in which a man was raised from degradation to respectability and self-esteem. The plot should center around a man who mistakenly believes he murdered someone, an idea Barrett had picked up from a short story entitled *Dead in the Desert* that he had read years before—a sort of *East Lynne* in reverse. Jones combined this idea with his own recent story about the remorse of a man who committed a crime of passion. After working for several months, he and Herman submitted a draft. There was potential in it, Barrett told them, but it was too loosely constructed. "I daresay Herman has told you that we are not quite satisfied with the melodrama," he wrote to Jones. "The story is a strong one, but it wants binding together."[2] Barrett assisted in the building-up of the entire dramatic scheme and insisted that some scenes be rewritten over and over again—an unheard of practice in the construction of melodrama. This melodrama, said one reporter later, "would have stood for a very curious and slipshod bit of stagecraft, and its authors might have been ridiculed for their constructive powers, if he [Barrett] had not come in and pulled it together."[3]

The new play, called *The Silver King*, was essentially a domestic melodrama; there was nothing remaining of the sensational Gospel of Rags in the story. The action centers around the character of Wilfred Denver, a rogue whose only redeeming virtue is his devotion to his family. He is taunted into jealous anger by his wife's former suitor, Geoffrey Ware, and threatens him before witnesses in a public house. Meanwhile, a subplot reveals that thieves led by Captain Skinner are planning to burgle Ware's home that same evening. Later, arriving at Ware's to carry out his earlier threat, Denver is surprised by the thieves and put to sleep with chloroform. When he awakens he discovers Ware's body on the floor before him and, not knowing the man was killed by the thieves, he mistakenly believes himself to be guilty. Escaping London by train, Denver speaks one of the play's memorable lines as he is gripped by guilt over the effects of his action on his family: "Oh, God! Put back thy universe and give me yesterday."—a line, incidently, which almost did not make it into the play because of Barrett's religious scruples. Denver jumps off the train short of his destination, then discovers the next day that the train was wrecked and that the authorities presume him among the dead. Thankful for the reprieve, Denver flees to America. Several years later, Denver, who has in the meantime made a fortune in the Nevada silver mines—hence, the "Silver King"—and has also reformed his dissolute ways, secretly returns home to catch a glimpse of his family. He wants to be assured that they are being well cared for through the agency of his secret contributions to their welfare, but he discovers instead that they are penniless due to the machinations of Captain Skinner. There follows a series of complicated events at the end of which Denver's identity is revealed and the whole story straightened out, enabling Denver to become safely reunited with his family.

What elevated this play above typical melodramas was Denver's uncommon remorse. Denver wanted *heavenly* pardon for his mistakes, not just civil dismissal, and in this way the play struck an important chord in the Victorian public. A popular fad for guilt pervaded late-Victorian society.[4] This was the time of countless tracts praising vegetarianism, damning smoking, and exhorting the public to avoid the dangers of inoculations, for example. It was also the time of Ernest Dowson's popular sex and guilt poetry, notably *Cynara*. In the character of Wilfred Denver the new play was to give to the public a tangible symbol of the guilt it seemed to crave.

The Silver King opened at the Princess's on 16 November 1882, marking "a new era in romantic melodrama."[5] Until this play, few major critics had paid serious attention to Barrett; he was, after all, a relative newcomer to London management and had yet to prove himself worthy of sustained and serious consideration. A few highbrow critics remained put off by the extraordinary success of the play and tended to ignore it because of its melodramatic form, but the majority of reporters and public were entranced. Among the most noteworthy dimensions of the play was the high quality of its literary craftsmanship, prompting Matthew Arnold to be drawn out of playgoing retirement to see the play and praise it. "Instead of giving their audience transpontine diction and sentiments," he wrote for the *Pall Mall Gazette*, "Messrs. Jones and Herman give them literature. . . . In general throughout the piece the sentiments are natural, they have sobriety."[6]

Playwright Bronson Howard was struck by the same literary precision of the play and wrote to Barrett,

> I know very few dramas in which the points necessary to sustain interest and carry on the story are so accurately and strongly emphasized. What particularly struck me throughout was the fact that whenever a point has been duly impressed on the audience no more words are wasted and the play goes on to the next milestone. This, it seems to me, is a rare merit.[7]

Even the American dramatic critic John Rankin Towse, no particular friend of Barrett's, had to admit that with this play Barrett had succeeded. It was a play, Towse wrote, that was "well knit, ingenious, continuously exciting, and full of adroitly calculated suspense." "A really good melodrama," he concluded.[8]

But the average playgoer was unconcerned with the technical details of the play's construction; to him the play was a radical departure from previous melodramas simply because of its high moral sentiments. Denver's frequent references to heavenly forgiveness, together with the singular lack of conventional melodramatic spectacle in the piece, placed *The Silver King* in a much higher artistic key than the ordinary melodrama of the day, wrote Clement Scott. *The Silver King*, he continued,

> must not be confounded with the sensational panoramas which nowadays so often pass for plays. The dialogue of the play is throughout clever and witty, and much of the language is lofty and poetic. Taken altogether *The Silver King* is one of the best plays seen for years and its authors may be congratulated upon the production of a work which will live and bear revival many years hence, a work which is thoroughly honest in purpose, dramatic, pathetic, full of human nature, and withal an original drama of English life, sentiment, and feelings.[9]

George R. Sims agreed, writing to Barrett, "You have done more than any man living to lift melodrama from the depths to which it has fallen."[10]

Given a better script to work with, Barrett could also demonstrate a higher level of directorial ability with this play. *The Silver King* contains five acts and seventeen scenes, of which over half are "set scenes," and the whole complex play was staged with such skill and attention to detail that critics began to speak of Barrett's directing in the exalted terms of art. "The real strength of *The Silver King*," wrote Austin Brereton, "the quality which attracts one to it a second and even a third time, when its mere interest of plot has evaporated, is the care with which the whole canvas . . . is worked over by the artist."[11] Moreover, carrying on the practices he had begun earlier in the two Sims plays, Barrett's work on *The Silver King* extended beyond mere visual spectacle and into artistic work with the entire company of actors. Each role in the large cast was rehearsed and performed with

5. Wilson Barrett as Wilfred Denver in *The Silver King*.

6. *The Silver King*. Princess's Theatre poster.

uncommon patience. Matthew Arnold had nothing but praise for what he termed "the high general level of acting" in the play. He continued:

> Instead of a company with a single powerful and intelligent performer, with two or three middling ones, and with the rest moping and mewing in what was not to be called English, but rather stagese, here was a whole company of actors, able to speak English, playing intelligently, supporting one another effectively.[12]

The light and brisk tone with which Barrett staged the play was another decided contrast to the typical practice of enveloping melodramas in sepulchral gloom. In fact, Henry Irving's well-known attraction for dark stage lighting and plodding rhythm made him recoil at the play's brightness, and he was driven to ask Barrett, "Wasn't that a little light, my boy?" To which Barrett answered, "Well, you see, it's eleven in the morning [in the train station scene]." Irving was not satisfied. "I should have had an eclipse," he said.[13]

Literary quality, high purpose, elaborate and detailed *mise en scene*, directorial skill, and ensemble acting were all dimensions of *The Silver King* which helped to raise it far above the standards of ordinary melodrama, but the emphasis in the play was on the acting, and it was this element that impressed most playgoers. Among the cast of thirty-one, Mary Eastlake, Walter Speakman, and George Barrett were singled out for their fine characterizations, and so was, once again, E.S. Willard. His portrayal of the calculating Captain Skinner, a mature artistic outgrowth of his two previous Gospel of Rags roles, began the tradition of faultlessly elegant stage villains, of which Conan Doyle's Professor Moriarty is a memorable example. Skinner was not a peer or a member of the gentry, but a West End societaire, a perfect representative of the kind of snobbish upper-class person so despised by members of the English working class.

Barrett's portrayal of Wilfred Denver was without doubt the high point of the entire play. His acting was one of those mysterious theatrical events that mark the turning point in an actor's career and place him a level above the majority of his peers. Denver was not just a common melodramatic reprobate; he was a deeply unfortunate man who had experienced life's hardships and was rapidly declining because he had no friend to stop him. He elicited true pity, not just pathos, because Barrett added a genuinely artistic perspective to the role. True, certain highbrow critics complained with exaggerated emphasis about Barrett's self-conscious policy of dignified melodrama. (It was acceptable, apparently, to produce melodrama, but not to advocate it.) The majority of playgoers, however, recognized in Barrett's acting the blend of personality and role that occurs only once in a generation. The playwright Charles Reade wrote, "I really do not see a fault in this gigantic performance."[14] "Rest assured that your impersonation has really thrilled and terrified whoever has seen it," Jones wrote to soften the remarks of some of the critics.[15] "As to your embodiment of the leading character," Bronson Howard declared,

> it seems to me the best protest I know of against that "tea-cup and saucer" school of acting. . . . I appreciate the "strength" of your performance at the striking points of the play, but the heartfelt earnestness you evinced from first to last is what I value most.[16]

Clement Scott was another critic who was impressed by Barrett's truthfulness: "Always human, always pathetic, always strong," he wrote.[17]

It had been some time since an actor had taken such a spirited role and made this kind of hit with it. There were mumblings in the press before the play that the new style of "cup and saucer" (Realistic, new school) drama being introduced was destroying England's classical (old school) acting tradition. E.J. West later referred to this phenomenon as "the disappearance of the old school actor with the concurrent development of the new school non-actor." He concluded by arguing that the dramatic renascence that occurred between the 1870s and the turn of the century was decidedly not one of playwriting genius, but "a floral wreath upon the grave of histrionic genius" by actors such as Irving and Barrett, who were living examples of the best of the past.[18] That contemporaries of Barrett recognized this is evident in the quality and degree of praise they reserved for his personal achievement in *The Silver King*. "At times," Clement Scott wrote, "his acting came little short of genius . . . a revelation . . . as welcome as it was unexpected."[19] "Had Mr. Barrett done nothing else," Austin Brereton wrote, "he would be entitled to be classed with the few really great actors of the century."[20]

Barrett's success as Wilfred Denver remained with him for the rest of his career because all the elements which best embodied his acting style were present in the role. He later revived the play hundreds of times, proving that the play was to be as longlasting as Clement Scott predicted. *The Times* declared that *The Silver King* was "the most successful melodrama ever staged."[21] The play remained popular even long after Barrett's death. It was performed at the Strand in 1914 for a command performance before King George and later was filmed by two different English companies and serialized by a third, each time very successfully. The last noted professional production of the play occurred in the 1940s, over sixty years after its premiere.

The Silver King played at the Princess's for thirty-nine weeks, 234 performances. Its operating expenses were enormous, over £1,100 per week, more than any previous Barrett play; but its receipts of over £1,500 per week left a profit of nearly £10,000.[22] Barrett had already made Sims wealthy; now it was the turn of Jones and Herman, who each made almost £3,000 in royalties for the initial London run of the play alone. Jones, for one, had suffered intense emotional strain during the preparation and rehearsals, during which time there was only £300 between him and poverty. After opening night, when he saw how successful the play was going to be, he felt much better, saying, "This play is going to make things easy for me."[23] Jones eventually accumulated over £18,000 in royalties for the play.

With the production of this play Wilson Barrett became at once a major London actor-manager. He had fulfilled his ambition of managing Charles Kean's playhouse and returning it to its former glory. *The Silver King* placed the popular theatre on the high level he and so many others had been waiting for, and the Princess's was now well supported because it had its audience back. Moreover, the audiences were not just trendy sophisticates, but a democratic representation of all English tastes. Even Matthew Arnold noticed it. "The Princess's," he observed, "is a representative public furnished from all classes, and showing that English society at large has now taken to the theatre."[24] This demonstrated that Barrett had achieved his third wish as well, to produce wholesome plays for wholesome amusement for an audience that was representative of English attitudes and tastes.

The play attracted managerial enquiries from abroad. Henry Jack received Australian rights, and U.S. approval went to Joseph Brooks and James Dickson. Earlier Barrett had sent out a few provincial tours of his plays, and the results had been very encouraging. In 1883 Barrett had three of his own companies on tour with *Lights o' London*, *The Romany Rye*, and *The Silver King* and had given permission for other designated companies to play these same hits. Barrett received from these about £1,500 each plus ten percent of gross receipts; his authors received a percentage of this based upon a sliding scale agreement. Tours brought in anywhere from £600 to £6,000 in royalties. Most of the money was made from *The Silver King*, which accumulated over £6,000 in profits for one year's tours. Total profits from all tours and royalties for Barrett in 1883-1884 amounted to nearly £18,000.[25]

Immense popularity now attended Barrett. Popular burlesques were staged to take advantage of the success of the new play, among them *The Silver Guilt*, by Warren St. Leger, at The Strand and *The German Silvery King*, by Walter Burnot, at the Elephant and Castle. There were also burlesques of *Lights o' London* and *The Romany Rye*. Moreover, thanks to the tours, Barrett's plays were popular in the provinces, where their wholesome sentiments enabled them to be seen by classes of people not usually attracted to the theatre. The characterizations created by E.S. Willard were especially popular there; Spider from *Lights o' London* even became a popular fad. Young boys were heard imitating Spider's secret whistle, an unusual run of notes invented by Willard and used as a signal to his criminal companions in the play. Barrett would have been exceptional had some of this popularity not gone to his head; vanity was the other side of ambition in his case. The role of Wilfred Denver so impressed him, and he became so closely identified with it in picture posters seen all over the country, that he took on something of the character's traits. He began to wear in private life the frock coat, slouch hat, and four-in-hand that Denver wore when he returned from Nevada a rich man.

Classic-Revival Melodrama

In March of 1883, after 100 performances of *The Silver King*, Barrett gave a speech on stage in which he said he hoped to use the profits from his first three Princess's hits to broaden his vision both as manager and actor.[26] He rededicated himself and his company to the task of elevating melodrama into the regions of "romance and poetry." Barrett already had a play in preparation that would introduce this second, higher phase of his management policy, and Henry Herman was the inspirational source. Early in 1883 Herman, who was always attracted to spectacular stage violence, fabricated an ingenious working model of a classical earthquake scene for the Princess's stage. He had been adjusting it for several months, and after he got it to work successfully both he and Barrett were encouraged to write a play for it. *The Last Days of Pompeii* was naturally the immediate thought, but Barrett decided to add to that story the parable of the wandering Jew, together with the repentance-pardon-peace plot development of *The Silver King*. The new play was to be another guilt drama. Herman was assigned the task of constructing a scenario, and, since Herman was not much of a writer, the dialogue was contracted to William Gorman Wills, who Barrett knew had a Romantic interest in the past. Wills was given £800 in installments in return for a finished play to be ready no later than six months after the signing of the agreement in July. The plot was to be polished by Herman and the whole written in conjunction with Barrett's wishes.[27]

This collaboration proved to be less troublesome than the previous one. Wills and Herman were two of a kind—both eccentric, impetuous, and used to working by flashes of inspiration rather than by careful method, as was Jones's way. "When I have knocked the plot out," boasted Herman, "the rest will be child's play comparatively."[28] There followed an intense, rapid, and often chaotic exchange of letters among the principals. Herman fed so many scraps of plot to Wills with his breakfast each morning that Wills often despaired of filling in all the prescribed action with appropriate dialogue. They began by writing a prologue to instruct the audience in the manners and habits of the play's locale and period. Barrett at first vetoed this, then approved it. Acts I and II progressed quickly, but the third act containing several "set scenes" and the earthquake was problematic. Herman declared it would be "bursting with scenery . . . a regular Princess's act,"[29] but Barrett expressed a manager's concern over the practical problems involved.

Herman assured him that "there will be very little or no noise of setting during the act." "But," he warned, "the interval before the act I'm afraid will be long."[30] Finally, Act III was complete. "It is very strong and swift," wrote the two authors, "quite an *Arrah na Pogue* or *Shaughraun* excitement about it."[31] The story was becoming too somber, however, and Barrett requested some humor to relieve what was proving to be a kind of unrelenting grimness in the play similar to that of Wills's *Juana*. Moreover, Barrett tried to make sure that proper sympathy for the hero was maintained throughout. The character of the hero was to be afflicted with a terrible curse, and Barrett sensed that because of this the sympathy for Claudian was tenuous. It would have been disastrous for the play if the audience were to lose pity for the hero in the last act. The new play, entitled *Claudian*, was complete in six weeks.

Ever since *Lights o' London*, Barrett's productions had been noted for their elaborate and spectacular scenery. In a play like this one, where the accoutrements of the past were to be be so important, it was imperative that the scenery be tastefully and accurately rendered. For this reason Barrett turned to a former colleague, E.W. Godwin, a close friend of Wills's who had helped with the "archeology" of *Juana* at the Royal Court. Godwin was passionately in love with the past. He had acted as historical consultant at the Prince of Wales under the Bancrofts and earlier worked in the same capacity with Phelps and Coleman at the Queen's Theatre. Though he was an amateur as far as the theatre was concerned, he had written at length on the archeology of Shakespeare's plays, a subject in which he was intensely interested. Godwin was a pioneer in the use of diagonal settings at a time when most other designers used a straightforward, easily shifted arrangement of parallel flats and drops. Godwin thought of scenery in emotional terms; he sought to evoke moods through arrangements of color, mass, and light as abstracted from the utilitarian nature of architecture.[32] He was also a pompous autocrat who demanded complete control over every aspect of his work. But this was more than mere ego, for he sought unification of all the arts of the stage and recognized that a single authority was necessary if this was to occur. His decision to work with the Bancrofts was based partly upon his understanding that their company worked together toward a unified conception and that his contributions would be considered important parts of the final production, not just adjunct decoration, as was the case in most other managements. Godwin learned during *Juana* that Barrett had respect for artistic unity in his productions, and he received from Barrett the same kind of artistic dedication in *Claudian*.

Oddly enough, Godwin contributed to Barrett's expenses for the Princess's at this time in a way totally unconnected with his designs for *Claudian*. He had for some time been concerned with the terrible backstage conditions in English playhouses. He and his architectural partner had performed several theatrical renovations and were appalled at the state of disrepair of many London theatres, including major playhouses. They jointly published a series of articles revealing their findings and stating recommendations for overcoming the problems. "Some common sense people suggested that it might be just as well," they wrote in one article,

> before we cried upon [the actors'] indecencies to look to their dwellings and give them the chance of living a little better than a pig, perhaps, though not as good as a horse. With equal reason we may suggest an enquiring into arrangement and construction of that miserable looking portion of the theatre which lies behind the footlights.[33]

The series of articles was so controversial that Parliament debated the issue and formed a committee to study theatre safety and the installation of new electric lighting in many playhouses. Late in 1883 the committee sent their recommendations to Parliament, which ordered local councils to undertake renovation injunctions against those playhouses failing to meet certain minimum safety standards.

No manager was more concerned about safety than Barrett; he proved it by his work at the Leeds Grand and elsewhere. Moreover, the Princess's had been renovated by Gooch in the late summer of 1880. Despite this it was among the theatres which did not meet the new standards. In fact, it may have been precisely these difficulties that Barrett was concerned about when he expressed his dissatisfaction with Gooch's plans at the time of the latest rebuilding. In any case, in 1884 Barrett was presented with an injunction. The Metropolitan Board of Works ordered that certain alterations be made immediately, the total cost of which must have been about £3,000.[34] Barrett could absorb these expenses, but other managers were not so fortunate. Soon a representative group of London theatrical leaders led by Barrett and Henry Irving arranged a meeting with the Home Office to oppose granting any more power in the supervision of theatres to the present Board of Works. Continued demands for extensive renovations would have severely hampered the financial health of the London theatre that season. Renovations at the Princess's occurred during the late summer and fall of 1883 while *Claudian* was being prepared.

Claudian is set in Byzantium 360 A.D. and deals with a rich sensualist who falls under a curse which consigns him to endless life, perpetual youth, and misery: his friendship and love are doomed to bring unhappiness to anyone who possesses them. The play contains a prologue and four acts in nine scenes, and among the locales are slave markets, ancient ruins, peasant farms, the splendid city of Charydos in Bithyria, and Claudian's gorgeous palace. Elaborate music for the play was composed by Theodore Jones, and Godwin's scenic ideas were expensively executed by Barrett's chief scene painter, Walter Hann. The play was originally intended to open at the end of

November; the date was pushed back until 6 December, however, due to understandable difficulties with the scenery.

Playgoers were impressed by the spectacle in *Claudian*. Godwin intended the scenery to make its own artistic statement and he succeeded, for critics thought the settings and costumes were splendid. "It is superbly mounted," said the reporter for *The Fortnightly Review*; "in certain scenes Realism is shown at its best—picturesque and not overaccentuated."[35] Moreover, the attention of certain artists testified that Barrett had struck just the right tone of "romance and poetry" in this classic-revival play. Oscar Wilde was charmed by it. "Mr. E.W. Godwin," he wrote,

> showed us the life of Byzantium in the fourth century, not by a dreary lecture and set of grinning casts, not by a novel which requires a glossary to explain it, but by the visible presentation before us of all the glory of that great town. . . . It was . . . a scene not merely prefect in its picturesqueness, but absolutely dramatic also, getting rid of the necessity for tedious descriptions, and showing . . . the whole nature and life of the times.[36]

John Ruskin was eqully impressed. In a detailed letter to Barrett he wrote,

> You know perfectly well, as all great artists do, that the [play] is beautiful, and that you do it perfectly. I regret the extreme terror [of the earthquake scene], but the admirable doing of what you intended doing, and the faithful co-operation of all your combination, and the exquisite scenery, gave me not only delight at the time, but were a possession in memory of great value.[37]

Ruskin encouraged Barrett to produce a series of classic-revival plays as educational experiences for English audiences. "And," he concluded, "with scene painting like that the Princess's might do more for art teaching than all the galleries and professors in Christendom—only you needn't do all the grapes in gold, always." A visiting German actor-manager who saw *Claudian* declared there were no scenic artists in Germany equal to the task.[38]

Ruskin's passing reference to the gold grapes was the key to some of the hostile criticism of the scenery. With characteristic pride in their accomplishments, Godwin and Barrett published a pamphlet describing the elaborate measures carried out to insure the historical accuracy of their work on the play. All this was a little too bookish for some, including the prestigious *Times*, which wrote,

> What has been done has been to collate authorities bearing on the period from which it would seem that Byzantine life in the fourth and fifth centuries was distinguished for gorgeous display. . . . The . . . play is accordingly somewhat lavish in colour and ornament—barbaric rather than classicial.[39]

Wilde, in turn, defended the scenery. "Only the foolish called it pedantry," he scolded, "only those who would neither look nor listen spoke of the passion of the play being killed by its paint."[40] All the same, some reviewers still could not help laughing at the desperate earnestness of the entire effort.

There were few, however, who laughed during the climax of the play, which contained one of the most frightening earthquake scenes ever seen on the English stage. H. Barton Baker, who saw a later production in which the effects were simplified due to the demands of touring, testified that there was still ample power in the scene. The setting, he wrote,

> reveals the gardens, the porticoed palaces steeped in the soft Italian [sic] moonlight, the groups of classic statues, the subdued music, the voluptuous dancing figures, the oppressive hush of the hot summer's night. Then all of a moment blank darkness, a vivid flash of lightning, a crash of thunder, the roll and rumble that shakes the theatre to its foundation; a few moments' deathlike silence, and the moonlight steals over the stage again and shows, where late were beautiful gardens and marble palaces, a chaotic ruin of broken walls and pillars. It was really terrifying.[41]

This earthquake was a very complex scene to carry off well, and one time a sixty-pound decorative lamp fell and clipped Barrett on the shoulder, knocking him to the floor. Most of the time, however, the scene played perfectly. It was, in fact, just one of many examples of the kind of elaborate staging Barrett was coming to be known for in London. *Claudian* also showed Barrett's increasing skill as a talented manipulator of crowd scenes. The actress Helen Faucit was especially impressed with this. "The grouping struck me as particularly able and artistic," she wrote in a letter to Barrett.

> So much to appear the effort of accident, which of course it always should. For the scene in Claudian's house this was particularly the case. The figures stood well out, they were not too crowded, and they were dispersed with the artistic knowledge which helps to make a fine picture. But of course the same might be said of all the scenes.[42]

The one glaring fault in the play was its construction, which showed evidence of Wills's propensity for looseness. *Claudian* started out strongly; the tension in the prologue was so great that the audience, who sat through it "with breath held," sighed in unison at the release of tension when the scene ended.[43] But the play's structure became more diffuse as the story unfolded, mostly due to the static nature of the dramatic idea itself. Some important plot developments, moreover, were not sufficiently understood by the audience, another fault of the flat story line. William Winter observed in a later production that following the powerful prologue the character of Claudian was able only to "exist," not to act. "He suffers," said Winter, he endures, he is acted upon, he is the cause of action in others, but he no longer stands forth conspicuous as the active agent of all that is done. There is either poverty of invention or inadvertence of judgement in allowing the hero of a play to do the same thing over and over again.[44]

Evidently Barrett's earlier concern over sympathy for Claudian was well taken. Wills's dialogue also aroused some criticism. Some reporters believed that it was best in the mournful passages but otherwise was often stilted, overstated, and overburdened with imagery. Nor was Barrett ever completely able to surmount Wills's sombreness, and the few humorous incidents that did make their way into the play only served to emphasize the dark tone because of their incomplete connection with the story.

The cast of *Claudian* was somewhat smaller than those of Barrett's first three Princess's plays, and the acting of the company was not on the whole as good as before. E.S. Willard, for example, was incapable of sustaining the power needed for a historical characterization. Mary Eastlake had the same problem. The acting of Thariogalus by Charles Hudson created an unwanted controversy. Hudson, a former member of Irving's company at the Lyceum, had evidently picked up some of his mentor's mannerisms. Irving's admirers in the audience interpreted this to be an unflattering imitation of their idol and hooted at Hudson each time he came on stage. Finally the matter was put to rest in a series of letters to the theatrical press in which Hudson and Barrett disavowed any intention of satirizing Irving. It was a small incident, but important because it revealed the hypersensitive nature of Irving's admirers and foretold in a vivid way future trouble for Barrett.

But if his company members received more than their share of criticism, Barrett, on the other hand, was praised. Most playgoers simply ignored the faults in the play's construction and concentrated on him. It was the first time since Mercutio that they saw him in a period role and many were pleased. "At last," wrote Clement Scott, "we get a part of intense importance, played with all the advantages that an actor should have—voice, presence, melodious utterance, and personal charm."[45] Barrett's grace in the role reminded Helen Faucit of classical statues she had seen. Furthermore, as Claudian, Barrett demonstrated the mysterious magnitude of personality that makes a star. William Winter recognized that despite the faults of the piece, Barrett's acting was the key to its success. He wrote,

In order to make the performance of Claudian noble, the actor must show, by the use of transparency in his art, that the nature of Claudian is inherently grand; that his life has been a dreadful outrage upon himself, as well as an impious and awful defiance of his Maker, and that his soul is worth the tremendous cost that must be paid for saving it. . . .

Wilson Barrett as Claudian conveyed that essential meaning of the part, with subtle intuition and affluent artistic felicity. To the eye, the ear, the imagination there was something in his presence, his voice, and his fine reserve that showed this ideal to be in full possession of him; not so much executive ability as spiritual significance.[46]

To some this star quality made Barrett a threat to Irving's dominance of the English stage, and they responded by refusing to recognize any merit in Barrett's acting at all. But just as Wilde defended the setting and staging, others defended Barrett's acting. Clement Scott said,

Claudian was not written with the idea of pleasing the doubtless excellent people who sneer at everything that soars above a commonplace intelligence. Such folk may be converted by and by when they have ceased to make broad their phylacteries like their ancestors the Pharisees. . . . They hate imaginative work, and they say so. They state in print that *Claudian* makes them laugh and only appeals to their sense of the ludicrous; so why should they not pour out the vials of their little wrath on the misguided individuals who see in such plays as those a great source of delight and pleasure?[47]

This, prefaced by the unuusal reaction to Charles Hudson's innocent actions, was the beginning of a reaction against Barrett's popularity that eventually damaged his career more seriously. As yet, however, the feeling against Barrett's populist policies was still limited in its effects, and *Claudian* was recognized by most playgoers as an appropriate continuation of Barrett's policies, a move away from tawdry, cheaply prepared melodrama. "*Claudian* lifts us into a different atmosphere than common-day melodrama," wrote the reporter for *The Illustrated London News*; "It has a loftier aim."[48] The *Fortnightly Review* agreed, saying, "The play is wholesome, of good tendency, and the public . . . are content to be led to the appreciation of better things."[49] Barrett, critics continued, was "a reformer with dauntless courage," and they pleaded that his work demanded public attention—"and strong public attention."[50] Winter also joined in praising Barrett's aims with the play. "The scheme is visionary," he said,

but it is to be viewed with requisite and fair allowance, and it may justly claim to be accepted not for its structure, tested by the prosaic standard of fact, but for its lofty and beautiful meaning, when judged as a poem.[51]

Claudian turned out to be the successful step into the region of "romance and poetry" that Barrett promised.

In February *Claudian* joined the ranks of Barrett's productions already on tour, bringing the number of Princess's plays on the road in 1883 to nine. Six were Barrett's own fit-up companies; three were arrangements with various American managers. Leeds and Hull continued to be more profitable each year. The London production of *Claudian*, however, did not make money. Barrett was spending over £1,200 per week on the show, a total of £47,800 for the entire run of thirty-nine weeks. In November Wills sold

Barrett his full interest in the play so that Barrett would have no royalties to pay, but average receipts of only £1,000 per week meant that *Claudian* lost nearly £6,500.[52] What was worse, in the provinces the play did not have Barrett's acting to make up for its weak structure; the tour lost over £500 in only six months. A combined loss of £7,000 was, of course, a considerable blow to the Princess's capital, but in itself did not cause immediate problems because profits from eight other tours remained good. American rights alone brought in almost £5,000, while provincial receipts for other Princess's companies in the provinces amounted to over £14,000.[53]

Barrett still could have gone on safely if another even more disastrous loss had not occurred at about the same time. In 1883, during the success of *The Silver King*, Barrett had invested £15,000 with his broker in Leeds. In mid-1883 the broker was missing; the affairs he controlled were so complex that the specific nature of the difficulty, if any, was not known immediately. By the end of the year, however, it was clear that Barrett had lost every penny. Now his losses amounted to nearly £27,000. This, combined with certain unforeseen events, would eventually prove fatal to the Princess's company.

Nevertheless, he had no immediate plans to close the theatre. He had made good profits in the last three years, and there was no reason to believe he would not continue to do so. Barrett's publicity campaign for *Claudian* remained as strong as ever; London continued to be besieged with posters picturing Barrett in one of Claudian's characteristic poses, stating "Wilson Barrett *is* Claudian." Burlesques of the play were staged, the most popular of which was F.C. Burnand's *Paw Claudian, or The Roman Way* at Toole's. In the burlesque the actor playing the lead was cursed to play the role of Claudian forever. J.L. Toole, who was a master mimic, called special attention to a dress habit that Barrett initiated with the play and that continued to be used by him in later classic-revival pieces: a bare chest. Actually, very little of Barrett's chest was revealed, but there was no denying that his muscular physique was an important part of his success as an actor. One story was circulated about two galleryites who were startled when they saw a poster of Barrett in his decolleté armor. "Eh," said one to the other, "I knew 'er when she were Connie Gilchrist."[54] This was all harmless joking that helped publicity for Barrett and the play. Appropriately enough, Barrett even had a marble bust made of himself as Claudian and presented it to a journalist friend.

Around this time Jones and Herman made a gift of a new short play, *Chatterton*, which they had secretly written for Barrett as a curtain-raiser for *Claudian*. *Chatterton* was "not a drama in the ordinary sense of the word," Barrett's friend Lord Lytton wrote, "but a dramatic presentation of character—the artistic development of one strong situation strongly conceived." Lytton also commented on the writing. "I think it by far the best piece of genuine dramatic *literature* I have yet seen upon the contemporary stage. . . . I feel strongly interested in its fortunes."[55] The story contained several tearful incidents, and the dialogue contained some carefully written and very moving speeches. One speech, Chatterton's tribute to poetry, Barrett performed especially well and became a trademark for him. *Chatterton* opened on 22 May 1884, and reporters thought the play deserved some praise because it would lead audiences "to think and use their brain and exercise their imagination."[56]

With losses mounting, Barrett was desperately looking for a big new play. His first inclination was to return to the successful partnership of Jones and Herman. Herman was already a member of the permanent staff of the Princess's; now Barrett presented the same opportunity to Jones, offering to make him playwright-in-residence. Barrett, of course, insisted that Princess's plays were both popular and artistic; Jones, however, would accept the invitation only if he could write on his own terms, meaning emphasis on the literary. "I will not disguise from you," Jones wrote to Barrett in March of 1883,

> that I think a large popular theatre like the Princess's is in some respects more difficult to fit, not with a successful play, but with a successful play that shall also be a real work of art, than a smaller theatre where it is only necessary to attract a small audience night by night.[57]

Jones's next plays, in fact, were not written for the Princess's. In 1884 he wrote *Saints and Sinners* for the Vaudeville and *Breaking a Butterfly* (an adaptation of Ibsen's play *A Doll's House*) with Herman for the Prince's. Jones was later to return to write for Barrett, but at the moment he wanted to get away from big melodrama and concentrate on social realism. In the meantime, Barrett received from Jones and Herman rights for a play called *The Golden Faith*, which they had written after *The Silver King*, but he never produced it.

Hamlet

Henry Irving had assumed management of the Lyceum in 1878. As was the case with Barrett at the Princess's, literary melodrama was the staple dramatic fare at the Lyceum, with memorable presentations of *Two Roses*, Tennyson's *The Cup*, *The Corsican Brothers*, and *The Lady of Lyons*, among others. But however often and successfully Irving produced such melodramas, it was nevertheless true that he maintained among the public the reputation of a Shakespearean actor. Critics agreed that this reputation was certainly not built on his acting as Benedick in *Much Ado About Nothing* or as Romeo, both done in 1882. Irving was not an effective *bon vivant* or stage lover; his mannerisms were too mysterious and eccentric. Perhaps it was built on the impression he made as Hamlet or as Shylock in his 1879 adaptation of *The Merchant of Venice*. Or, as some had observed, it may have been the result of careful cultivation of his public image through effective, occasionally even self-serving, manipulation of the theatrical press. But whatever the real cause, by 1883 Irving was considered to be the preeminent English theatre artist of his time. His next move, a logical one under these circumstances, was to give his London audiences a short time away from him to avoid the possibility of overexposure and to attempt to broaden his reputation on an international scale. He accomplished both of these goals by undertaking in the 1883 season his first American tour.

Barrett quickly exploited Irving's decision. It would have been too self-consciously competitive for him to attempt to play Shakespeare while Henry Irving was in town; but now that Irving was away in the United States, Barrett felt the time was right to produce *Hamlet*, a play which had been on his mind ever since he saw Charles Kean's production at the Princess's in the 1860s. This was a controversial decision. Barrett was acting during a time when every new Shakespearean portrayal was scrutinized to an extraordinary degree by a very stage-conscious public. Besides, Hamlet would draw attention no matter who played it. Henry Herman was among the first to warn Barrett of the consequences if he should fail. There were also warnings in *The Era* stressing the fact that the Princess's was a melodrama theatre and not a place for Shakespeare. Some reporters were hopeful, however. Clement Scott thought that undertaking *Hamlet* would be "the best thing that Wilson Barrett could possibly do, not only for his popularity, which is personal to himself, but for his influence, which is everything for the playgoer."[58] There was probably no personal battle between Irving and Barrett at this time, but to each actor's admirers the possibility of such a clash was real, especially since the styles of the actors were utterly different. George Bernard Shaw reported that Irving was "afraid" of Barrett; perhaps Barrett's decision to undertake Shakespeare was one of the reasons behind Irving's concern.[59]

Barrett opened his surprising and unconventional production on 16 October 1884.[60] Except for the mediocre performance at the Princess's by the aging Edwin Booth in 1880, Barrett's was the only new *Hamlet* to be seen in London since Henry Irving's at the Lyceum ten years before. Prior to Irving there was Fechter, an unconventional Prince, sensitive, pathetic, graceful, and natural. Miss Heath had acted with Fechter in other plays and may have informed her husband of certain elements of Fechter's performance. And before him there was Charles Kean, one of Barrett's favorites, whose pervading melancholy in the role made him almost too sentimental. Edwin Booth was a very great actor, full of fine scholarly intelligence and mature execution, but he failed in London as Hamlet because he displayed too much

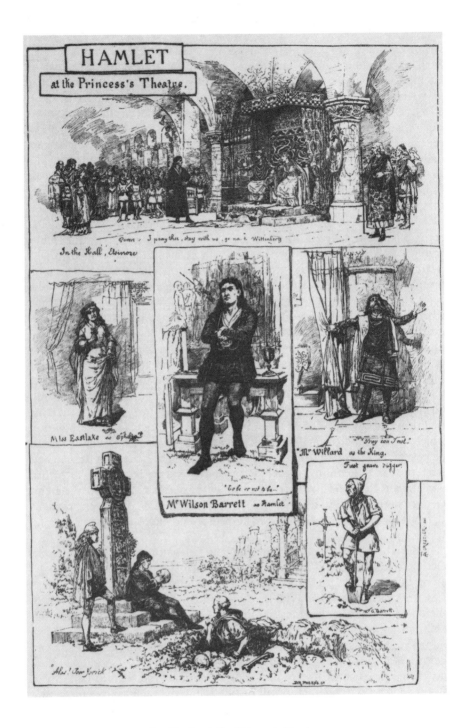

7. *Hamlet* at the Princess's Theatre.

PRINCESS'S
THEATRE.

Lessee and Manager - Mr WILSON BARRETT

7.45 EVERY EVENING 7.45

SHAKESPEARE'S TRAGEDY OF

HAMLET

The Archæology of the Play by Mr E. W. GODWIN, F.S.A.
The Scenery by Messrs W. R. BEVERLEY, W. L. TELBIN, STAFFORD HALL & WALTER HANN.
The New Music by Mr. EDWARD JONES.

Produced under the Sole Direction of Mr. WILSON BARRETT.

Hamlet	Mr WILSON BARRETT
Ophelia	Miss EASTLAKE
Claudius (KING OF DENMARK)	Mr E. S. WILLARD
Ghost of Hamlet's Father	Mr JOHN DEWHURST
Polonius	Mr CLIFFORD COOPER
Horatio	Mr J. R. CRAUFORD
Laertes	Mr FRANK COOPER
1st Actor	Mr WALTER SPEAKMAN
2nd Actor	Mr WILLIAMSON
Rosencrantz	Mr G. R. FOSS
Guildensterne	Mr C. FULTON
Osric	Mr NEVILLE DOONE
Marcellus	Mr H. EVANS
Bernardo	Mr W. A. ELLIOTT
Francesco	Mr H. DE SOLLA
1st Gravedigger	Mr GEORGE BARRETT
2nd do.	Mr H. BERNAGE
Priest	Mr M. CLEARY
Messenger	Mr H. BESLEY
Sailor	Mr LENNOX
Gertrude (QUEEN OF DENMARK)	Miss MARGARET LEIGHTON
Player Queen	Miss MARY DICKENS

Lords, Ladies, Soldiers, Players, Sailors, and Attendants.

DOORS OPEN AT 7.15. BOX-OFFICE 9.30 TILL 5 DAILY.

PRICES OF ADMISSION :—Private Boxes, 1 to 9 Guineas. Stalls, 10s. Dress Circle, 6s.
Upper Boxes, 3s. Pit, 2s. Amphitheatre, 1s. 6d. Gallery, 1s.

BUSINESS MANAGER - - Mr J. H. COBBE

Musical Director, Mr EDWARD JONES. Assistant Stage Manager Mr B. BULWER
Acting Manager ... ... Mr C. KNOX FURTADO.

All Applications respecting the Bills to be made to THE MANAGER.
[WALTER SMITH, Printer, High Street Bloomsbury.

8. *Hamlet.* Princess's Theatre poster.

old school technique. Irving, on the other hand, was considered to be the Hamlet of the age. His Prince was a pale, poetic, despairing man, and most playgoers felt this was the perfect embodiment of all that Hamlet was intended by Shakespeare to be. But none of these characterizations was the model for Barrett, who returned instead to the first folio and quarto, introducing a new version of the play that included many innovations. He discarded the traditional act divisions in favor of new ones that clarified the action. He also allowed the neglected roles of Laertes and Claudius to blossom into full-grown acting parts by restoring many deleted lines of their dialogue. Equally important, with Godwin's help, the classic-revival scenic style was continued at the Princess's. Barrett even agreed to pay for a trip to Elsinore, where Godwin and his staff gathered detailed information about the period of the story. Significant as all these elements were, they were eclipsed in importance by Barrett's original conception of the Prince. He introduced to London playgoers a very young Hamlet, an energetic hero capable of addressing challenges forcefully and free from ambiguous Romantic yearnings. The revenge motif, so long subservient in theatrical tradition to poetry, was restored to a prominent place in the play.

One further dimension of Barrett's interpretation of the role that appealed to audiences was his unique approach to the acting. The roots of English realistic acting tradition lay with the "gentlemanly melodramas," especially those performed by Charles Kean. These plays were relatively new to the English stage in Kean's day, so no formal acting tradition existed for them as it had for Shakespeare and other classics, and they could therefore be approached more prosaically than the traditional classical style. Miss Heath was a specialist in this manner of acting, probably learned while acting in Kean's company at the Princess's. Barrett himself excelled at this kind of melodramatic acting, and it seems likely that he was attempting to carry on the traditions of Kean and Fechter by adapting the style of his acting in *Hamlet* to that of middle-class melodrama. Barrett's approach was exemplified in his manner of speaking, particularly in the soliloquies. Those critics unable to perceive the style called it spiritless and unpoetic, that is, untraditional. They complained that Barrett's delivery "jarred the ears of Shakespeare lovers."[61] On the other hand, a few reporters recognized that he was doing something different and reviewed the production more disinterestedly. The critic of *The Illustrated London News*, for example, observed that "the magnificent speeches [he] delivers easily, gracefully, and, as it were, incidentally."[62] Barrett's speaking style was actually an extension of his approach to the acting of the entire play, which was easy and natural. Representative illustrations of this occurred during "To be or not to be . . .," which Barrett delivered leaning untraditionally against a table, and during Hamlet's philosophical discourse with the gravedigger, which Barrett spoke reclining on the stone steps of a large cross. The critic for *The Nation* commented that Barrett "ventured far more freely than his predecessors upon the use of the familiar style; he is more of a man like ourselves than an incarnate psychological problem."[63] Playwright Bronson Howard perceived the same thing and wrote in a letter to Barrett: "For the first time in my life I felt last night that Hamlet was one of us—a real, breathing and feeling human being—not a poetic-philosohical myth."[64]

Yet for some influential observers, a production of *Hamlet* with this kind of human sympathy in the leading role was too popular and coarse; this, in effect, was the direction taken by much of the criticism leveled against the play. Despite the warm reception of the interpretation in many quarters, sophisticated commentators generally disliked it. *The Era* missed the old-fashioned declamatory style of acting. Barrett, the reviewer said, "puts away the poetic side of the character [and] ignores the reflective, melancholy, philosophical prince."[65] *The World* complained that Barrett's production demonstrated only "patient intelligence, conditioned by commonplace personality."[66] *The Saturday Review* picked up on the same theme, and the vituperative tone of its criticism suggests that there might have been motives here beyond objective dramatic criticism.

> [Barrett's] Hamlet is a highly respectable and serious person, trying to look younger than his age and taking himself with the solemnity of a perfect householder. He is touched with the vestryman; he has notes of the Churchwarden. He is not stately, but pompous; not dignified, but respectable; not melancholy, but dull; not gentlemanly, but decorous; with the passion, the invention, the imagination, the petty fogging ingenuity, of the complete Philistine, and withal, the distinction of being absolutely, irremediably commonplace.[67]

Edwin Booth blamed his own recent failure at the same theatre on his unwillingness to reproduce Irving's fashionably melancholy interpretation. "I don't care to waste my efforts on Londoners," he growled when he returned to America; "*fashion* alone secures success there and nothing could make me fashionable."[68] Booth's lesson was not lost on Barrett, who knew that the impact of Irving's interpretation would make it hard to see the part in any other way. "The playgoer forms his conception of a character upon that of the first actor he sees attempt to play it," he lamented. "Most playgoers are not grateful to the man who wantonly disturbs [their preconceptions]. Any actor who does so," he concluded, "places himself at an enormous disadvantage."[69] Barrett set about creating a production that would attempt to reduce this disadvantage as much as possible. He prepared *Hamlet* and executed it with an attention to detail unmatched even by his own previous productions and hoped that his interpretation would be imaginative enough to satisfy sophisticated tastes, warm enough to please the masses. But he did his work well, and the result was too imaginative and too popular for its own good.

Godwin's scenery, heretofore one of the Princess's genuine claims to fame, and even in *Hamlet* widely praised by the majority, was not saved from antagonistic criticism. *The Stage* regretted that "picturesque effect [had] been sacrificed in order to obtain absolute [archeological] correctness."[70] This was in agreement with a few others who wished that the nineteenth-century scenic tradition had remained intact. *The Era* declared that Barrett's adventure into antiquity was "ugly" and "grotesque" and that the costumes and scenery completely destroyed the play's intimate poetry.[71]

Actually, there is more to be gained from an understanding of the production's implications than from analyzing the specifics of the performance, imaginative as they may have been. Perhaps the main characteristic of the interpretation was that Barrett abandoned tradition, took up the play new, and settled scores of perplexing questions for himself with intelligence and insight. Almost all of his ideas were good, and what straining aftereffect there was may be said to have come from his desire not to be a slave of tradition. As Charlotte Porter declared in *Shakespeariana*, his *Hamlet* was "the boldest and most triumphantly successful" that had been seen for many years in London.[72] *The Times* observed that Barrett had taken a tragedy which to many had become stilted, artificial, and even dowdy on stage, and transformed it into "an interesting panorama, full of colour, movement, and human nature."[73] The result was that unlike other *Hamlet*s rooted in tradition and, in effect, isolated from the world, Barrett's production had about it some of the atmosphere of change taking place in the theatre of the day. According to Clement Scott, Barrett's interpretation was the kind for "which the taste of the day was pining."[74] In short, Barrett's *Hamlet* was the perfection of the popular and artistic policy for which he had been searching. "For a season," declared George C. Odell, "it seemed as if a new tragic actor had arisen and a new force had been brought into the dying places of the drama."[75]

Hamlet played at the Princess's from 16 October 1884 to 21 February 1885, a total of 110 performances. Unfortunately, the extraordinarily high production costs, coupled with Barrett's very understandable desire to extend the run beyond the magic 100 nights, resulted in losses of nearly £5,000. Weekly expenses of £1,200 were several hundred pounds more than *Lights o' London* or *The Silver King*, and average weekly receipts were significantly below Princess's standards.[76] Barrett would have lost considerably less if he had stopped the run at the end of sixty nights, after which time the attendance dropped drastically.

In several ways this play was a major turning point in Barrett's career. After curtain calls on opening night he addressed the audience, mostly well-wishers, who received his original interpretation with great enthusiasm.

Twenty-five years ago a poor and almost friendless lad stood outside the walls of the theatre that once stood here, and determined to devote his last sixpence to the enjoyment

in the gallery of one of the celebrated revivals of Charles Kean. Coming out of the theatre
he swore to himself that not only would he become manager of that theatre, but that in the
distant future he would play Hamlet in that very spot. Ambition is in this instance
justified, for the little boy was myself, and I have played Hamlet to you this evening.[77]

Hamlet was the pinnacle of Barrett's hopes and ambitions—and the
beginning of his descent. His success with the play fueled the fires of
competition with Irving that had been smoldering for some time among
Irving's admirers. Rumors started which claimed that Barrett wished to
surpass Irving in acclaim. Word spread that immediately following that
appealing curtain speech, Barrett walked through the parted drapes and said
to his waiting cast, "Where's Irving now!" All this was exaggerated still
further by two burlesques of the production that were exceptionally severe in
their satire. These were *My Little Hamlet*, by William Yardley, at the Gaeity
in November and *A Fireside Hamlet*, by J. Comyns Carr, at the Prince of
Wales at about the same time.

Accumulated losses after *Hamlet* amounted to £32,000, and the organization was beginning to show the effects. All of Barrett's fit-up companies
were canceled at the end of their scheduled runs late in 1884; there was not
enough money to finance them. In order to get some capital, Barrett
mortgaged the rights of most of these plays in return for sums to keep the
Princess's operating. Samuel French loaned Barrett £1,000 for *Claudian*; in
an odd twist of fate, Henry Arthur Jones loaned Barrett £1,000 in return for
the rights to *Lights o' London* and *The Romany Rye*.[78] Since the provincial
tours and overseas royalties were now gone, the playhouse was by the close
of *Hamlet* running almost on its own. Without the safety of other profitable
productions to support him, Barrett's popular and artistic policy would
degenerate into merely popular work simply to survive, and his entire empire
would be undermined.

Throughout all the bad press and financial distress Barrett remained as
sanguine as ever. As if in defiance, he had a large portrait painted of himself
as Hamlet by Frank Holl of the Royal Academy, in which Barrett looked
very much the successful actor-manager. And like the good manager he was,
he had plans for a production to follow *Hamlet* even before *Hamlet* opened.
He had decided to take Ruskin's advice and continue for a third time his
series of classic-revival pieces designed by Godwin. This time Barrett had
another surprise ready: *Brutus*, an undiscovered play by the popular mid-
Victorian writer Bulwer-Lytton. Lytton's *Richelieu* was one of the most
popular star vehicles in the early nineteenth century. Irving and Booth had
given fine impersonations of the leading role, as had Macready, for whom it
was written and who was another important model for Barrett.

The unfinished script for *Brutus* had been discovered by the author's
grandson, who then offered it to Barrett. One of the first changes Barrett

made in the script was to remove the politics. Lytton was not persuaded that this should happen. "My impression," he wrote to Barrett in July 1884,

> is that the pathos . . . of the domestic interest will be enhanced in proportion as the audience can be inspired with a certain [wider political] consciousness. . . . I think we should be careful not to tone down too much the heroic note whenever it is strongly sounded.[79]

Lytton finally consented, as he did regarding Barrett's other advice on the play, but by February, immediately prior to the opening, Barrett still was nervous about his role, worrying he might not be able to fill it out the way he had with *Claudian*. Lytton tried to reassure him by appealing to his pride:

> It is a complex part which requires constant acting—and careful acting. It won't act itself if it is let alone. The whole effect must be put into it by the actor. It is full of by-play and frequent changes of tone, and above all of *facial* expression . . . and the variations of sentiment which it exhibits throughout the piece are such mere manners so slight and yet so important that the part of course requires great flexibility. . . . All this is exceedingly difficult—for the author seems to have set the actor a great task without clearly indicating how it is to be done—he has only furnished the actor with all the elements out of which to make a great dramatic creation of his own.[80]

Barrett accepted. But the name was changed from the original *Brutus* to *Junius, or The Household Gods*, a title which pleased Barrett because it sounded newer and because the subtitle contained the idea of the play. The story is set in ancient Rome and centers around Junius Brutus, a conservative statesman who refuses to move against a rebellion until the sanctuary of Rome's household gods is formally broken.

Junius opened on 26 February 1885. It was a gloomy script and found little support among either critics or audiences despite the elaborate efforts on scenery and costumes. The play did not even provide Barrett with potential for good acting as Lytton suggested it might. Barrett never seemed to be emotionally committed to the role, and this was noticed by critics used to praising his earnestness. The nobility of Claudian, the humanity of Hamlet were missing. "Mr. Barrett is, throughout, oppressed by his consciousness of his intense classicality," said one observer, "and never has his eye off the imaginary photographer, or allows the future pictorial advertisement to be lost to the view of his mind's eye."[81] Some reporters tried to help Barrett by stressing the educational value of the new play, but it was no use. *Junius* played only five weeks.

Characteristically, *Junius* was mounted with all the resources available to Barrett and its running expenses amounted to a very high £1,500 per week. Receipts were not sufficient to cover even the initial costs of production, however. The play lost nearly £2,500.[82] Lord Lytton generously offered to return his royalties, but Barrett refused, adding still more to his growing burden of debt. Clearly, Barrett had not expected such a large failure so soon after the opening of the play. Princess's productions had a history of running for several months at worst; the failure of *Junius* caught him off guard and he had no play ready. In desperation he put on revivals of earlier Princess's hits until a new script could be found. First, *The Silver King* reopened on 2 April and ran until 19 May. It lost £1,500. Next came *Lights o' London*, which reopened on 20 May and closed one month later at a loss of £500.[83] It was now near the end of the theatre season and audiences for revivals were hard to find in London. The Princess's closed for July.

Junius was the last play in Barrett's initial classic-revival series of melodramas. He returned to this style once more before he left the playhouse, but only after going back to more reliable domestic fare. The string of bad luck that started before *Hamlet* was eroding Barrett's usually positive and hopeful nature: he would not star in his next play. Instead, he would return to the safety of former practice by featuring an actress, this time his leading lady, Mary Eastlake. Back in June, Barrett had asked for help from Henry Arthur Jones, who had recently produced two successful dramas for other playhouses. Jones now agreed to work with Barrett on a new script they hoped would bring the Princess's back on an even keel.

Coauthorship

Mary Eastlake had been Barrett's leading lady for the last six Princess's plays, steadily improving her talents under Barrett's training. In the new play that was to follow *Junius* onto the boards, Miss Eastlake would be given a starring role almost equal in importance to Barrett's. The script was provisionally entitled *Nancy Newman*. In it Eastlake was to play two dramatically different roles: a kind young girl and her evil sister. The plot was adapted from Frank Harvey's 1881 melodrama, *The Workman*, but there was in the new Princess's play a deeper note than present in its model because of Jones's increasing social consciousness as a dramatist.

The play was to take place in a peaceful rural village in modern day England; the action revealed, however, that the pastoral charm of the setting was only a facade for the pettiness, gossip, and slander of the characters. In other words, the new play would display some of Jones's recent fascination with the new school "problem play." Moreover, it can be shown that this renewed Barrett-Jones partnership was an example of the atmosphere of paradox existing in the theatre at the time. Jones was an ardent Ibsenist; Barrett a traditionalist. Eventually Barrett would come to terms with certain elements of modernism in his plays; for now the dispute was to remain unresolved, as evidenced by the struggles between action-minded Barrett and literature-minded Jones. During the writing Barrett encouraged Jones with suggestions from various traditional melodramas. Barrett had to remind him, for example, of the traditional practice of alternating "front scenes" and "set scenes" and of the concomitant necessity of introducing minor characters to fill "front scenes" with significant action while the full stage was being set behind. Barrett also made other suggestions to stir up Jones's imagination, tricks of traditional dramatic construction, such as adding papers, letters, or documents to a scene, or proposing that some character overhear another at a critical moment, or that a particular person should enter sooner or later than Jones originally conceived.[84] In April 1885 the play was finished, and Barrett purchased it outright from Jones for £500 plus one-thirtieth of the gross receipts in London.[85] The title was changed to *Hoodman Blind*, a reference to the child's game, which implied the deception in the story. Later Jones admitted that he felt the play was "a waste of time" as far as he was concerned, but in June, just before the opening, Barrett was unaware of his partner's feelings. Barrett was optimistic, and in a letter to his still ailing wife he wrote, "Our new piece is quite ready for rehearsal—the few alterations wanted can be done at any time. I am sanguine over it and so is everybody else. I hope that the long strain will be over and that success will come with it."[86]

Hoodman Blind opened at the Princess's on 18 August 1885. Critics liked the play's modern approach. "The best characteristic," said *The Athenaeum*, "is perhaps its full-bloodedness. Genuine passion is exhibited and other motives by which characters are influenced, though extravagant at times, are at least human."[87] *The Theatre* agreed that the authors handled the story truthfully, not in a distorted manner.[88] The drama was staged in Barrett's typically excellent way, with strict attention to detail in all the roles. "The whole is an excellent ensemble," observed *The Athenaeum* further.[89] Moreover, Barrett's acting of the simple countryman Jack was surprisingly effective. Critics were used to seeing him in roles with more stature and were pleased to see that he had a wider range than they thought. "The acting of Mr. Wilson Barrett here is at its best," said Scott, "it is fervent, passionate, eloquent, and natural. He thoroughly arouses the sympathies of his audience."[90] *The Illustrated London News* was also taken by Barrett's newly discovered acting versatility:

> As a picturesque and romantic actor Mr. Wilson Barrett has no rival. He looks the young farmer to the life, and plays the part with refinement, energy, spirit, and good taste. In his home with his wife and child he is the most lovable of men—a delightful figure in a series of true English pictures. And he understands the chords and vibrations of the human heart. His passionate laments of jealousy, the isolation of the widowed heart, the sense of still loving that which is apparently so vile, the lamentable wreck of manhood, are admirably conveyed.[91]

Other dimensions of the play were not so well appreciated. Mary Eastlake was only "steadily improving and winning more favour."[92] The play itself was overburdened with scenery. Barrett wanted to impress the public with visual display but lacked the time to make sure that all the shifting was as smooth as his earlier plays. Critics complained that the scenic investiture inhibited the dramatic action.[93] Perhaps the most damaging criticism had to do with the play's dramatic action; though it was well constructed and true to life, some of that truth was excessive. Mark Lezzard, the antagonist of the piece played by E.S. Willard, was too raw. He boasted of "gnawing out the heart" of the woman who refused to marry him. And, Jack, the hero, raged about pulling Lezzard's body from the grave, stamping on the dead flesh, and casting the pieces around the earth. Jack actually concluded by throwing Lezzard to a pack of bloodthirsty hounds. Critics complained that such extreme actions were "not Christian."[94]

Hoodman Blind attracted reasonably good houses for nearly twenty-four weeks. Some money was made from the rights sold to other managers, and altogether the new play reduced Barrett's losses at the Princess's by a few thousand pounds. Barrett wisely closed the play the moment receipts started to decline; he was sorry to do so, for he liked the play, but he couldn't risk extending it. "No indeed," he later wrote to Jones, "*Hoodman Blind* has not gone badly. In fact if the firm had continued firm and not gone flabby, we might have done well, really well."[95] Actually, as a blend of "problem play" and melodrama, it was a little ahead of its time. Barrett never produced it again himself, but after his death it was made into a successful silent film.

Just before the revival of *The Silver King* in April 1885, Jones's renewed partnership with Barrett stirred up two controversies. One involved Henry Herman's claim in a few newspaper statements that he was solely responsible for the writing of *The Silver King*. Jones never had much respect for his own work with Barrett until he heard about Herman's claims. The disturbance lasted for several weeks until it was finally agreed, with Barrett's assistance, that Jones had written the dialogue, Barrett most of the situations, and Herman a small share in both dialogue and situation. Jones's overreaction to the whole incident and the timing of it suggests that Barrett's publicity consciousness, and not Jones's vanity, may have been behind it all. Barrett certainly knew that press controversy meant free advertising.

Newspaper interest in Barrett's writing associations continued through the fall when attention was turned to *Hoodman Blind*. Influential new school critic William Archer wrote an article in *The World* that condemned the contract method of playwriting. He singled out the Barrett-Jones partnership as especially despicable because Jones, Archer alleged, was being forced to write plays he did not like. This led to a second battle of letters in the press within one year regarding Barrett and his authors. In a letter to *The Era* Jones admitted that he did not care much for what he was writing, but he declared strongly that he was not being forced into anything.[96] Of course it is possible that this incident, too, may have been another Barrett publicity stunt; whatever the motive, these arguments regarding *The Silver King* and *Hoodman Blind* also suggest the growing power of the press in theatrical affairs in England.

Meanwhile, Barrett and Jones had been working on another play with an important part for Miss Eastlake. Jones's agreement with Barrett stipulated that he should write two more plays for the Princess's, and both he and Barrett thought it best to write them simultaneously in order to save time. The second play was another historical piece, but not set so far back in history as to be considered classic-revival. It was entitled *The Lord Harry* and was set in seventeenth-century Puritan England. The story deals with the adventures of the Royalist leader Captain Harry Bendish and Esther Breame, the daughter of the Puritan commander. Later, author William Allingham accused Barrett of copying his play *Ashby Manor*, which he had sent Barrett back in 1880, but which Barrett refused because it needed too much work. This criticism was never resolved. The new play was to contain lots of action, and Barrett was once more suggesting action scenes. By the time the writing had reached the third act, Jones was worried about this. Barrett wanted to add "the sack of the city" to the end of the act; Jones feared that too much activity would destroy the "love and duty" struggle he felt to be important to the drama. Furthermore, Jones continued to have trouble with minor characters. Barrett insisted that they be there in order to facilitate scenery changes necessary in spectacular melodramas; Jones, on the other hand, was never fully committed to them and merely tacked them on to the story. Barrett refused to allow this and made sure that all the characters, no matter how small, were "worked into the play."[97] Jones also had to be reminded of melodrama's need to contain certain loosely written scenes for the hero and heroine that permitted freedom of invention and soliloquies that allowed for the display of vocal skills.

The Lord Harry opened at the Princess's on 18 February 1886. Critics were disappointed that this play and *Hoodman Blind* had come from the same author as *The Silver King* and severely condemned the results because of this. "The story is thin to the extreme," complained one, "and could be told in a breath, while the action, which hardly ever carried the spectator out of himself, practically finishes in the third of five acts, leaving scene after scene of little relevancy to be presented."[98] *The Lord Harry* was also accused of lack of originality, lack of true dramatic action, and even lack of stirring incident. It was condemned for its lack of good acting potential, for neither Barrett nor Miss Eastlake, whom it was intended to feature, had much to work with in their roles.

Many were also dissatisfied for another reason. In order to generate more income from seating, Barrett removed some inexpensive pit seats and replaced them with several rows of more costly stalls. On opening night loyal followers were upset and interrupted the play with cries of "Where's the pit?!" Rumor had it that Barrett had changed his strict policy of appealing to popular audiences and given these seats to his friends from the press. The cries were so vehement that Barrett was forced to stop the play and address the audience. He claimed he would charge anyone who had gotten in free and that he would do whatever he liked with his theatre's seats since it was his own money he was risking. This straightforward reply subdued the protestors, but the effects of their uproar badly damaged the opening, perhaps even the entire run. Barrett's voice tended to speed up and assume a staccato rhythm when he was nervous; the opening night disturbance made him so tense that his articulation suffered and he hurried his speeches, thereby reducing their effect and ruining much of the play.

The new drama did have some merit, however. The scenery and costumes were excellent, and Barrett staged the whole with his typical good taste. This satisfied critics who expected little more from melodrama. *The Lord Harry*, said the reporter for *The Athenaeum*, was "managed as Mr. Wilson Barrett manages such affairs, whatever the nature of those engaged [and] will rivet attention."[99] There was even enough interest to generate at least one burlesque, *Oliver Grumble*, produced at the Novelty Theatre. But on the whole, *The Lord Harry* would not hold and closed with a loss at the end of ten weeks. It was the last play Jones wrote with Barrett. The large sums of money Jones made and the important playwriting lessons he learned at the Princess's enabled him to advance autonomously into more modern dramatic interests.

Next, a series of unfortunate and unpleasant events began to take shape, all of them apparently calculated to make continued success in London impossible for Barrett. Memories of Barrett's alleged remark about Irving after the *Hamlet* premiere in 1884 were still fresh, and now fuel was added to this fire in the form of a couple of slanderous pamphlets that exaggerated Barrett's personal rivalry with Irving. It was further alleged that Barrett had a secret business partnership with the influential critic Clement Scott, who was being cast at this time as Barrett's apologist. There was enough that was almost true in the pamphlets to give credibility to the entire affair. After all, Barrett was ambitious and did envy Irving, as did most other actors. And he and Scott had formed a loose business partnership with Samuel French, called the Dramatic Bureau, although the group dissolved because not enough authors could be found to support it. The whole unfortunate affair was probably instigated by an overzealous group of Irving's supporters, who sensed a threat in Barrett's success and then took it upon themselves to defend their idol. Barrett responded with scorn, as he always did to the intrigues of the theatre. When *The Era* began to publicize the incident, Barrett reacted appropriately enough by banning it from his theatre. "Such journals as those which fill their columns with false and indelicate theatrical tattle," he raged, "and serve to bring the dramatic profession into disrepute, are not to be admitted to the green room."[100] Nevertheless, many professionals were convinced of the truth of the anonymous accusations.

Barrett's reputation among London's theatrical leaders had been tarnished, and he was finding it increasingly difficult to locate good new authors who would work with him. William Archer also made it hard for Barrett to find new plays by writing a series of articles that condemned contract playwriting. The Princess's had thrived on innovative plays in the past; now such plays were becoming almost impossible to secure. At a speech given to the Dixey Supper in May 1885, Barrett publicly announced his anger at the situation that seemed to be forcing him out of London management. He complained that good plays could not be found and that authors' decisions of what to write and for whom were too often guided by "cliquism, friendly feeling, traditional vogue and notoriety."[101] Fortunately, at this point Barrett's difficulties remained professional only, for the public still loved him. Even Archer had to admit that in 1885 Barrett was the most important manager in London.[102]

Throughout the last two seasons Barrett had toyed with the idea of producing another play by Shakespeare, possibly *Othello*, but he put aside this wish and decided instead to continue featuring Mary Eastlake. E.W. Godwin was once again engaged as designer, and a new writer for the Princess's, Sydney Grundy, was hired to prepare the dialogue. Grundy was a lawyer from Manchester who discovered in the 1870s that he had a talent for adapting French farces. In the summer of 1885 he had sent Barrett his first serious play, *Clito*, a period drama set in classical Greece. Barrett had immediately recognized it as a potential classic-revival production for Miss Eastlake. A contract with Grundy was subsequently arranged, and the two began work immediately, completing the play in the winter of 1885, while *Hoodman Blind* was on the boards. Barrett was not so generous with Grundy as with his previous writers, and the fact that he used the old style fixed scale of royalties for this new piece indicates that he now needed all the funds he could get. *Clito* tells the story of Athens under the domination of the female despot Helle, who entices the renowned sculptor and statesman Clito away from his liberal political cause. The play was written in verse, which gave Barrett many fine opportunities to display his voice, while the scenery gave Godwin the chance to create another *Claudian*.

Clito opened on 1 May 1886, and Clement Scott observed that Grundy's first attempt at verse did amazingly well because of its color, wit, and sarcasm.[103] The scenery was also praised. Settings included a market in Athens, palaces, courtyards, and magnificent gardens; Godwin even put in goats fitted with their own costumes to look like satyrs. All this was too baldly reminiscent of *Claudian*, however, to suit the taste of some critics, and there were complaints that more money was on stage than talent. The reporter for *The Saturday Review* lamented that the production of *Clito* was too unimaginative and commonplace in a management previously noted for its innovations—a sure sign that Barrett was changing his policy to make enough money to keep afloat.[104] Barrett was under terrible stress during

Clito; his acting showed the usual faults: he "snapped" and occasionally spoke in the kind of staccato utterance heard in *The Lord Harry*. The particular night when this observation was made, though, may have been the performance during which Barrett was almost killed when he was accidentally stabbed by an actor during a fight scene. The best acting in the play was Mary Eastlake's, who finally reached the level of work Barrett had envisioned for her. "Miss Eastlake took her greatest admirers by surprise," said Scott, "she rose to such unexpected heights that the attention was riveted by the great art of her personation."[105]

The frank and brutal cynicism of the play led to its failure. Usually an optimistic person, Barrett decided with *Clito* to throw in with the modernists and dwell on the hidden sores of society. (Something of the same had been done in *Hoodman Blind*.) *Clito* consequently purported to show the debauchery resulting from excessively jaded living. Princess's playgoers, used to being consoled and entertained, were instead harassed and depressed by the new play. Some of the dialogue describing the relationship between Clito and Helle, for example, was very explicit for Victorian ears. And excellent as Eastlake's acting was, it was nevertheless overplayed with regard to her character's bad habits. When she groveled on the ground in terror, beating the floor in agony and fear, it was to much for weak hearts. Barrett was trying to inject modern ideas into his productions, but he lacked the spiritual sympathy with them to make them convincing.

This was the third play which Barrett officially coauthored and the third successive Princess's failure. William Archer blamed it on the contract system. "My conviction," he wrote in a personal note to Barrett,

> that you would act more wisely in giving authors a free hand (subject of course to such modifications as might be agreed on at rehearsal) is founded entirely on my own observation of the three plays in which you have collaborated and on my general theories of the principles of playwriting.[106]

Barrett, however, was simply not as interested in dramatic literature as Archer was. Here was the fine but important distinction that was making it so hard for Barrett to find new dramatists: younger authors were more interested in literature than in acting or production.

There were also grave personal problems which exacerbated Barrett's growing professional and financial difficulties. This was a time in history when many prescription drugs still contained morphine or laudanum. Caroline Heath's long-term dependence on such drugs to ameliorate her illness had apparently led her into addiction. Friends were quiet on the subject, as if by mutual agreement, but the children suffered badly. Miss Heath's position as hostess of Barrett's gala dinner parties at The Priory was gradually assumed by their oldest daughter, Nellie, while the younger children frequently found themselves on extended visits to relatives. Lacking a stable home life, the two boys, Alfred and Frank, began to become problems themselves. Barrett must have seen that he shared some of the blame for this state of affairs. He would have been superhuman if his acting and managing responsibilities had also not suffered during this time.

Early in 1885, the American tour agent Henry E. Abbey, the first manager of New York's new Metropolitan Opera House who had also arranged Henry Irving's profitable U.S. tour, offered to arrange a tour for Barrett, who was about £45,000 in debt. Barrett had no choice but to close the Princess's and take his company to America to recoup some of his losses, despite the personal and professional sacrifices that would have to be made. He placed revivals of *Claudian* and *Hamlet* on the stage, and gathered together his creditors, telling them frankly how much he owed, how much he hoped to make in the near future, and how much he would need for his new productions. He refused to consider bankruptcy. Barrett's creditors had such faith in him that a "letter of license" was drawn up which stated that creditors would not ask for any repayment until April 1888, at which time Barrett was to begin clearing his debts.[107] Barrett then leased the Princess's to the actress Grace Hawthorne and signed over his power of attorney to Alfred Pearpoint as a precautionary measure in case of accident on the journey. He mortgaged his home for £1,600 and mortgaged the rights to the remainder of the plays still under his control for another £2,000.[108] Now he had enough capital to finance the tour.

Barrett officially closed the Princess's on 23 July 1886 with a farewell benefit attended by hundreds of admirers. After the last scene, Barrett stepped before the curtain and spoke the following words:

> You cannot imagine how hard it is for me to say goodbye. Only an actor knows how a professional learns to like his audiences. I have worked hard to please, and have made many friends. Doubtless I have made some enemies, but I do not feel enmity towards anyone. I feel that I am not going among strangers, but among friends. Not an American brother or sister has been here but has encouraged me. Even American strangers have written, promising a good greeting and giving me excellent advice. My prayer is that our meeting next spring will be pleasant, as our parting is tinged with sadness.[109]

Barrett and his company spent the next few weeks touring the provinces; then they left Liverpool on 21 September aboard the liner *Wyoming*, bound for New York, where they would open in October.

By this time Barrett had matured as an actor, director, and producer. In these dimensions of his work he would never exceed anything he had done at the Princess's, though he later often matched it. He had turned to play-writing in his last seasons in London due to the difficulty of finding authors to work with him the way he wanted. From now on Barrett took a more active part in this art. In a few years he would return to London as star, director, and author of a play destined to lift him back to the top of his profession. But for now a period of new life for the Princess's was ending. For the last six years its audience once more had been made up of Englishmen from all walks of life. Barrett had set a standard there for high quality theatrical production that few managers were capable of matching.

4

International Wandering (1886–1894)

First American Tour

By 1885 it was common practice for English and American actors to appear in each other's countries. The old xenophobic theatrical prejudices were dying out, and it was more likely than ever that foreign actors would be received with an objective eye for their talents. The usual plan was for a single actor to undertake a tour supported by an established company in the host country. A few managers, such as Augustin Daly, Henry Irving, and Barrett, made their reputations at home working with their own carefully rehearsed companies, and they chose instead to take their companies along on foreign tours rather than incur the risk of working with entirely new colleagues. Irving had already toured American cities twice, in 1883 and 1884. On his first tour, due to the rigorous traveling conditions during U.S. winters, Irving decided to return most of his Lyceum scenery and technicians to London. Then, at each of the remaining cities on the tour, he hired local carpenters to build scaled-down settings to which were added Lyceum costumes and props. He followed the same plan for the second tour, displaying his complete Lyceum productions only in New York. It was the only way Irving could make a profit. Barrett, of course, knew about Irving's activities on tour, but even though he knew he might lose money, he chose to use full Princess's productions for each city where he played.

The contract stipulated that Barrett and his company would tour in America for one full season through May 1887. Barrett was required to act in every performance, but never more than once a day, and for this he would receive fifty percent of the gross receipts. Abbey paid all travel and transportation expenses to and from London and within the United States; he also supplied supers in each city, hired and paid for first-class theatres and appropriate advertising, and provided a specially equipped Pullman car for Barrett's personal convenience. Barrett would not be asked to travel any more than five hours at a stretch or to travel after one o'clock on any performance day. The repertoire would include three of Barrett's classic-revival plays, *Hamlet*, *Claudian*, and *Clito*, and three curtain-raisers, *The*

Colour Sergeant, A Clerical Error, and *Chatterton.*[1] It was Barrett's first foreign tour; he did not wish to burden himself with too much variety.

The steamship *Wyoming* arrived in New York on 27 September, six days after leaving Liverpool. On board were Barrett and his company of sixty-three actors and technicians and about ninety large baskets of costumes and accessories. On the next day, the liner *City of Chester* reached New York with the scenery, twenty tons of it. Barrett was met at the dock by journalists who reported that he was very cordial, not distant or difficult to speak with.

Barrett's debut production was *Claudian,* presented at the Star Theatre beginning on 11 October. Abbey thought he had publicized the engagement well and, expecting a sellout, raised the prices to $2.00 for stalls and $1.00 for gallery, but by curtain time seats were selling for half price. Abbey was usually good arranging tours, but he apparently did not advertise this one well enough. Moreover, New York was not accustomed to productions of the Princess's scale. Theatres there were equal before the footlights to any in London, but stage, rigging, lighting, and dressing rooms were inferior to their English counterparts. Dion Boucicault warned Barrett to expect this in the United States. "Mr. Barrett will have a hard time giving *Claudian* in this country to his own satisfaction," he wrote "as the number of stage hands employed in the theatres is so limited and the conveniences for scenic display so slight."[2] Boucicault was correct. *Claudian*'s scenic effects—the selling point of the play—were carried off badly in New York. The audience plainly saw all the wires and gadgets Henry Herman had carefully arranged to create the illusion of an earthquake.[3] Barrett had to tone down the entire scenic effect to a scale far below that of the Princess's with the result that the play was only half as effective as its original. One New York reporter even declared that the quake in *Claudian* was vastly inferior to the one done at humble Niblo's Gardens several years before.[4]

Barrett failed as well to make a strong acting impression in his early performances, and Mary Eastlake, complained one critic, was "no Ellen Terry." The play itself was reported to be a "pretentious, very pseudo-classic thing."[5] As if these were not enough problems, the old London scandal appeared again, and some observers believed that Barrett was simply cashing in on Irving's success in America. This time events were triggered by Charles Hudson's pronounced similarity to Henry Irving, an effect some New York playgoers again interpreted to be a mockery of Irving's style. This criticism hurt Hudson deeply and angered Barrett, who could not seem to escape Irving's spectre. Barrett made it known that Hudson had already been absolved from such accusations in London. The hissing soon stopped, but the damage was done. Next, anonymous hints about the ridiculous London pamphlets appeared, and further harm to Barrett's reputation occurred when carefully edited extracts from U.S. reviews sent back to London gave the impression that Barrett was a failure in the United States. The alleged Barrett-Irving rivalry was carried so far that one New York newspaper felt obliged to remind New Yorkers of good manners.

American theatrical readers have long been accustomed to see the names of Henry Irving and Wilson Barrett written together, but such readers are not devoid of a discriminating knowledge that, while the former is the leader of the English tragic stage, the latter possesses a great following in his native land, and is in no respect an imitator or an opponent of his famous compatriot. Thoughtful acceptance of Henry Irving does not stand in the way of equally thoughtful acceptance of Wilson Barrett. . . . This should be said with distinct emphasis now. . . . Nothing could be more unjust . . . than to suppose that American favor towards Henry Irving . . . would oppose the progress of Mr. Wilson Barrett. The existence of this obstacle has been insinuated, . . . but it may be dismissed as an utter delusion.[6]

Actually, after the problems of moving in were solved and after playgoers were given time to become used to Barrett's unique style, he eventually did very well. William Winter, the dean of American critics, gave his hearty approval. "The foremost attribute of Wilson Barrett's acting," Winter wrote in the *Tribune*, "is simplicity, and yet it is not easy either to define its distinctive character or to specify its charm." Winter went on to say that Barrett possessed "extremely physical" assets, but that he seemed to be restrained in their use by a sense of beauty. Barrett's strength, Winter continued, was refined by gentleness. "It is the . . . prominent and distinguishing peculiarity of this actor that his ingenuous nature and simple dramatic method appeal involuntarily and directly to the spirit of comradeship in other men, and to the average public conception of art." Winter concluded that Barrett was a genial, simple, kind-hearted, and generous man, as well as a forcible, sensible, picturesque and thorough actor—an English John McCullough.[7]

Barrett's congenial personality proved to be a further asset on the early part of this tour, for he was naturally gregarious and took to public life easily and gracefully. Americans have always loved accessibility in their stars. Barrett endeared himself to them by appearing in numerous benefits, one for a recent flood in Charleston. Americans were also stirred by his encouragement of their own dramatic efforts. He asked them to have faith in native theatrical enterprises and not to depend on the English, whose style, he admitted, could not help but be foreign to them. He further advised about an American national theatre.

There should be in one of the large cities, a theatre which should be managed by a man whose knowledge, honesty of purpose and artistic skill should be unquestioned, and whose position should be unassailably safe from financial troubles, no matter what the receipts of the theatre were.[8]

He proposed that such a theatre be supported by private subscription, however, and not by government subsidy. After playing initial runs in the home city, Barrett concluded, this theatre's plays would then tour the country, and the American public could depend upon dramas being "pure and wholesome." Barrett seemed to be describing dreams he had for himself back in England.

After several weeks in New York, Barrett continued his limited repertoire on tour, playing a few weeks each at Boston, Chicago, Kansas City, Cleveland, Washington, D.C., and Philadelphia, returning to New York once in the middle of the season and again at the end. He was received well everywhere and feted by local government and artistic dignitaries. From the capital in February he wrote to Caroline Heath,

> Washington has received me with great acclamation. No such reception ever given to a foreign artist, they agree. And they vow I am the greatest actor England has ever sent to America. . . . It was a very swell audience last night—I wonder they took to me so for my voice was (to me) very dreadful and I could not do Hamlet justice. I made money in Chicago and lost it in Cleveland—although the success artistically and socially was wonderful.[9]

Barrett's comment on his voice referred to a nagging sinus infection that would continue to plague him on future tours through radical changes of American climate.

Newspapers declared the tour to be a great success. "Since his opening here," the reporter for *The World* wrote, "Mr. Barrett has made the theatrical circuit of the larger cities of the country, playing to immense audiences and followed by a furor of enthusiasm. His progress was one great triumphal tour."[10] As for money, he seems to have profited about £8,000 ($40,000 in 1887 dollars) for his twenty-eight weeks of touring, an average of about £300 per week.[11] The company returned to England in mid-May. Irving, in turn, left for his third U.S. tour a few months later.

Earlier, Barrett had negotiated with Henry Arthur Jones for another drama, a play "full of home interest and some very touching and original situations . . . and a powerful character," Jones wrote.[12] He admitted that there was little opportunity for scenic display, but, he continued, "perhaps we could fit in a big London scene."[13] After the recent failures with Jones, however, Barrett felt the author no longer had his heart in his work. Besides, Barrett already had plans to open in London in late fall with a new play written in collaboration with another former colleague, George R. Sims. On hearing this, Jones wrote to Barrett that he had "washed his hands of melodrama, anyway."[14]

After he left the Princess's following *The Romany Rye*, George R. Sims had gone on in 1885 to write another successful lowlife melodrama, *The Harbour Lights*, which starred William Terris and Jessie Milward and played at the Adelphi for over 500 performances. Then Sims teamed up with still another Barrett associate, Sydney Grundy, to write *The Bells of Haslemere*, which Terris made popular at the Adelphi in 1887. Clearly, Sims's and Grundy's playwriting had benefitted from their effort at the Princess's with Barrett. The new Sims-Barrett drama would open at the Globe Theatre because the Princess's was still under lease to Grace Hawthorne. Barrett and Sims spent most of the early part of the summer working on the script at Poppyland Mill resort north of London.

Miss Heath's condition continued to deteriorate. When her illness was originally diagnosed eight years before, her doctor confined her to home. She remained there until a relapse occurred, at which time she was placed in a rest home in Hampstead. In the summer of 1886, prior to Barrett's departure for the United States, Miss Heath suffered a stroke and was sent to Worthing where she could be looked after by her brother, Reverend Frank Heath, and her daughters. Reverend Heath had a parish at this southern seaside resort, and it was hoped that the quiet and clean life there would do Miss Heath some good. On 22 July, while writing with Sims at Poppyland, Barrett received a telegram from his daughter, Dorothy, saying that Caroline Heath had suffered another relapse. Barrett immediately dropped his work and boarded a train for London, then went on to Brighton, where he hired a private rig to take him to nearby Worthing. He arrived too late. Miss Heath had suffered a brain hemorrhage and had died almost immediately. She was fifty-three. Caroline Heath was buried at Shoreham-by-Sea.

Barrett's personal and artistic debt to his wife was enormous, but her demise at this time could not have been unexpected, and circumstances allowed him little time to mourn. Early in September Barrett took the company on a tour of the provinces for three months, then in late November he moved to the Globe, preparing to present a new work. Few theatres in London had so frequently changed managers and styles as the Globe. Built in 1868, the house had passed through at least half a dozen ownerships, and would continue its variegated course long after Barrett's engagement ended. Barrett took over the theatre from Charles Hawtrey. According to the lease arranged with the owner J.H. Addison, he intended to stay there at least until October of the next year. Located in Newcastle Street on the Strand, *The Globe* seated 1,000 and rented for £4,000 yearly. Receipts from the three-month tour in the provinces offset this cost a little, but even so, nearly half of the U.S. profits were already gone.

The new drama, entitled *The Golden Ladder*, opened at the Globe on 22 December. Its theme was not an especially new one for Barrett; it was, in fact, another melodrama in the vein of *The Silver King*, but an unusual twist made it memorable. The hero was a parson. *The Golden Ladder* concerns penniless Reverend Frank Thornhill, who chooses to live in Madagascar as a missionary rather than inflict his poverty on the wealthy heiress he loves. The role of a parson was new for Barrett and a rather daring experiment, for despite some precedent, clergymen were seldom subjects for plays. Nevertheless, the new play had the potential to be a fine spectacular melodrama of the sort Barrett had made so successful earlier. His acting, a reporter wrote in *The Theatre*, was enough in itself to secure a long run for the play.[15] "Mr. Barrett was a very muscular Christian," said *Dramatic Notes*, "manly, earnest, and in the prison scene his pathos was such to draw tears from many eyes."[16] Moreover, the acting of the company's villain, Charles Hudson, was praised and filled a large gap left when E.S. Willard departed for his own career before the American tour. The plot, though, was considered by some to be "rather disjointed and uneven," because "the interest of various scenes was not as closely knit together" as it might have been.[17] Some reporters referred to the occupation of the hero as another source of trouble for the play. The acting of Miss Eastlake in one particular scene caused further alarm. She was exceptionally tender and sweet throughout her role, but in the fourth act she was found at Millbank Prison, and here the agony of her portrayal was so intense "as to become painful to the beholders."[18] Evidently Miss Eastlake had not yet learned Miss Heath's techniques for drawing the humanity, not just the suffering, out of such scenes.

Opening night was a success. Loud applause greeted all the actors at the final curtain, and Barrett made a cordial speech. He was happy to be back among his friends, he said, and was thankful that he was so well treated in the United States. He also expressed the wish that the Globe, being a smaller theatre than he might have wished for such an occasion, might nevertheless serve in the future to draw him that much closer to his friends and supporters.[19] *The Golden Ladder* underwent several rewrites before it settled into a comfortable twenty-week run. It made an enormous profit of nearly £17,000 because Barrett cut expenses to the bone, only £730 per week, as compared to twice that for *Claudian*. Average weekly receipts were a healthy £1,790.[20]

In December Barrett moved from The Priory, with its sad memories, to a new home at 21 Maresfield Gardens, Haddingham, in South Hampstead. Augustin Daly recalled that Hampstead then was a lovely rural area, but also that it was dangerous by night. There were long stretches of unlighted paths; in fog and darkness thieves had an easy time of it. In fact, shortly after Barrett moved to this three-story house, he was plagued by a recurring dream of burglary, which later turned out to be true. His house was burgled a short time after by the notorious criminal Bill Kemp.

In February 1888 Barrett learned that Grace Hawthorne was leaving the Princess's, and that it was consequently appropriate for him to return there for a season-long engagement. He thought that going back to the Princess's with the success of *The Golden Ladder* behind him might prove advantageous. He subleased the Globe, received in return £2,000 of his original rent, and used the money to begin work on a new play for the Princess's. While waiting to begin at his old theatre, Barrett decided to revive Bulwer-Lytton's drama *The Lady of Lyons*, a former Macready vehicle, during matinees at the Globe. Barrett and Miss Heath had performed the play hundreds of times in the provinces, and he had come to respect the play due to its continued popularity there. His experience since then had led him to believe that the play could be considered in more modern terms by bringing to it certain ideas about new school acting he had learned in *Hamlet*. Surprisingly, Barrett's production met with widespread approval. Reviving Irving's 1879 hit at a major London playhouse was risky, but Barrett's fresh, modern interpretation caught audiences pleasantly off guard. If some critics would not seriously consider his work in Shakespeare, then at least Barrett could undertake other Victorian stage classics and get a fair hearing with them. *The Lady of Lyons* was an artistic *success d'estime*; Barrett continued to produce it for several weeks at the Globe and thereafter on his tours. Other matinee performances at this time included *Hamlet*, *A Clerical Error*, *The Colour Sergeant*, and *The Silver King*.

Barrett concluded his tenure at the Globe in mid-May. His U.S. tour had been modestly successful; his renewed partnership with Sims was very successful. According to the account books, he had restored approximately £25,000 to his depleted capital, enabling him to show good faith to his creditors and allowing him to return with some confidence to the scene of his past successes. He had made good progress during the past two years towards getting his operations back in order. More important, *The Golden Ladder* proved that despite the failure of his first three attempts at playwriting, he had the potential to write good plays. Finally, it was rumored around this time that a romance existed between Barrett and Miss Eastlake, and that they were waiting until a proper time had elapsed after the death of Miss Heath before they would announce their engagement.

Hall Caine and Folk-Revival Melodrama

Hall Caine, who was the literary advocate of the Manx nation, wished to do for the Isle of Man what Dion Boucicault had done for Ireland: change it from a subject for comedy to one for tears and appreciation. His first two novels, *The Shadow of a Crime* and *A Son of Hagar*, were written while he lived at the Isle of Wight and dealt with native life there. After the success of these he began his Manx mission in earnest, starting with his novel *The Deemster*, published in 1887. Caine's work was immediately popular. He was a careful, conscientious craftsman, though his plots tended to be crude and his characters overly simple for the detail required of the novel form.

Barrett first made Caine's acquaintance on the occasion of an earlier

Princess's play when Caine criticized him in *The Liverpool Mercury*. Barrett wrote a reply, but the main reason behind the letter was his perception of a special kind of talent in Caine's writing, even if it was just a play review. "And now that I've told you what I think of your article, I wish to tell you what I think of yourself," Barrett wrote. "I think you could write a play and if someday you should hit on a subject suitable for me, I shall be glad if you will let me hear of it."[21] Caine had such a subject with *The Deemster*, but this was years after Barrett's letter, and consequently it took a note to Caine from the critic Theodore Watts to remind him of Barrett's earlier interest. In 1886 Caine had sent Watts excerpts from *The Deemster*. Watts wrote back, "*The Deemster* is precisely the passionate and powerful plot for Wilson Barrett to do wonders with."[22] Caine then sent excerpts to Barrett, pointing out where Barrett might find them "picturesque" and where he might find "big scenes for dramatic passion."[23] In 1886, however, Barrett was virtually broke, and with his plans for the U.S. tour he was forced to put aside Caine's idea. After the success of *The Golden Ladder* Barrett thought of Caine again, and Caine responded pleased. He was sure, he wrote, that a play adapted from *The Deemster* would prove to be "the strongest play of *passion* that has been seen in our day."[24]

Of course, Barrett had coauthored before, but the task of tinkering with a published piece of popular literature proved to be riddled with unforeseen difficulties. When Caine heard what was involved in adapting his story for the stage, he was shocked and pleaded that he needed time for the new ideas to "cerebrate."[25] While Caine was adjusting, Barrett set about learning all he could of Manx life, particularly the religious customs so important in the novel. Caine advised that Barrett read the story very closely because it contained in itself "much that is practical and valuable on Manx costume, scenery, dialect, etc."[26] Barrett recognized the exotic qualities of Manx life and wished to understand them since they would be part of the play's appeal. By March Caine was at work on the dialogue; he was helped by Barrett's frequent testing of each scene to make sure the language would "act as well as it reads."[27] Barrett had a keen ear for dramatic emphasis.

Later that same month the authors ran into some problems consolidating some of the novel's important action in order to keep the number of characters within the limits of stage necessity. After a few days of fruitless trials, Barrett at last hit upon the idea of making one character in the drama perform the actions of several characters in the novel. Caine said this was an "inspiration," and the drama was now free of the last vestiges of the novel that restrained it.[28] Caine was jubilant and appreciative. He had learned much about dramatic construction from Barrett, while Barrett had treated him respectfully throughout the entire affair. Caine felt that his talent and his work were trusted and responded by offering Barrett formal coauthorship on the program "*with your name first.*"[29] A few days later he wrote to

Barrett, "You have written fully as much of the text as I have, and planned the incidents from first to last, whatever my share in concocting them."[30]

Caine and Barrett evolved a more formal pattern of work for the remaining drafts. Barrett offered ideas, then Caine constructed larger events around them using material from his novel. Next, Barrett arranged the events while Caine wrote dialogue. Barrett then tested the dialogue. This last step was critical now, and Barrett spent much time polishing speeches, especially those surrounding the climactic moments of the drama. Caine seemed to have difficulty understanding that good dramatic dialogue changes its structure imperceptibly at these moments in a play. Barrett referred him to classical poems and plays in order to sharpen his attention to these dimensions. At one point Caine wrote, "I have read up *A Fair Quarrel* by Middleton and Rowley to see how the same situation was treated by the old dramatists." He continued,

> One thing I find is that the dialogue grows brisk and sharp before the fight. The lines I send you intended to carry the effect of a fight before the fight begins—to make the audience see that the fight is inevitable. Short, sharp, epigrammatic lines like the clash of swords ought to have a stirring effect when spoken.[31]

Finally, to insure clarity and to advertise a point in the play's popular appeal, Caine wrote program notes which explained Manx laws and customs and the effects of the island's strong Church courts in the story. Rehearsals began in early May.

The title of the play was changed first to *Dan*, then to *Ben My Chree* ("Girl of My Heart" in Manx language) in order to maintain the distinct identities of the drama and the novel. The story as it eventually evolved dwells on one of Barrett's favorite themes, a self-sacrificing hero. Dan Myrlea, a reckless Manx vagabond, is tricked into committing manslaughter and is condemned by Church law never again to speak to anyone on the island under pain of death. At the climax of the play Dan chooses to speak and die in order to protect the innocence of the woman he loves. Settings in the drama included domestic scenes, sea coasts, quaint Manx cityscapes, judicial halls, and Church meeting rooms.

Ben My Chree opened at the Princess's on 17 May 1888. For several years now personal and professional fortune had not been especially kind to Barrett, and he had for some time displayed in his productions a subtle but significant vein of modernist despair, notwithstanding the superficially happy endings. *Jane Shore* capitalized somewhat on this theme, along with the more recent *Hoodman Blind*, *Clito*, and *The Golden Ladder*. *Ben My Chree* continued in this same direction with a little more force. At the conclusion of the drama both Dan and his sweetheart, Mora, are condemned to live the rest of their lives as social outcasts, pathetic victims of villainy and

Manx law despite Dan's heroic sacrifice. This dark conclusion, combined with the already mysterious tone of the setting itself, created a production altogether too somber for traditional optimists. "There is a good deal that's fresh, powerful, and poetically suggestive," said the critic for *Dramatic Notes*, "together with much that is productive of disappointment and depression. The play is a gloomy one throughout."[32] Barrett and Caine capitalized artistically on the "weird solitude of the old Celtic places" and created a tone of "brilliant melancholy which makes a haunting undertone through the play."[33] But W.W. Kelly, Grace Hawthorne's partner and one of Barrett's backers for *Ben My Chree*, was among those who were uneasy with the tone of the play criticized by the reporter. Kelly was also nearly bankrupt. He wanted the offending dialogue and action deleted and the ending made softer. "Rubbish!" Barrett replied, "I know my public. Wait 'till tomorrow morning and you'll find columns of unadulterated praise and the box office besieged by a public mad for seats."[34] Nonetheless, Barrett did back down. His creditors were on his mind too, and during the first few days of production the ending was altered so that Dan is forgiven by the Church and he and Mora are united in marriage.

The acting, ensemble, and staging were all up to Barrett's high standards. As Dan, Barrett displayed the "power, impetuosity, and tenderness" of which he was past master. Mary Eastlake, though, faltered; her "emotional resources [were] hardly equal to the strain which she so constantly puts upon them," said one reviewer.[35] Miss Eastlake was soon to leave Barrett's company and begin a career of her own. Taken all in all, *Ben My Chree* was a success, just as Barrett said it would be; even more so after the rewrites and changes inevitable at the beginning of any new play. Clement Scott was pleased. "The production of *Ben My Chree* will rank as a red letter day in the annals of Mr. Wilson Barrett's triumphs," he wrote in *The Theatre*. "To welcome him back to his old house was itself an occasion of much moment to his friends and admirers; that hearty cheers, applause, calls, and floral tributes should be showered upon him was but natural."[36] Scott proved to be correct about the importance of the play to Barrett's career. *The Times* gave the production an entire column of praise and *The Daily Telegraph*, *The Morning Post*, and *The Standard* each gave it at least as much. *Ben My Chree* became a staple on Barrett's tours at home and abroad for years to come. Somehow success seemed to come to Barrett at critical times in his finances. The reason was that he held fast to his innate affinity with popular taste and trusted his public to prove him right, and in the end they always did.

Ben My Chree ran for nine weeks at the Princess's, until 14 July. Receipts were £4,300 against equal expenses; since he was booking the theatre he had to pay only half the running costs, and his profits therefore amounted to £2,150.[37] This was by no means an elaborate play in Barrett's patented manner because he had to be fiscally conservative now. He had overproduced before and run his plays too long; now he closed at the first sign of a decline in receipts. The day after the opening Kelly hurried to the theatre to find out if the box office would be besieged by patrons, as Barrett said. To his surprise, he discovered that the queues were indeed there, but they consisted as much of creditors there to take their share of the success as of audience members.[38]

No new play was immediately available following the success of *Ben My Chree*. Barrett decided to tour the provinces again rather than risk the possible losses involved with producing revivals in London. Profits were sure to be made on tours, while at the same time he could prepare new plays he planned to produce at the Princess's next season. In the meantime, since Kelly and Hawthorne put up a play of their own at the theatre in the interim, Barrett needed storage and scene-building space to prepare new plays, more space than either the Leeds or Hull playhouse could provide. He mortgaged *Ben My Chree* to Pearpoint for £700 and used some of this money to lease a large converted bath house in Lambeth for the purpose. From now on he would use this as the scene-building and storage headquarters for his company.

On the provincial tour, Barrett played *Ben My Chree* in a limited repertoire because he wanted no additional burdens to interrupt his writing. He was preparing two new plays. The first, with Caine again, was entirely new: *The Good Old Times*, written from Barrett's original ideas. He wrote to Henry Arthur Jones in September, "I am hard at work on two plays which promise well. *Good Old Times* is of good old metal, I am sure."[39] The second play was to be his first solo playwriting experience since *Twilight* in 1870. Barrett and Jones also had been corresponding again about another partnership between them. Jones continued to disparage his work with Barrett; he wanted no more to do with melodrama. But Barrett, as always, had great respect for the genre and reminded Jones of the difference between cheap melodrama and his own more dignified brand. "Dear Jones," he wrote, "I didn't say a melodrama—but a play. Do not be unjust to *The Silver King*, it will outlive many a better praised work and continue to draw when they are forgotten."[40] Barrett concluded his provincial tour at the end of December, accumulating nearly £8,000 in profits.[41] He then negotiated a booking with Grace Hawthorne for *The Good Old Times* and the other play beginning in January 1889 at the Princess's and continuing twelve weeks. He was to receive fifty percent of the gross receipts, but Hawthorne stipulated that the contract must terminate if receipts fell below £1,000 per week. Barrett had the option to renew only if his receipts exceeded this amount at the end of the contractual period.[42]

The Good Old Times opened on 12 February 1889 and carried on the revival of interest in English folk culture begun with Hall Caine's play. This time Cumberland life was the focus. The incidents in the play were familiar to Barrett fans: John Langley bravely assumes responsibility for the pistol assault committed by his wife against her former suitor, then he and several villainous types are sentenced to prison in Tasmania. There follows a spectacular series of scenic displays, escapes, robberies, and brawls, the last scene resulting in the capture of the culprits and the reunion of John and his wife. This sort of highly energetic plot was perfectly suited to the physical dimension of Barrett's acting style, and Miss Eastlake made her regular contribution as the virtuous and long-suffering woman. The entire company was once more praised for the meticulous care with which every role was played. Barrett was welcomed back to his old playhouse enthusiastically. "The numerous wreaths and floral offerings," reported one critic, "presented at the close of the performance testified that [Barrett and his company] had once more been most successful in their efforts to harrow the feelings of their audience."[43] Despite this welcome, the play itself was weak, its story was hard to follow and its dialogue needed condensing. *The Good Old Times* played for only two of the three weeks planned in the contract because receipts were beginning to fall dangerously close to the minimum.

Ever since his association with Henry Arthur Jones during the 1885-1886 Princess's season, Barrett seemed to be moving toward autonomy as a dramatist. *The Golden Ladder* was an important step in this direction, as was Barrett's next play at the Princess's this year, *Nowadays, or A Tale of the Turf*. Besides being highly traditional, as many good first efforts in art tend to be, this drama was another which confirmed Barrett's interests in folk-revival themes, focusing on Yorkshire life as well as on the favorite English pastime of horse racing. Several years back Barrett had contacted the novelist of English racing, Robert Merivale, to determine whether he would consider writing a play. When nothing came of this, Barrett undertook the task himself. *Nowadays* is a comedy about a stern Yorkshireman whose misanthropic attitudes lose him friends until he discovers the value of forgiveness. The play contained many stirring scenes, central to which were the abduction of a championship race horse and the assault by an aristocrat on the commoner woman who loves him. *Nowadays* opened on 28 February 1889, and the combination of Yorkshire charm with horse racing proved to be a successful one. It was observed that

> the horse-loving British public, from the sporting butcher with his shilling sweep to the noble Duke who plunges in five figures, might reasonably be counted upon to take some interest in a play in which all the action was made to revolve around a high-mettled racer.[44]

A much earlier play by Boucicault, *The Flying Scud*, had previously assumed the position as prototypical English racing drama; *Nowadays* threatened to replace its popularity. "Since the days of *The Flying Scud* we have certainly had no sporting drama that has taken greater hold of the public than Mr. Wilson Barrett's *Nowadays*," reported *The Theatre*.[45] The critic for *Dramatic Notes* added that Barrett's playwriting deserved a great deal of the credit: "The characters are human, the dialogue terse and natural, and the situations naturally worked up to."[46]

Nowadays was the first play since 1881 in which Mary Eastlake did not play opposite Barrett. Perhaps there was a falling-out due to Barrett's indecision about their plans for marriage. The exact reasons, however, are unclear. She remained with the company for some time yet, but it could not have escaped Barrett's notice that she would never grow into the actress he hoped. *Nowadays*, consequently, may also have been a first delicate effort on Barrett's part to see how the company would work with another actress in the female lead (Grace Hawthorne as Jenny), or it may simply have been that the role itself was not of sufficient importance for Miss Eastlake. Whatever the cause, the change did Barrett no harm; his portrayal of John Saxton was some of the best acting he had ever done, deserving, as Scott said, a "thoroughly bestowed double honour" on the actor-playwright.[47] Barrett had never before played a warmly humorous part like this shrewd York-shireman; it revealed that he was becoming a polished character actor and that some of his work was developing interesting new dimensions. Dan Myrlea in *Ben My Chree* was the first tentative step in this direction; now John Saxton was actually a full-grown character part with many comic overtones. The reporter for *Dramatic Notes* wrote,

> Mr. Wilson Barrett, clever as he is, has never done anything so good as John Saxton, the canny, obstinate Yorkshireman, hard and gruff and determined to have his way outwardly, but with a world of kindness and warmth under his rough exterior. There were little touches in his performance that were absolute perfection, and the whole was conceived and carried out with a fidelity to nature that showed the highest art.[48]

Nowadays closed on 14 April after one and a half months of success and was followed on the Princess's stage by revivals of *The Silver King* for one week and *Claudian* for two more. Earlier in January, Barrett produced two plays at matinees that proved to be of some interest. *The Lady of Lyons* began a short run on the thirtieth and was welcomed as warmly here as it had been during its first performance with Barrett's new adaptation a few months earlier. This play was followed by Barrett's first performance of *Hamlet* in London since 1885. Except for Barrett, Miss Eastlake, and George Barrett, few of the cast members were the same as in the original; as a result the production was only a pale reflection of its prototype.

Barrett completed this, his last Princess's engagement, on 18 April. Total receipts for the twenty-week run were £15,700, and the receipts for his last two weeks were significantly under the £1,000 agreed limit in the contract. Average receipts for the entire run were £785, meaning he made a profit of £4,000 after his share of the expenses was met.[49] As far as Barrett's other income was concerned, the picture was only a little brighter. Receipts available for the Leeds Grand this year indicate a profit of only £350 and at Hull only £120—money which was doubtless used up on the yearly maintenance of the buildings alone.[50] Of course, a number of road companies played Barrett's other hits in the United States, Australia, and the British provinces. However, he was still very much in debt, and the receipts from these productions went to the plays' various mortgage holders, principally Alfred Pearpoint, Barrett's attorney. Records show that for 1889 a total of £2,400 in royalties was contributed to the solvency of Barrett's debts, ranging from a low of £31 for *Hoodman Blind* to nearly £400 for *Lights o' London*.[51] Barrett could not hope to repay his debts as long as his profits remained so marginal.

Another arduous tour was immediately scheduled. Unfortunately, Barrett had to borrow money even to do this and went into debt for another £7,000 to Pearpoint. He could look back on the interval since his last extended tour with some pride, however, as the debts were decreasing slowly, and he was growing in several promising directions as an artist. He discovered new dimensions in his acting with the roles of Dan Myrlea and John Saxton, and he had embarked on a lucrative new adventure adapting a play from a successful novel. He had also experimented with dramas dealing with the popular revival of interest in English folk culture. But most important, he could begin to look forward to the day when he would be an autonomous theatre artist. Now that his playwriting skills were sharpening, he would soon be free from the difficulties of working with recalcitrant authors and the necessity of paying royalties. He was on his way to becoming actor-manager-dramatist.

Second American Tour

In 1886 information about the costs of theatrical production in the United States compared with those in England was not readily available to Barrett, and he had to arrange his tours there with Henry E. Abbey, who knew the territory. In other words, Barrett accepted a reduction in his share of the profits in exchange for Abbey's knowledge of American theatrical conditions. In 1889 Barrett decided to take an active hand in the arrangements for his second U.S. tour and scheduled a full season of short dates at cities not usually considered attractive to foreign actors. To solve the problem of lack of familiarity with the country, he hired an American advance agent, Clark Sammis, at a salary of $50.00 per week plus a small percentage of the receipts. Sammis was responsible for engaging supers at various cities along the tour; his major task was to arrange for printing, advertising, and posters, and to perform the actions of a first-class publicist. Sammis also acted as an intermediary to confirm all the bookings.

After a twelve-week British provincial tour, Barrett and his company sailed for America, arriving in Boston in late September, where Barrett was immediately met with a financial omen that warned of greater difficulties ahead. Until now foreign theatrical scenery and costumes arriving at American ports had been admitted duty free as "tools of trade." By 1889, though, American actors' concern over the increasing numbers of English tours arriving resulted in the Actor's Order of Friendship of New York putting political pressure on U.S. Customs. The organization thought that a duty on foreign scenery, costumes, and properties would help to create a more appropriate balance of trade between American actors and their British neighbors. Consequently, when Barrett arrived he was levied with a tax of $10,000 on 300 tons of production supplies. If he did not pay, his materials would be confiscated and sold to pay the tax. Barrett paid $6,000 to show his good intentions, then filed an appeal to the Department of the Treasury in Washington, D.C., which, after several days of wrangling, settled in Barrett's favor. Barrett received his deposit, and foreign companies were allowed free access for their supplies, for the time being at least.[52]

The company opened at the Star Theatre in Boston on 14 October, and during the next few weeks played *Ben My Chree*, *Hamlet*, *The Lady of Lyons*, *Claudian*, *The Silver King*, *The Lord Harry*, and the "Triple Bill" (*A Clerical Error*, *Chatterton*, and *The Colour Sergeant*). Barrett did very well, drawing $2,570 for closing night of his first appearance there since 1886, the largest sum Barrett had ever drawn for a single performance in America.[53] One thousand dollars at the Star was a very good house, especially since seats were priced at only 25¢ to $1.50. By comparison, Bronson Howard's landmark play *Shenandoah*, produced by Charles Frohman at the Star the same year, grossed only slightly more than $1,000 nightly.[54] Things changed after Barrett moved to New York, where memories of the old scandal remained; nevertheless, poor receipts did not prevent Barrett from performing in several benefits, his usual practice, thus carrying on the social success, at least, that he had begun there in 1886. The rest of the first leg of this tour was nearly the same schedule in the midwest and east as last time, including Philadelphia, Chicago, Cleveland, and Washington, D.C.

When spring and warmer weather arrived, Barrett was in a buoyant mood because audiences away from New York were enthusiastic and profits seemed to be steady. In January he received a letter from a friend back home who wanted to help him eliminate some of his debts. He suggested that since musical reviews were popular, Barrett might return to London with one of his own; an idea, he assured Barrett, that was sure to solve his financial distress. Barrett responded with a humorous and satirical reply. "Dear Brainerd,"

Thanks for your "tip." I am going to study the song and dance business and put all my young women into very short frocks and have them practice high kicking. I am going to write a piece called *A Wooden Ladder*. The great fun of the thing will be that all my short coated young women will have, in turn, to get half way up that ladder—while the lover who will also be on it (the wooden ladder) but below the young woman will in that position declare his passion for her. The tag of the play will be a grand march of the characters up this ladder to the tune of *Climbing up the Golden Stairs*. You will see that there is a suggestiveness about this idea—that *Ben My Chree* does not possess. One of the songs will be How Seductive are Suspenders When They're Looked at From Below. How does the thing strike you?[55]

In April the company paid a return visit to Washington, D.C., where Barrett had become a political as well as a social and artistic attraction. He wrote home,

I have had a splendid week here—both in and out of the theatre. Mrs. [Benjamin] Harrison made me quite the "Belle of the Ball" at the White House on Wednesday and they all came to *Hamlet* on Thursday. Mrs. McKee, Mrs. Harrison, and the President having a little chat with me after the play. In fact doing all they could to make things pleasant for me.[56]

The second leg of the tour began at St. Louis in late April; early May was Denver, and by mid-May Barrett had reached San Francisco. The support of the railroad magnate Jay Gould that Barrett had gained in New York now paid off, and as Barrett moved westward, he was treated like a visiting potentate on Gould's trains. "Jay Gould has given orders all along the line that I am to be treated with special care," he wrote in May, "and I am."[57] The 1890 half of this tour, however, did not turn out to be as profitable as Barrett might have hoped. He failed to take into account American distances, and now that he was his own tour manager, he discovered that the costs of shipping his company and all their equipment were enormous. Besides, there was a financial depression in the country; theatres west of the Mississippi River were hit hard. Worse still, these theatres were small. In San Francisco in May he wrote, "We began last night to £170—the theatre holds about £250."[58] Barrett's plan to visit cities outside the regular itinerary strongly backfired on him in California, where from Los Angeles in June he wrote back a pessimistic letter to his brother-in-law, now his business manager.

I am in a very bad way indeed and at present moment have no idea how I can get out of it. I am nearly two thousand pounds short of the amount necessary to clear me to London. I shall make two or three hundred pounds here I hope, but that is a drop in the sea only. I am terribly depressed, but keep well. The changes of climate seem to keep up everybody but me. Tour [members] were ill [all] at once in San Francisco. I dread to think of what's happening to you or what's happening to me. I suppose I shall get through.[59]

Barrett went on to describe the "terrible state of depression" the country was in; concluding on an upbeat note, he wrote how easily money could be made on land speculation in California. The relative security of a life away from theatrical pressures was beginning to appeal to him. "I should never repent this trip. I have learned more this last seven weeks than you could imagine," but he added, "I wish we could all come over here and settle."[60] Then, a week later, from San Francisco again,

> We have no time to go to hotels. I am living on the train. Tropical heat, mosquitoes, tarantulas, cockroaches, and beetles the size of lobsters—dressing rooms without ventilation—inconvenient theatres, *Hamlet* and tinned provisions—how does that strike you?![61]

By the end of June the company, who had already agreed to half salary, was on its last legs, but there were still a number of small towns to play before returning home. Barrett wrote to Frank Heath,

> Gradually I am moving east. We have now to give nine more performances—all in small towns—where a hundred pounds is a fine house. I get 75% of the receipts and I am £2000 short up to now. I have no idea how to pull through. You will just get this in time to answer it—which is a blessing for it shows how near I am to returning.[62]

Frank Heath borrowed money at the end of July and sent it to Barrett in order to pay for the company's return. They arrived back in England in August, completely broke.

In 1890, at age forty-four, Barrett was faced with three alternative paths of action, none of which promised much success. American tours were proving too expensive and too exhausting. Provincial tours were not as expensive, but involved about the same amount of effort. A major London theatre offered the most potential, but it was the most expensive alternative. Barrett swung this way and that, hoping to find along the way a new hit that would make him solvent once more. Toward this goal, Barrett now borrowed money to book another London theatre, the New Olympic, today the Aldwych, on Wych Street in the Strand.[63] There would be no difficulty with receipts here as there had been at the much smaller Globe in 1887. Moreover, the New Olympic had a reputation for being a popular playhouse despite its expensive trappings. There were no stalls, and pit benches for two or three shillings were still the order of the day. Barrett also must have remembered that he had played *East Lynne* briefly at the New Olympic with Miss Heath early in 1879.

After a short provincial tour, Barrett opened at the New Olympic, on 4 December, with a play he wrote in collaboration with the popular novelist Victor Widnell, *The People's Idol*, a play the authors had been at work on since September. The idea for the drama was Barrett's, and Widnell was hired exclusively to write the dialogue for a flat fee of £350 in several £50 installments,[64] most of which was covered by a £500 advance Barrett received for the play from Samuel French for American rights. French always made money with Barrett's plays in America, and it was a tribute on his part to Barrett's work that he continued to negotiate rights for each new play that Barrett produced. Barrett, of course, would have made money on them too, but all of his royalties were still being used to pay debts.

The People's Idol is a "problem play" dealing with the conflict between labor and management, a relevant topic due to the devastating dock strike the year before. The hero, Lawrence St. Aubrey, falsely believes himself to be a murderer in an episode reminiscent of *The Silver King*. The play was costumed by the new fashion team of "Elita et Cie" on Bond Street, a firm run by Barrett's daughters and bought for them by their father after he returned from his second foreign tour. The girls had first approached their father about the shop back in 1885, but Miss Heath opposed the idea. Now Barrett consented, hoping that the business would offer his daughters security at a time when his own financial prospects were poor. Ellen was the designer, Katherine the business manager, and Dorothy the bookkeeper. Around this time it was discovered that Ellen was suffering from tuberculosis. Barrett, incidentally, had also been supporting his widower father for many years.

The People's Idol was scoffed at by the usual critics, but received warmly by Barrett admirers; if for no other reason, Barrett's desperate attempts to reestablish himself had gained him a following on the merit of his stubbornness alone. One reporter observed,

> The audience were eager to welcome back to London an actor whose services to the native drama have been valuable, whose personal character is high and unblemished, and whose elevated rank in his profession has never been in dispute.[65]

English playgoers were finally beginning to see that they had in Wilson Barrett a theatre artist of the first rank. In response to this, Barrett lowered ticket prices to reaffirm his allegiance with popular audiences. This action caused some concern that Barrett might also lower his production standards, as *The People's Idol* was actually not a very good play. "The work will, in all probability, greatly please the frequenters of a house which is to be conducted on the basis of popular prices," warned the usually supportive Clement Scott.[66] *The People's Idol* played for a meagre twenty-eight performances, including matinees, and this thanks only to judicious rewriting, which toned down Barrett's ubiquitous remorse as St. Aubrey. It was followed at the New Olymic by a lengthy series of revivals that seem to have been the real purpose of Barrett's tenure at the theatre this year. Eighteen-ninety was certainly the period of lowest income for Barrett since the early 1870s, and revivals may have been the only alternative with no new script ready. Whatever the motives, the revivals seemed to work reasonably well, contrary to past practice. *The Lady of Lyons* ran for four afternoon performances in mid-December, followed by *The Silver King* and *The Colour Sergeant* for thirty-one evenings and afternoons beginning on 3 January.

One significant dimension of the New Olympic season was the introduction of three new members to Barrett's company, all of whom went on to significant achievements and fame: Franklin McLeay, Winifred Emery, and Maud Jeffries. McLeay had been introduced to Barrett by the American actor James E. Murdoch, who saw Barrett's production of *Ben My Chree* in Boston the year before. A Canadian actor with a large popular following at home, McLeay began work as a teacher at a Canadian university, later turning to the stage. At Murdoch's urging, Barrett saw McLeay at a matinee in Boston and then invited him to join the company. He was a statuesque actor with a robust style. Winifred Emery had actually begun in Barrett's combination company in the late 1870s, but after a few appearances at the Royal Court, she went on to join Henry Irving at the Lyceum. She was the daughter of comedian Sam Emery and the wife of actor Cyril Maude, and was an instinctively good actress noted for her impressive bearing on stage. She was also an excellent dancer. Later, she would go on to success in *The New Woman*, Cazenove's criticism of feminism; still later, she was to find fame in several plays by Arthur Wing Pinero.

The most important of the new company members was Barrett's new leading lady. At the end of the 1890 provincial tour, Barrett and Miss Eastlake finally parted company. She was given the rights to *Clito*, which she took on a provincial tour financed by Barrett. The separation seemed abrupt after nine years of close association, but Miss Eastlake said that it was prompted only by simple business and artistic considerations and that she and Barrett continued to be the best of friends. After this she went on to establish her own career, though she never achieved on her own the kind of success she had with Barrett. Eastlake's replacement was American actress Maud Jeffries, the daughter of an American plantation owner. She began her stage career at age seventeen and in 1890 was playing supporting roles with Augustin Daly's company in New York. There she saw Barrett in *Claudian* and was so impressed that she applied to him. Jeffries was a far better actress than her predecessor; in fact, after her tenure with Barrett's company, she became actor Herbert Beerbohm Tree's wife and leading lady.

A string of older plays, mostly associated with the name of the actor William Charles Macready, were next at the New Olympic. Barrett and Macready were similar in several important ways. Both were primarily old school actors whose forceful stage presence allowed them to play heroic roles with great effect. Moreover, Macready, like Barrett, perceived himself to be the victim of a press conspiracy. Even more coincidental at this time was the fact that both men experienced high achievement only to find themselves at the bottom of the profession soon afterward, and each actor went through a subsequent period of fluctuating fortunes (in Macready's case, for thirteen years, 1823–1836). Barrett was aware of the similarities between himself and the great tragedian and carried a large painting of Macready with him wherever he toured, placing it prominently in his hotel rooms. Barrett's formal identification with Macready had actually begun with *The Lady of Lyons* at the Globe. He renewed this identification more seriously now when he introduced at the New Olympic his version of Kotzebue's play *The Stranger*, a very famous Macready vehicle, for two performances late in January. The purpose was to establish copyright for his adaptation of the script in order to use the play more extensively on later tours. Barrett had a talent for pumping life into these older plays; despite the stilted language and the "oppressive lugubriousness" of *The Stranger*, he made a success of it.[67]

On 9 February Barrett reintroduced *Lights o' London* evenings and afternoons, while later in the run the play was accompanied by various curtain-raisers—*Tommy*, a new comedy by Rachael Penn (Mrs. E.S. Willard); *A Yorkshire Lass*; and *Father Buonaparte*, by Charles Hudson. *Ben My Chree* was revived for two matinees in March, and in April Barrett brought back *Hamlet*, with Jeffries as Ophelia and McLeay as Claudius. Reporters paid very little attention. Another revival of an older script received more commentary when on 21 April Barrett presented his version of *Belphegor* by Paillasse, here entitled *The Acrobat*. First produced in London at the Adelphi in 1851, the Romantic story of the famous mountebank with the faithless wife since then had a notable stage career with Charles Fechter and the eccentric Charles Dillon, among others. Barrett had been thinking about this play as far back as 1887, when he wrote to Henry Arthur Jones asking for an "Englishized" script which Jones refused.[68] Clement Scott observed,

> There is a mingling of light heartedness, pathos, and complete honesty in the character of Belphegor exactly suited to Mr. Wilson Barrett, and from the time that he enters on the scene in the showman's van . . . until his scene with the Duke in the last act, [he] held his audience.[69]

A few critics saw too much of Dillon's style in Barrett's acting and condemned the play for being too old-fashioned. A short play, *The Miser* (a fantasy), was presented during matinees in May.

This miscellaneous season at the New Olympic also witnessed the first and only time Barrett thought of moving away from melodrama when he considered producing Henrik Ibsen's play *Pillars of Society*. Jeffries and McLeay may have had something to do with this, but the main impetus probably stemmed from the popularity in London of the Independent Theatre in 1891. Significantly, *Pillars of Society* is one of Ibsen's earlier works and contains an uncharacteristic happy ending. All the same, Barrett's March plans for the play never amounted to anything, for in the end Barrett's whole artistic tone was antithetical to modern social drama.

Barrett closed his New Olympic season in May. The complete financial picture is not known, but scattered accounts indicate that his expenses were in the area of £19,000, an average of £800 for each of his twenty-four weeks there. At two-thirds, he probably accumulated around £12,500.[70] Tours and the two provincial playhouses reduced his debt this year an additional £3,500.[71] Barrett's total indebtedness therefore must have remained about what it was when he came back from his last U.S. tour. Besides the addition of two new revivals of older plays together with various inconsequential short plays, Barrett's major victory this year in London was the advantage of keeping his name before the public and hiring several important new actors.

The company toured the provinces from June 1891 through June 1892, their repertoire consisting mainly of Barrett revivals. Nevertheless, the tour proved to be extremely profitable and brought in nearly £7,000 in twelve months. This, together with another £400 this year from the provincial theatres in Leeds and Hull, reduced his debts some, but still left him considerably in arrears.[72] Of all Barrett plays on tour with other companies, *Jane Shore* remained the most consistently profitable, returning about £1,100 in 1892.

Othello

Barrett's most significant accomplishment on this tour was his new production of *Othello*, another Macready success, which he first produced at the Royal Court Theatre in Liverpool. It seems probable that he would not have thought of undertaking this difficult play without the inspiration of Jeffries's potential as Desdemona. In fact, her unique new school acting style contributed significantly to Barrett's interpretation of the play. First of all, Barrett clearly showed in his Othello the military zeal and discipline and the Moor's impulsiveness, all the parts of the role as acted traditionally. After all, these were dimensions which Barrett could portray with little difficulty. His new school contribution to the part was a tender, almost naive credulity generated by a sincere and tender devotion for Desdemona, which she reciprocated. In fact, Othello's love for his wife turned out to be the most important dimension of his interpretation. Barrett's Othello clung to his belief in Desdemona, and his gradual disillusionment became the central interest in the play. He was not immediately suspicious and eager for revenge. First, he met Iago's hints with scornful disbelief; then he began to doubt, which was followed in turn by self-hate for doubting his own wife.

This led to fury, but aimed at Iago, not Desdemona, for daring to suggest infidelity. Finally, there was the arrival of belief accompanied by a complete abandonment to Othello's hidden superstitious nature. Barrett planned and staged the play with the same thoroughness, honesty, and artistic self-sacrifice that he had applied so successfully to *Hamlet* in 1884.

Othello opened on 22 October, and the praise was loud and virtually unanimous. Critics approved of Barrett's clear plan of development in the action. *Othello* was "well worked out. The design was clear, bold, and impressive," critics reported.[73] Added to this was Barrett's new school natural acting. The traditional majesty and stateliness of the warrior were there, but these dimensions were less in evidence than they had been even in Charles Fechter's new school interpretation in the early 1860s. Fechter's performance was called "natural" and human; critics thought Barrett's was even more so.[74] "His reading is a very human one," it was observed. "Daring touches of realism here and there throw a flood of light upon Othello's inner life, and his scenes with Desdemona had so 'husband-like' a tone that they appeared entirely new to seasoned playgoers." "There was no approach to melodrama," the same critic continued, "Everything was 'noble, simple, tragic.'"[75]

This critic's mention of melodrama at this time was more than a passing reference to Barrett's well-known love for this style of play; it was a hint that Barrett's acting had slipped some in the eyes of critics during the interval since he left the Princess's in 1886. His early successes, *The Silver King* and *Hamlet*, were anything but cold, but the unremitting repetition of roles before undemanding provincial audiences may have led to a tightening of Barrett's technique. Weak scripts also probably played a part. Barrett's acting in recent years had begun to show too much formality and not enough belief. *Othello* reversed the downward tendency in Barrett's acting of important roles. This was most evident in the play in Act III with its unfolding of Othello's doubts. Addison Bright was among the first to see the change. Writing in *The Theatre*, he observed,

> The [third] act is played certainly as no English-speaking actor of our age has played it. Those scenes are justly said to be the test of the tragedian. . . . Barrett's execution is masterly: nobly and profoundly tragic. Time was when Mr. Barrett's acting was anything but masterly. Unsightly excrescences appeared, encumbering a style once singularly pure and lucid. The ringing voice *would* make for head notes, in which no passions, no emotion ever lay. The art was not of that kind which is able, or perhaps careful, to conceal art. Gestures, tones, and method rapidly grew mannered and mechanical. And the actor over and over again in recent years has saved his performance only by some fine vigorous outburst in the eleventh hour. With the donning of Othello's robes Mr. Barrett has put on a natural method and tones to suit. He seeks no effect from the outside. . . . There is no whine of self-pity in his pathetic tones, . . . and the spectacle he presents is one of superb artistic achievement and fearful human significance.[76]

9. Wilson Barrett as Othello.

The artistic success of *Othello* was the first of its kind for Barrett since *Hamlet* in 1884, but in itself the production did little to restore Barrett's economic condition. It was more important as a harbinger and reminder that Barrett had by no means dwindled into an insignificant force in the English theatre. Unfortunately, it would be several years yet before the final effects of this rejuvenation would be fully felt, but *Othello* proved that Barrett's decision to introduce the talented Maud Jeffries was a fortunate one.

In 1891 the influence of William Archer and Ibsenism was growing very strong; it was a style that would hold great attraction for Henry Arthur Jones, Arthur Wing Pinero, and George Bernard Shaw, whose earlier play *Widower's Houses* was produced at the new Independent Theatre. Many who adhered to the new school principles espoused by these artists and their followers believed Barrett's persistent theatrical conservatism to be anachronistic. On the other hand, Barrett believed that the new social drama was alienating the middle class. Barrett did not think that new school artists were unskillful, but that their dramatic temperament was simply un-English. He believed, perhaps with some reason, that Ibsen, for example, was a powerful and intelligent playwright who had a strange grasp of a special part of the human mind, but that he lacked sympathy with virtue. Ibsen recognized no heroes, Barrett said. As for Ibsen's English counterparts, they were clever, Barrett stated, but

> they are frankly cynical and almost contemptuous of virtue, honour, and truth; and the teaching conveyed may be summed up in a few words: viz.—Truth and falsehood, virtue and vice, purity and impurity are almost entirely the result of temperament, heredity and circumstances. Morality is unpleasant, but immorality is *not safe*—therefore it is, on the whole, better to be good, unless you can *sin without being found out.*[77]

Barrett was, of course, far from alone in these beliefs. As a star actor, Henry Irving, for example, disliked modernism in drama and acting, though more for reasons of personal style than aesthetics. The majority of Victorian playgoers opposed the new style, and the contemporary theatrical press often carried articles criticizing Ibsenite modernism. Today we find these conservative ideas reactionary, but it is helpful to point out opinions like those contained in Sydney Grundy's influential antimodernist essay "Marching to Our Doom" that suggest there were genuine reservations about dramatic modernism in the minds of many intelligent people who were pesent at its birth. "It is the tendency of the contemporary serious drama," Grundy wrote,

> to become less and less a play and more and more a study of character, and that in proportion to this tendency its popularity is declining . . . and that our serious theatre is being destroyed by a coterie of enthusiastic eccentrics, who represent nobody's opinion

but their own, and who have no sympathy with the drama or with anything that is dramatic.[78]

As some observers saw it, modernism was undermining the renewed popularity theatre artists had worked so hard to achieve in the last generation; the new drama was becoming an entertainment for the select, only now it was the intellectuals and artists who were the select instead of, as in the past, the wealthy and royal. Moreover, this pattern would continue as long as new school English dramatists were attracted to Ibsen's style.

For Barrett, the result of this understanding was that he began now to stress even more the popular dimensions of his work, yet without changing in any way the nature, quality, or style of the productions themselves. He did this by appealing publicly to people who were beginning to feel themselves cut off from the theatre against their will, and he used the power of the press to disseminate his ideas. Articulate and appealing spokesmen like Archer and Shaw were writing weekly articles advancing their cause. As a popular actor-manager, Barrett already had access to the press wherever he traveled, and from now on, in interview after interview, he assumed the unofficial position of "leader of the opposition" while advancing his populist policies. Barrett was a formidable adversary; he spoke strongly and clearly. And if he lacked the depth of style of Shaw, he nevertheless had the advantage of espousing ideas already current among a large class of playgoers. When he spoke about the needs and wishes of average people, he had a ready audience.

These populist principles were probably in Barrett's mind when he undertook his first solo playwriting adventure in four years, another classic-revival piece, *Pharaoh*. He wrote the new play during the 1891-1892 provincial tour, and since Egyptology was a hobby of his, it took him only six weeks to complete the entire drama. He selected his time frame from the period of Egypt's greatest wealth and power. The setting was Thebes, and the dialogue was written in a kind of "high prose" similar to that of *Claudian*. The central role is Prince Arni, who is caught between the decadent atmosphere of the court (represented by the character Tuaa) and his own noble nature (represented by Princess Latika). The theme of a man struggling between two moral extremes was not new for Barrett, but it was more obvious in this play than in any of his earlier works. Psychologists might see in its idea something of the popular *versus* artistic paradox that was deeply a part of Barrett's entire career; Barrett probably saw it only in terms of clear-cut dramatic situations. At any rate, the effect was the illustration of court passion, treachery, and revenge—a deadly serious drama of manners that would have been reminiscent of Ibsen's cynical plays except for the historical setting and lack of subtlety.

Pharaoh opened at the Grand in Leeds in mid-September 1892. The utter strangeness of a play about Egypt presented in Leeds in 1892 caught critics off guard. Worse, because of the death of his daughter Ellen from tuberculosis in May, Barrett was not up to his usual acting powers. Critics did see, however, that Barrett was as skillful an actor and director as he ever was.

Third and Fourth American Tours

After the premiere Barrett arranged for another tour of the United States, this time with a different manager, John R. Rogers, husband of the American actress Minnie Palmer. Barrett and the company would leave from Liverpool in late October for a full year's tour, and it was hoped that there would be no recurrence of the financial disaster that resulted from the second tour. Barrett would spend a carefully planned thirty weeks in the American east with his full company, then travel west for ten more weeks with a smaller troupe, hiring local help when he needed it. He hoped that a smaller company would offset the expenses of traveling long western distances. One and two night stands of the kind he lost so much money with before were to be eliminated.

Barrett's first U.S. tour opened in New York, his second in Boston; in 1892 he began in Philadelphia, where, to his dismay, he encountered the same difficulty with U.S. Customs he thought he had solved in Boston. The company's freight, arriving in early October aboard the steamer *British Prince*, was attached again for duty. The weight and volume of the material was less than that which arrived in Boston for the last tour, 100 tons in 163 trunks instead of 300 tons, but continuing pressure by American actors forced Congress to reevaluate the laws regarding such activities. Barrett was required to pay $20,000 in taxes. He and his lawyer reminded officials of the Boston decision, and a compromise was reached in which Barrett paid a $7,000 deposit and took an oath that all this scenery, costumes, and properties were "tools of trade." He could then have use of the supplies while his lawyer continued to argue the case before the U.S. District Court in New York. If he lost, he would have to pay the remaining $13,000; if he won, he was still out legal costs, but at least he would have his supplies and the assurance that the entire affair would soon be permanently resolved.

A large deficit was not an auspicious beginning, but Barrett was more buoyant now than he had been for years. He had regained completely the optimistic, cheerful nature he was known for and suffered difficulties more easily now. An argument with his tour manager over some obscure real estate deal occurred in Philadelphia in December, but the disagreement was over almost as soon as it began. Barrett's distress over audience complaints in Philadelphia of increased general admission pit seating during an opening performance of *The Lord Harry* also passed without effort.

In January the company moved west, playing a large repertoire of plays that included *Pharaoh, Hamlet, The Lady of Lyons, The Acrobat, The Silver King*, and *The Lord Harry*. In Pittsburgh Barrett added *Othello* to the list, and for the first time Franklin McLeay played Iago. He had been a serviceable company member in England, but Barrett had not wanted him on this tour because his methods were extremely robust even for English tastes. His voice was often strained, his muscles tight, and his movements artificial. Since Barrett was to play in Canadian cities for the first time, however, McLeay desperately wanted to come along, agreeing to allow Barrett to train him like a novice for the privilege. The acting lessons proved to be to McLeay's advantage. Barrett preached the advantages of relaxed muscles, a natural voice, and especially the absence of strain when making an entrance in a strenuous role. McLeay's Iago became one of the high points of Barrett's *Othello*, a production already celebrated in its two other major roles.[79] The company reached Montreal in January, and when they produced *Othello* there, along with *Hamlet* and several other of Barrett's best plays, Canadian audiences were impressed. Here was a famous English company producing excellent plays with a popular Canadian actor. Barrett found himself a celebrity. After one especially popular performance of *Hamlet*, he was "abducted" from the theatre by a large contingent of college students and given an elaborate celebration that included a "bounce" in a blanket (a college fad at the time). The evening concluded with a sleigh ride through the streets of Montreal pulled by a "team" of students.[80]

Back in England, before Barrett left on the tour, he had produced for copyright a play called *Our Pleasant Sins* at Leeds. Charles Hannan, an obscure writer, gave Barrett the idea for the play, and for several weeks Barrett fed him suggestions until a completed script could be given its copyright production. But a difficult structural knot had developed in the Leeds version; Barrett kept the play with him during the following tour and worked on it when he had the chance. By February it was ready to be tried again, and Barrett introduced it in Chicago on 23 February at the McVickers Theatre. *Our Pleasant Sins* is a slight comedy whose easy demands and derivative nature seem to indicate that it was intended primarily as a diversion piece in the repertoire. In four acts, the play has a complex plot centering around two brothers (Barrett and McLeay) who are trustees of an estate and guardians of an attractive ward (Jeffries). One brother gambles away the money entrusted to him; the other assumes the debt and the hand of the ward. The play was warmly received in Chicago and elsewhere on tour, as it was the next year at home in England, but it was never a major piece in Barrett's repertoire and tells little of his development as a play-maker. In fact, the play never solidified into a permanent script, being amended almost everywhere it was produced.

Later in February Barrett began the brief westward leg of his tour with a reduced company. In Denver he was again in high spirits. The theatrical entrepreneur F.B. Leavitt managed to gain something of a monetary advantage over Barrett there during the engagement, but Barrett characteristically turned the tables and congratulated Leavitt on what he termed his "persistency and superior judgement."[81] Leavitt was pleased to receive both a profit and a compliment from a manager whose skills he admired so much. After short runs in Los Angeles and San Francisco, Barrett returned to Philadelphia where the tour ended in early April.

This was a more successful tour than the last U.S. affair, resulting in nearly £10,000 in profits, not including the $7,000 returned to him when U.S. Customs finally ruled in his favor.[82] Moreover, Barrett's new mood of hope and confidence shined through everything he did. Even the attack of "grip" he encountered in Philadelphia and a slight injury he received when he was brushed by a train while waiting to board there did not seem to prevent him from enjoying himself. Throughout the tour, in newspapers and other periodicals, he expressed his opinions to journalists on a wide range of subjects, both theatrical and otherwise. He showed a keen interest in American architecture and politics. He praised American theatre, especially its character actors, though he lamented the lack of sound schooling in diverse theatrical companies that prevented the country from having as many successful poetic actors as England. In his new role as theatrical leader he also found time to criticize certain new school acting methods. He did not admire, he said, young actors' nonchalant manner of walking on stage, their habit of smoking at every available moment in the play, their careless sitting, or their frequent twirling of moustaches. But after all, he added, these new plays demanded little else of them; consequently, young actors both in America and England had no poetic appreciation of the stage.[83] What did he think of the American accent? The nasal twang, he pronounced, was due to a drying up of the nasal passages on account of the dry climate. He had awakened on tour many times with a dry nose that badly affected his own speech. Maud Jeffries was probably the inspiration behind Barrett's renewed contentment at this time. At the end of the tour he sent the company home, and with her he traveled to the American south, a region he had never visited before. They went to Memphis to see her family, then toured Mississippi. Barrett took in everything he could. He even attended a revival meeting and later wrote a story about it for a Leeds magazine.

Back home in early May, Barrett continued his gregariousness when in several interviews he gave his views on questions of labor and management, reasserting his belief that social concerns might be well served in plays, as in his own drama *The People's Idol*. Barrett was taking his new leadership role so seriously that he began to sound like a politician. He was a man with broad travel and management experience, and rumors persisted at this time and hereafter that Barrett was interested in public office. He was obviously courting wide responsibilities.[84]

In August Barrett made plans for a fourth U.S. tour, but before this he hastily revived another old Macready play, Sheridan Knowles's *Virginius*, a long-time favorite of heroic actors. Written in 1820 for Macready, *Virginius* became one of the most popular Romantic plays of the early half of the century. The subject of the play, a father's relationship with his daughter, was obviously close to Barrett around this time. The idea of producing it was suggested to Barrett in the United States by the actor John McCullough, a close friend of Macready's. Barrett began studying *Virginius* in August; since he planned to produce the play on a scale comparable with his other work, he started at the same time on the settings with designer Lawrence Alma-Tadema. Alma-Tadema was an English artist who had worked extensively with Irving. He was as much a perfectionist as Godwin had been, and both he and Barrett spent the next month consulting various period sources in the British Museum before they began elaborate designs. As for the updating of the script, Barrett turned to Addison Bright for help. Together they rearranged the first three acts and adjusted the endings of Acts III, IV, and V, simplifying them and making them more intensely dramatic. As with *Hamlet*, these revisions were actually closer to the original text than the generally accepted stage version; Barrett used scenes that had not been seen on the stage in twenty years.[85]

Virginius opened at the Grand in Leeds on 19 November 1893 for a brief copyright run. Critics' responses were similar to that for *The Acrobat*, *The Lady of Lyons*, and *The Stranger*: Barrett could effectively lift these old plays out of their dusty pasts and breathe new life into them. His trick was to play some heretofore insignificant dimension of the play "against the grain." In the case of *Virginius*, he was helped in this regard by his inspiration to play Virginius not as an old man, but as a man in the prime of life.

Barrett's fourth U.S. tour began in November 1893 and lasted a full season until June 1894. By this time he was an efficient producer of foreign tours. He budgeted his money carefully and by doing so could profitably visit again small American towns eager for polished entertainment. The company left Liverpool early in November on the steamship *Teutonic* and arrived in Boston a week later after a very rough crossing that made most of the actors sick. This time Barrett did not have to pay duty for his supplies. The company played four weeks in Boston at the Globe Theatre, 20 November through 9 December, their repertoire for the tour including *Virginius, Claudian, Othello, The Silver King, Ben My Chree, The Stranger, Hamlet, Nowadays, The Lady of Lyons*, and *The Acrobat*. The financial picture of this first engagement was excellent. Barrett received payment from the Globe management based on a sliding scale: fifty percent of the first $4,000 per week, sixty percent of the next $2,000, eighty-five percent of everything over $6,000, plus fifty percent of the gross at all matinees.[86] The first week Barrett received $3,403, followed the next week by $2,740, then $2,141, and finally $1,275. The salary list he used in Boston and for the rest of the tour noted that Barrett received $500 per week; Maud Jeffries and the stage manager-actor Austin Melford $150; while the rest of the company's salaries ranged from a high of $95 to a low of $14. The median was $70. The total salary list each week (minus supers) amounted to $1,382. Other expenses in Boston, including costume repairs, supers, props, lights, and publicity (a high of $70 per week), raised the expenses another $275 to $1,607.[87]

When profits fell below costs Barrett, as manager, cut his salary before anyone else's, but fortunately this was seldom the case this time. George C. Odell relates that Barrett made less with each successive U.S. tour.[88] Actually, the opposite was true. Certainly the second tour was a disaster, but since then Barrett had made substantial profits at almost every theatre he played, as indicated by the following financial breakdown of this particular tour:

Theatre	City	Duration	Profits
Park	Brooklyn	1 week	$1,883
Chestnut	Philadelphia	2 weeks	$1,762
Queen's	Montreal	1 week	$4,309
Grand	Toronto	1 week	$3,233
Grand	Hamilton (Ont.)	1 day	$495
Grand	London (Ont.)	2 days	$1,128
Star	Buffalo	4 days	$1,010
Duquesne	Pittsburgh	1 week	$2,540
Walnut St.	Cincinnati	1 week	$4,338
Hooley's	Chicago	2 weeks	$1,448/wk
Grand	St. Lous	1 week	$5,116
Masonic Temple	Louisville	2 days	$367
Grand O.H.	Nashville	1 day	$184
New O.H.	Chattanooga	1 day	$222
O'Brien's O.H.	Birmingham	1 day	$237
New O.H.	Meridian	1 day	$104
Grand O.H.	New Orleans	1 week	$2,201
Fremont	Galveston	1 day	$403
Sweeny	Houston	1 day	$543
Grand	San Antonio	1 day	$375
Millet's	Austin	1 day	$238
Greenwall's	Ft. Worth	1 day	$355
O.H.	Dallas	1 day	$544
Grand	Memphis	2 days	$1,332[89]

Similar profits were made at the remaining cities, which included one day each at Helena, Arkansas, and Alton, Illinois; and one week each at St. Louis, Pittsburgh, Washington, D.C., Baltimore, Jersey City, Brooklyn, and New York. The tour concluded with a final three-week engagement in Boston in May 1894. In large towns Barrett used a sliding scale similar to that in Boston; elsewhere he used a flat seventy-five percent of the gross.

Balance sheets indicate that profits for the entire forty-week tour amounted to a healthy $69,683 or £13,936 in exchange rates.[90]

Touring was now as much a part of Barrett's artistic responsibilities as major London engagements, but tours had to be carefully planned since Barrett used his best actors and, as much as possible, complete productions. (In this respect Barrett had much in common with the successful American producer Charles Frohman, a close friend of Barrett's who might have given him advice.) Barrett usually traveled with a company of about 100 and supplies that required nearly a dozen freight cars. Daily administration was handled by several company members who doubled their responsibilities. Foremost among these facile artists later in Barrett's career was Austin Melford, the stage manager. On tours Melford's headquarters was simply a room in the theatre or perhaps at his own hotel. The "office" was contained in three large wicker hampers holding three typewriters, accounts books, various contracts on file, press books, letter books, and an alcohol-fed copy press. Melford's job was strenuous; each Monday began a brand new round of affairs. Some theatres, mostly those in large cities, had sufficient in-house storage space, but a large proportion of playhouses that Barrett toured had little or no storage space. In the latter case Melford had to arrange a complete change of production with each new program; even then there was frequently not enough room for an entire setting on stage. Some of this difficulty was overcome by using certain large scenic pieces in different configurations for several productions. During the plays Melford stayed at the prompt corner; he yielded control to his assistant on the other side of the stage (another actor-technician) when he had to go on to act. In Barrett's company the call boy was completely responsible for an actor's entrance. This resolved any possible trouble between the actors and the stage manager as it was never an actor's fault if he missed an entrance. The call book, Melford recalled, looked like a shooting script for a modern film. The whole operation "worked splendidly," he further remembered. "I can't remember anything untoward happening. . . . W.B.'s system was sound, [especially] when one remembers the entrances, lighting, changes, supers' entrances, sound effects, etc."[91] Other technicians on tours were a master carpenter and second carpenter, property master, baggage man, hairdresser, wardrobe mistress, and business manager.

Barrett's penchant for careful organization was also evident in his treatment of actors. He belonged to the Old Days, and every colorful trapping of the grand manner surrounded him on tour as well as at home. He always engaged special train coaches—one just for himself—and made sure each actor's belongings were correctly stowed in each compartment. Moreover, again like Frohman, Barrett wanted his actors to be warm on stage but aloof in public. The reasons for this had to do with the sensitivity of a Victorian public who might misinterpret the actions of theatre folk traveling and living together thousands of miles from home. Hence, each compartment was carefully guarded and bestowed with its own nametag, while certain older members of the company were designated to act as chaperones. Barrett carried this so far that his actors were not even allowed to speak with other passengers except when absolutely necessary. Leisure time also was organized, and on Sunday evenings the actors would be summoned to Barrett's rooms to hear him read or talk to them about various theatrical topics. Even the books they read were chosen by Barrett, The Chief. The American actress Lillah McCarthy, who joined the company on their next U.S. tour, recalled that Barrett was a "school of discipline and authority. . . . It was an autocracy of the theatre and Barrett insisted that we should have little or no life beyond the stage and his vigilance." "I revolted against his methods then," the actress concluded, "and I believe in them now."[92]

If the young actors chafed under such heavy discipline, Barrett thrived on it, showing more of his outgoing nature on this tour than ever before. Newspaper interviews continued to be far-ranging in their topics, and Barrett participated in philanthropic benefits whenever he had the opportunity. He was in a good humor, joking about his travels through drought-ridden Texas, where rain seemed to follow each day after *Claudian's* thunderclaps. And he took up a hobby. If any one thing points to a change in his mental outlook at this time it was his enjoyment of a newly discovered gadget: the camera. He loved his "Kodak" and used it extensively, taking thousands of pictures of architecture and scenery. He calmed himself, he said, by going into his darkroom and developing photographic plates, relieved from the pressures of theatrical affairs. Later he used the camera in his directing work, criticizing both his acting and that of the company by use of pictures.

Barrett returned home in May with several ideas for new plays. He was working in collaboration with the American author Alexander W. Thompson on a play about an inventor, Dr. Stephen Emmons, who resembled Barrett in appearance. Emmons, an Englishman who had emigrated to the United States, was widely known at the time for his experiments with electricity and batteries. In fact, he was instrumental in introducing electric light onto the London stage in Charles Reade's *Love the Money* at the Adelphi and in a pantomime at Drury Lane. He was a man of formidable will power, unhampered by traditional scientific thinking or fear of failure. Barrett met him in Boston and was immediately struck by his character. Nothing came of the play, however, because Barrett met another writer in the meantime, and both of them were inspired to write a play about a contemporary social problem. This writer's first suggestions to Barrett for a play about Savonarola or Benvenuto Cellini were rejected, even though Barrett probably would have done well with these picturesque subjects. Instead, they chose the daring theme of prostitution. Barrett's collaborator in this new work was Louis Napoleon Parker, a multilingual dramatist and musical composer who was also a member of the Royal Academy of Music. Parker's first play, *A Buried Talent*, was produced in London in 1890 and was the occasion of Mrs. Patrick Campbell's debut. He became a full time author in 1892 but was most successful as a play adapter and translator.

Barrett intended their new play to be a psychological study of a social problem. He wanted to "teach those who are growing up, not merely the broad lines of right and wrong, of honesty and dishonesty, but something more."[93] The play tells the story of Ralph Ainsley, a philanthropist who anonymously endows a refuge for unmarried mothers ("The House of Peace") in atonement for his own past, which involved a disastrous love affair. Ainsley falls in love with Sybil, the adopted daughter of his business partner, and marries her, later to discover that she was the woman of his "past." Of course, she is reformed now, and besides, the mitigating circumstances of "drugs" excuses her earlier actions.

Ironically, this play, *The Black Kitten*, is reminiscent of Ibsen's *Ghosts*. Ainsley's "refuge," for example, can be associated with Mr. Alving's orphanage; it was built for the same reasons and hovers over the action of the play in the same symbolic way. Moreover, Barrett intended that Sybil, like Mrs. Alving, should not be blamed for falling into a trap and getting into trouble because of it, for even though the trap was one into which her own inclinations may have drawn her, nevertheless "knowledge of the existence of such traps [had] been carefully kept from her."[94] The censor, however, didn't see it that way; he banned the play. Barrett was not deterred. He published the play and sold the rights for American production. Barrett normally was cautious as a producer, and he certainly knew that those who read this play would be shocked. Yet he persisted in using his valuable time to complete and publish it. Significantly, he demonstrated the same kind of persistence with an uncharacteristic play about another topic later in his career, and at that time his reason for attachment to the play was deeply personal. There is no evidence of this with *The Black Kitten*, though the tone of the play is so different from most of Barrett's work that the implication is left open to debate.

Published plays might satisfy personal or artistic needs, but Barrett was still substantially in debt and needed produceable dramas. To this end he turned once more to the novelist he had so much luck with in 1888, Hall Caine, who was about to publish his third novel about Manx life, *The Manxman*. Barrett had previously adapted without much success Caine's second novel, *The Bondman* (1890), producing it for copyright at the Park Theatre in Philadelphia, where the play was introduced briefly among Barrett's more successful plays during the 1893-1894 tour. *The Bondman* was accused of displaying all the gloomiest excesses of *Ben My Chree*. *The Manxman*, on the other hand, had more potential as a human drama. The action revolves around a woman who is torn between love for her husband, Pete Quilliam, and for the father of her child, Phillip Christian. Caine was afraid that Barrett's preference for virtuous heroines might lead him to reject the play. "One thing I must say to you," Caine warned, "the heroine is not in a good position at the beginning. . . . A blameless woman is no longer interesting on the stage. . . . Make your reckoning with that fact before going farther."[95] By this time, however, Barrett had adjusted to this idea, having used it himself in *The Black Kitten*, and he approved.

But from the start there was trouble concerning the novel's capacity to be transformed into either of two plays. First, it could have been an impressive drama with court scenes, renunciations, and the pangs of conscience of a haunted man, like *The Deemster*. In this case the play would have Phillip Christian as its central character, but it would have an overall tone of depression and cynicism—modern. On the other hand, the same novel could also be adapted into a more pastoral play, a warm drama with tragic overtones. In this case Phillip's friend Peter Quilliam would be the most important figure. Caine, along with members of Barrett's company, voted for the first version; Barrett held out for the second. The dilemma was resolved when Caine agreed to cooperate on a "Pete" version for Barrett, while Barrett consented to collaborate on a "Phillip" version for Caine. Barrett planned to produce his version of the new play abroad and in the provinces, and he agreed to allow Caine the rights to the "Phillip" play for London.

This settled, Barrett began working on *The Manxman* scripts while he was in Boston in 1894. Act I was completed there; Act II was written on the steamship *City of Paris* while Barrett was returning home in May. Then another difficulty arose. When Barrett arrived at Cardiff he was served with a civil suit filed against him by Caine regarding, of all things, *The Manxman*. Caine alleged that he had never allowed Barrett to play the "Pete" version in London. To make matters worse, Caine had signed a contract with two other managers for the "Phillip" version, knowing all along that Barrett would soon be playing the "Pete" drama. Barrett, who always despised double-dealing, was furious and wrote to Caine saying so. Then he put the matter in the hands of the firm of Lewis and Lewis, theatrical lawyers, hoping that the managers who had contracted with Caine would honorably recognize the difficulty and also that Barrett's right to eventually play his version in London would be verified.[96] The affair was finally settled in Barrett's favor, and the managers agreed to rescind their pledges, albeit with payment from Barrett for their losses. The provincial manager involved, Maurice Bandmann, was allowed to produce the "Phillip" version wherever it did not conflict with Barrett, and Barrett was given all the rights to the "Pete" version forever, even in London, if he produced it there before February 1896.[97] Caine was to destroy his version if Barrett's London production ran over fifty nights. In the meantime Caine was allowed to sell his "Phillip" version to Lewis Waller, a former member of Barrett's company, who produced it at the Shaftsbury in London in June. Barrett had actually written this version, too, but unlike his own, in this one he followed Caine's suggestions to the letter. Barrett knew this play would not succeed, and it did not, being doomed from the first rehearsal. "It has been a most unpleasant episode," Barrett wrote to Clement Scott, "and I fear the end is not yet."[98] For the moment, however, the legal decision ended the difficulties, and Barrett continued writing. Caine was simply naive, not malicious; he and Barrett were soon reconciled.

The third act of the "Pete" version was completed in a village in Buckinghamshire where Barrett was recuperating from the stress of the tour. Act IV was completed on location at the Isle of Man, where Barrett escorted the company in order to help them "realize [the play's] action more vividly than by many rehearsals."[99] The final act was finished during the first week of a two-week engagement at Leeds.

Barrett disliked the tedious process of adapting novels for the stage and had promised himself after *Ben My Chree* that he would never do it again. However, he was too ambitious to allow other managers to cash in on Caine's success. After all, he had given Caine his start as a dramatist and taught him all he knew about playwriting. So it was with some reluctance that Barrett went to work on *The Bondman* and especially *The Manxman*. The great amount of prejudice that an adapter had to face from a public in love with the novel was a major drawback to success. By the same token, there were the problems of the technical differences between drama and fiction as well as persuading literary authors that their work needed revision if it would ever make it successfully to the stage. In Caine's case, this was doubly difficult because he had the habit of drawing characters from several generations into his novels. Barrett recognized the need on stage to get right to the point and to incorporate previous action (play action which took place before the rise of the curtain) within stage action as much as possible. "On the stage," he wrote, "personality is the be-all and end-all, and words must logically be secondary; here, at least, actions speak louder than words."[100] Barrett's version of *The Manxman* differed from the novel in some important ways because of this understanding on Barrett's part. The locales were changed and consolidated, and the ending was changed as well. In the novel, Phillip, the child's father, goes off with Kate, condemned by Manx law to permanent exile. Barrett thought this implied sympathy with Phillip's and Kate's actions, so in his version he saw to it that Phillip and Kate were punished by being forced to live apart forever. The final curtain descended on the departure of the tragic figure of Kate's husband, Pete, the real victim.

The Manxman opened at the Grand in Leeds on 15 November 1894. Critics were surprised that the actor who played Claudian, Othello, and

Hamlet could play the part of simple Pete so well. A fine, delicate human touch was seen in Barrett's acting, reminiscent of the best of Joseph Jefferson. "There's been nothing seen like this Pete for many a year," wrote the reporter for *The Yorkshire Evening Post.* "We have seen Mr. Barrett in many parts, but none in which he more loses *himself* and becomes the character he impersonates."[101] All of the traces of formalism that had been creeping into Barrett's acting were gone, but once again it was the inspired natural acting of Maud Jeffries that provided the catalyst both for the play's action and for the believability of Pete's suffering. As Kate, she successfully portrayed the delicate balance of love for Phillip and sympathy for Pete that allowed Barrett to draw so much pathos out of his character's actions. If the audience would not sympathize with her character, Pete would be thought a fool instead of a victim; but as it was, the result was a carefully planned ambiguity precisely suited to Barrett's acting talents. The only negative criticism of the play was its tendency to be overelaborate, creating a slow tempo that occasionally made the action drag.

Sad personal events also occurred this year for Barrett, events which continued to remind him of Macready. In August Barrett unexpectedly lost his second daughter, Katherine Margaret, to meningitis. Later the same month Barrett's brother, close friend, and long-time company member, George, died of a spinal and kidney disease—sadly, only nine weeks after his marriage. George had been ill ever since his disastrous solo tour of the United States a few years before, when he lost all of his savings. Brother Robert had died of tuberculosis the previous October (Barrett generously took responsibility for his wife and four children). This meant that Barrett had lost two daughters and two brothers in three years. His family now consisted of his two sons and a third daughter. One boy, Frank, was in Los Angeles philandering; the other managed a Leeds printing firm. "Those two lovely girls gone," he wrote to Jeffries, "and those two blackguards of sons still living."[102] Dorothy was living with her uncle in the south. He took all these deaths hard and attributed the insomnia he began to suffer about this time to this cause.

Barrett's mood was saddened still more by the necessity this year of relinquishing the management of the Grand Theatre, Leeds. He was on tour too often to guide it as carefully as he had in the past, and its expenses were becoming an intolerable burden to him. As early as 1888 the directors of the theatre, wanting a resident manager, had tried to remove him, but when the shareholders heard the news they called a meeting and decided to keep Barrett. Since then he had tried to resolve the situation (and perhaps solve certain family problems as well) by assigning first son Alfred, then Frank as managers. However, this year the directors managed to get enough votes to end the lease. The Theatre Royal in Hull had been given up in 1891 for precisely the same reasons.

10. Wilson Barrett as Pete in *The Manxman*.

Barrett deeply regretted losing these playhouses. Recognizing this, and the fact of Barrett's recent personal losses, the people of Leeds gave a farewell benefit and celebration for Barrett to commemorate his long tenure at their playhouse. The theatre was elaborately decorated for the celebration, and after the performance Barrett received many tributes and telegrams from playgoers, actors, and managers all over England thanking him for his contributions to the artistic life of the country. His company, the typical member of which had been with him for an average of fourteen years, presented him with a silver plate inscribed for the occasion. The climax of the evening came when the Bishop of Truro made his presentation. Back in 1875, when Barrett first undertook management at Leeds, the Bishop solemnly admonished him "to endeavor to give Leeds people something to elevate them, something to take away which will help to make them better men and women." Everyone felt that Barrett had carried out that pledge, and the Bishop offered Barrett a silver commemorative vase inscribed with these words: "In grateful acknowledgement of a promise nobly kept."[103]

The termination of Barrett's management at Leeds was almost the end of his period of international doldrums. He was still in debt but making steady financial progress, and the day was ahead when he would at last be solvent again. He had gone through numberless calms, the worst of which were his family losses and disastrous second U.S. tour; he had encountered squalls with Henry Arthur Jones, Hall Caine, and others; and he had experienced the light winds of periodic success that never seemed to last long enough. In November 1894, as he embarked on his fifth American tour, the wind of his fortunes was rising again.

5

Prosperity (1894–1904)

Fifth American Tour: *The Sign of the Cross* and Religious-Revival Melodrama

An idea for a new play began to grow in Barrett's mind during his last two tours of the United States when he was impressed by the popularity of Colonel Robert Ingersoll's public lectures on the subject of "Atheism *versus* Christianity." Ingersoll, an American lawyer and orator, was known as The Great Agnostic; his lectures won him wide attention wherever he traveled. Barrett had it in mind to write a play that would embody a revivalist mood of religiosity in his own country, a drama to counteract the secular modern trend. His play would refute the ideas of people like Ingersoll and especially of new school dramatists. Later Barrett recalled the specific reason for writing this new work:

> I did it by prolonged reflection upon the best way of combating the unwholesome tendencies of the so-called "problem play." These "sex pieces" were frightening family people from the theatres. I wanted to bring wives and daughters to it, and at the same time bridge the gulf dividing regular theatre goers from the class which avoids the playhouse from religious motives.[1]

By the middle of the 1893–1894 U.S. tour Barrett had decided that the new play would be about a woman with a future instead of a past; someone who would be admired, not censured.

The immediate cause of the inspiration for the play occurred when Barrett was traveling with his company on a train between engagements. He was intrigued by a mark carved on numbers of large rocks which the train passed from time to time. The porter informed Barrett that they were assayer's marks used to designate the site where certain minerals were located. The mark was a crude cross, and the porter referred to it as "the sign of the cross." Stafford Smith, the business manager, related that this phrase seemed to have an unusual effect on Barrett, who repeated the words over and over. What was happening was that Barrett's unshaped ideas about the new play were crystallizing. The assayer's mark and the porter's comments triggered Barrett's well-known interest in the past. Earlier Barrett thought the new drama might be a personal one; he rejected that idea now in favor of a religious-revival drama with a larger scope called *The Sign of the Cross*. By the time he returned to England the scenario was fixed in his mind; Jeffries's importance can be seen throughout:

> My heroine is emblematic of Christianity; my hero stands for the worn out paganism of decadent Rome. She is strong with the faith of a woman; he, strong with the self-reliance of a man. As I see her, she is beautiful with a half-divine loveliness, and an exquisite soul looks out through a beautiful face. She has given up the world for the sake of her new found faith, in which she lives, and is resolved, if need be, to die. Nero is on the throne, and has decreed the extermination of the Christians, the execution of the decree is entrusted to my pagan Patrician, and thus he is brought into contact with the Christian girl. In her, he at once recognized an almost sacred beauty, a beauty of holiness, and voluptuary that he is, he sets himself to win her. Twice he stands between her and death, and she is consequently moved to regard him with a tender interest, but his persuasive pleadings and soft arts are of no avail. Steadfast in her faith, she resists all temptation, and he is driven in spite of himself to seek a reason for her sovereign power and his crushing defeat. He finds it in the uplifting and ennobling influence of her creed. And, his soul quickened by the breath of her spirit, and kindled into something of a likeness to itself, he flings honours, wealth, all to the winds, and hand in hand with her meets the martyr's doom.[2]

Anyone familiar with Barrett's previous plays would see another important similarity here besides the progress-toward-salvation theme. This would be the importance to the plot of an imperiously self-indulgent ruling class which generated an oppressed condition in the common people and gave dramatic momentum to the entire play. *The Sign of the Cross*, like so many other of Barrett's dramas, was an exceptionally well-conceived story. At home, during the early fall of 1894, Barrett informed Clement Scott of the new drama and asked him to help complete the dialogue and polishing. To his credit Scott declined, saying that the play was essentially complete already and that he could not add anything anyway, it was too good as it stood. Scott was especially pleased because he was a recent convert to Catholicism and welcomed the play as a significant contribution to his new faith.

Barrett's financial trials had developed in him a keen sense of the administrative operations of the English theatre, and for several years now he had abandoned the idea of reestablishing himself permanently in a major London playhouse as he had at the Princess's. That era was past; it was better now to go to London with a success than to try to make one there. By the same token, Barrett, said J.B. Booth, had a "fixed belief" that *The Sign of the Cross* would be the turning point in his up and down career.[3] He would not endanger this golden opportunity by hastily throwing an untested new play at the London public. Barrett's plan was to open the play during his next U.S. tour, 1894–1895, rewrite it as he moved homeward, then open in

London with a polished hit. Before he departed for America he left plans for the stage designs with his staff and arranged for the construction of the settings in well-equipped shops in Leeds and at the Lambeth Baths. Afterwards, the completed scenery would be shipped to a prearranged city in the United States, where Barrett would meet it and begin final rehearsals.

After a rough crossing on the *Britannic*, Barrett's fifth U.S. tour began at the Star Theatre in New York on 20 November 1894. His repertoire for the next twenty-two weeks included *The Manxman, Hamlet, Virginius, Claudian, Othello, Ben My Chree*, and *The Silver King*. The first weeks were spent entirely in the northeast: one month at the Star, another at the Park in Brooklyn, then two weeks at Boston's Globe through February. This lengthy engagement within one small area of the country gave Barrett the time he needed to complete the new script; he also had the opportunity to avail himself of east coast theatrical supply houses. After Boston, Barrett traveled to Montreal, Toronto, London (Ontario), Woodstock, and Hamilton (Ontario); then he went on to Buffalo, Milwaukee, and finally Chicago, where he wrote home that he was not doing as well here as last year. "I had hoped to make a lot of money this season [to underwrite *The Sign of the Cross*] and under ordinary circumstances I should have done so. . . . In advance one never knows in America what will or won't do."[4]

By the time Barrett left Chicago *The Sign of the Cross* was ready to open in St. Louis, the company's next tour stop. During their last tour, Barrett had done exceedingly well in St. Louis, but there were other reasons for choosing to open the new play there. "Why did I choose St. Louis?" he said.

> For this special reason that the early settlers . . . were French, and that consequently the Roman Catholic element was strong. So also was the Protestant community, for it is a large city. Now I had designed my piece in the days of the early Christians in order that it might be absolutely unsectarian. The attitude of a St. Louis audience and of the St. Louis press would tell me at once whether my work was as I wished it to be . . . free from sectarianism in any shape or form.[5]

The Sign of the Cross opened in the middle of the week, on 27 March 1895, but the effect of the new play was not immediately apparent at the box office, which showed a first night increase of only $20. But as the play ran during the next three days, Barrett's grand hopes for it proved to be true. He wrote home,

> The effect of *The Sign of the Cross* has been electrical. I never played a piece yet that has had the same strong hold upon an audience. Now it is the talk of the city—and men are debating it everywhere—they speak in the wildest terms of praise. "The grandest play ever produced," etc., etc. The reading gives no idea of the . . . acting value of the play. The audience in the three performances were breathless throughout except when roars of applause would come—this was the case not only on the first night, but yesterday

afternoon and evening. I can hardly write of the scenes for fear you would think I was exaggerating. What the results will be elsewhere I hardly know—but if St. Louis is any guide—I need play nothing else for the next five years. It was expressed that compared with *The Manxman—The Sign of the Cross* was an arc light to a tallow dip. . . . The scene of the Christians in the woods brings tears to the eyes—and the feeling is almost awe inspiring when as they are being slaughtered they raise their hands to God and sing a hymn until they are struck down. The third and fourth acts are tremendous in the effects. I wish I could get others to tell you what they tell me. The absolute reverence paid by the gallery is most remarkable. If I could only get it to London—!![6]

There was some press criticism that the hero and heroine did not become friends until much too late in the play; otherwise, praise was enthusiastic. The comments of the reporter for *The St. Louis Republican* echo those of other St. Louis newspapers:

The state has never witnessed such free and daring use of sacred things as the new play develops, but the theme is worked out with such skill that only the sublime results. Mr. Barrett's purpose was to divert the popular mind from the dramatic trash of the day. If he can but get the notion abroad that his new piece is not a slow-going lecture, but a spirited human play of an unusual sort, he will succeed.[7]

The one distressing thing was that Barrett was nearly broke due to the excessive cost of the play. He wanted to pay off the production expenses before he arrived home with the piece and had little money left to continue the tour. Moreover, he had been plagued throughout the tour by requests for money from his son Frank in Leeds, who was fast becoming a monetary liability. "The other side of the question is galling," as he described it.

The £300 that I sent to Leeds has left me unable to pay salaries and unless I had borrowed £100 last night we could not have got to Memphis [Jeffries' home]. Memphis will be bad—the £100 is to be repaid next week—and then another long journey. I have had the influenza all the week. It came on Tuesday and I have suffered horribly all the time. Last night I must have been semi-delirious. I have just turned the corner this morning—but the pain and the weakness is hard to bear. . . .

On no possible chance can I send another shilling to Leeds.

The best of my tour is over. I have paid almost all the cost of the production and it is beautiful.[8]

Barrett soon recognized, however, that worry about money on this tour and hereafter was quite unnecessary. As he moved eastward reviews for *The Sign of the Cross* continued to be extremely favorable and houses consistently full. Dispatches about his success preceded him from town to town, assuring him of a warm reception when he arrived. After Memphis, there were nine weeks left on the tour, which included the cities of Nashville, Louisville, Cincinnati, Pittsburgh, Baltimore, Washington, D.C., Philadelphia, Jersey City, and Brooklyn. By June, the end of the tour, profits had risen to $55,622 (£11,124), all of which was accumulated after the St. Louis date.[9]

Barrett and the company returned to England in July eager to continue to London. To this end Barrett arranged with William Greet to find a London playhouse as soon as possible. Meanwhile, Barrett began a four-month provincial tour, from which press releases to London about each performance generated interest in the new play. The provincial debut occurred at the Grand in Leeds on 26 August, and the response was even more enthusiastic than in the United States. According to a critic for *The Idler*,

What I then beheld was an audience, notoriously addicted to the frothiest and most frivolous forms of entertainment, hushed to silence, spell-bound and thrilled by dramatic pictures of the gradual purification by love and faith of a licentious Pagan, and the ecstatic exaltation of the early Christian martyrs. The whole house, it was apparent, was unable to resist a certain undefinable but undeniable spiritual charm evolved from an atmosphere of unassailable purity, simplicity and faith, pervading the crucial scenes of the drama. The exquisite language of Holy Writ—frequently pressed into the dramatist's service—was listened to with a reverence that bordered on awe. And as for the note of solemn reality struck during the final scene—of the gentle maiden martyr's last moments on earth—affected the vast throng as never before in my life I had seen a theatre audience impressed. Certainly, a deep and abiding impression might justly have been hoped for. In the amazing simplicity of the scene; in the pictures of the inspired martyrs going gladly to their doom; of the shrieking, terrified boy, strengthened by the grace of God to win his immortal crown; and of the final trial and temptation of the Christian girl; lastly in the triumphant calm of the last moments of the woman and the man, strong in faith and love, everything was so beautifully felt, so simply conceived, so classically treated, that any impression was possible. But for the classic and sublime there has not hitherto been a demand, and the author's daring at this point, I feared, had overshot the mark. It was not he, but I, who had done that. And when the curtain fell, and after a moment's silence a great roar of cheering went up, I was convinced that Wilson Barrett had that evening rendered the stage a signal service, and given it a memorable play.[10]

It was decided after some difficulty that the play would open in London after the beginning of the new year at the Lyric Theatre on Shaftesbury Avenue in Westminster. Barrett originally wished for the Princess's, but in recent years that playhouse had run into hard times. The Barrett Company could not profit at the new low admission prices there. Next, Daly's, the Lyric, Drury Lane, and the Shaftesbury were considered but found wanting. Following these, good terms were offered at the large Imperial until the owner discovered that Greet was negotiating for Wilson Barrett, then the price rose sharply. This was October, however, and Barrett was forced to accept the high terms. Barrett then learned to his dismay that the Metropolitan Board of Works required £3,000 and two months' worth of repairs before the Imperial could be allowed to open. At this point Greet, who may have been manipulating the whole affair to his advantage all along, announced that the Lyric could be leased if Barrett would grant him provincial rights to *The Sign of the Cross*. Barrett had no choice but to accept this gentle extortion at £200 per month plus rates for thirteen months. He was to receive sixty percent of the gross.

The Sign of the Cross opened at the Lyric on 4 January 1896; from the start it was clear that London audiences admired the play. Barrett's earnest and virile acting style suited the role of Marcus, the Roman centurion, while Maud Jeffries as Mercia showed that she possessed the innocence and stature that her important role demanded. Another popular actress in the play was young Haidee Wright, who played Stephanus, the young boy who suffered martyrdom. Wright's shriek offstage as she was thrown to the lions never failed to shock. In fact, it was not long until audiences came to anticipate the event. Erroll Sherson reported that one playgoer, hurrying to arrive on time for the opening curtain, asked the ticket man, "Has she shrieked yet?"[11] But there was more to the production than theatrics. A mysterious public reaction was at work. The play had *meaning*, being the complete theatrical embodiment of late-Victorian religious-revival feelings. "I rejoice to hear of the wide and warm approval which the piece has received," former Prime Minister William Gladstone said after seeing the play, "most of all because its popularity betokens sound leanings and beliefs in the mass of the people."[12] "I believe you have done more for the drama (and not merely British drama) than it's possible at the moment to estimate," playwright J.M. Barrie wrote to Barrett.[13] Even George Bernard Shaw liked the play, though, of course, modernists led by William Archer were appalled by it.

For over a year "House Full" signs were constantly on display in front of the Lyric, and posters with a large red cross against a black background were seen all over the country. By the end of the year, the play was being seen by nearly 70,000 a week in Great Britain alone. Later performed in Russia, Holland, Germany, Austria, South Africa, Canada, New Zealand, and the United States, by 1904 *The Sign of the Cross* eventually would be staged over 10,000 times. Seventy-nine thousand copies of the popular song of the Christians in the play would be sold. The play began a vogue for religious-revival melodrama that eventually became one of the mainstays of the infant film industry; Cecil B. DeMille produced a version of the play starring Frederick March that is still occasionally seen on television. The original production ran for 435 performances until 30 January 1897. Profits from the play, both during its premiere provincial tour and in London, were so great that as early as December 1895 Barrett was able to renegotiate the mortgages for several of his plays. By July 1896, through the agency of a syndicate formed by Greet and William Englebach, he had completely settled the £40,000 worth of debts, regaining the rights for all of his plays, which enabled him to send out profitable companies of his own once more. He also straightened out several personal financial affairs. Barrett put aside the royalties from William Greet's tour for his daughter Dorothy, "so that if

11. Wilson Barrett as Marcus in *The Sign of the Cross*.

anything happens to me Dolly would be all right as with very moderate business this should bring in £100 a week. . . . She must be protected against [the spendthrift natures of] the boys [Frank and Alfred]," he pronounced.[14] In January Barrett gave his stage manager, Austin Melford, three years' of provincial rights for *The Silver King* in return for back salary owed him. Besides these tours, others arranged on a strictly professional basis included three of *The Sign of the Cross* (north, midlands, and south), two of *The Silver King* (A and B), and one each of *Ben My Chree* and *The Manxman*. In all, eight Barrett productions began touring in 1896.

The general profit picture, after payment of all debts, looked something like this: £7,227 for the London production of *The Sign of the Cross* (sixty percent of the gross), plus £4,548 for provincial tour royalties—a total of £11,775.[15] A closer look at the account books for the London production reveals that receipts varied from a low of about £446 a week in July 1896 to a high of £1,702 late in January, an average of about £985 per week. Expenses were a high of £1,307 in early January to a low of £500 in mid-July, averaging about £768 per week. Advertising cost nearly £2,700 for the London run, indicating the importance of this dimension in Barrett's theatrical affairs. Evidence of the scenic quality of the production was shown in the high designers' salaries. Walter Hann, chief scene painter, received £650; Stafford Hall, who stayed with the play during its run to keep the scenery in repair, received £20 a week, or a total of £1,080 for the entire production.

Alfred Pearpoint, Barrett's solicitor, had been in charge of handling the mortgages for the last ten years, and in March he demanded repayment of £3,000 in personal loans he made to Barrett. Barrett felt that Pearpoint had already received all of this in royalties held for collateral; he called upon William Greet and William Englebach to look into the matter. After examining the accounts, they offered Pearpoint £1,500, which the solicitor refused. Barrett then undertook a full-scale investigation of Pearpoint's dealings with him. A ten-year record of bungling and mismanagement of funds was subsequently discovered, and in a dramatic reversal of events Pearpoint ended up returning £200 of overpayment.

Barrett's national theatre academy dreams also returned at this time. He instituted a training school and a series of revivals at matinees, he organized dramatic contests for actresses in his company, and he offered lessons in fencing and in stage movement. Then, so that young actors could see classic productions not often seen in London since the demise of the stock system, he began matinee revivals of older plays. The long runs were killing the acting traditions of these plays, and since he was one of the few remaining actors who could act them appropriately, the responsibility fell to him, he believed, to produce them. Among others, his Macready plays were performed at these matinees.

Professionally, Barrett resumed something of the high position he held ten years before. He attended important benefits, one honoring Charles Wyndham's twenty-year connection with the Criterion and another for Sarah Bernhardt, where he presented her with a personal gift of a silver wreath. He presided over the 1896 meeting of the newly established Actor's Association, though only 1,250 of England's 20,000 actors were members in 1896. Barrett stopped short, however, at supporting an actors' hospital, which he believed would lower the esteem of actors in the public eye. This did not stop him from being charitable himself, however. Always a generous man, his weekly subscription list, which accounted for a sizeable three percent of his weekly expenses, included the cost of outings for his staff and stage hands, loans to company members, donations to countless benefits, occasional funeral expenses, and other charitable help of various kinds. When Maud Jeffries's father was ill in Memphis this year, for example, Barrett paid for his medical bills and provided a private nurse for him. He also started his own charity fund for an actor accidentally killed while playing Tybalt in the provinces. Barrett's personal life once more took on the appearance of a successful actor-manager. He abandoned the slouch hat, velvet coat, and four-in-hand that had been his dress since *The Silver King* and assumed now a top hat, frock coat, and flannel shirt with a "Roman" neck. Also there were rumors of an impending marriage to Maud Jeffries.

In July Barrett received a request from Hall Caine regarding *The Manxman*. Dissatisfied with the production of his own "Phillip" version at the Shaftsbury some time before, Caine wanted to save face by having Barrett produce the "Pete" version on his own. Since Barrett was legally required to stage this play in London prior to the end of 1896 or lose the rights anyway, he consented. *The Manxman* opened at a matinee performance at the Lyric on 20 November and played for a few weeks; for three evenings per week it took the place of *The Sign of the Cross*. The play proved to be even more successful in London than it had been in the provinces. Shaw said he loved it. "A very excellent piece of acting," he wrote,

skillful and well judged in execution to the last degree, with just the right feeling and the right humor, and built, not on a virtuous hero formula, but in a definite idiosyncratic character conception. Add to this central attraction such effects of Mr. Wilson Barrett's unrivalled managership as the quiet certainty of business and effects, the excellent lighting of the stage, the simple touches of verisimilitude just in the right places, the filling of small parts apparently by picked character actors (though really only by young people who have had a competent adviser instead of being left to themselves or deliberately set wrong, as they are at most theatres), and you have the materials for a success out of all proportion to the merits of *The Manxman* as a serious modern play.[16]

Even William Archer recognized the quality of this performance, saying that Barrett's Pete "is a really excellent piece of popular character acting, robust, spirited, pathetic, and thoroughly alive. . . . [The role is played with] beautiful simplicity, the deepest pathos, and supurb force." Pete, said Archer, was Barrett's "best role."[17]

Barrett's writing activities and plans for the future continued unabated throughout all the activities of 1896. Reversing the novel-into-play pattern of his work with Hall Caine, he was preparing a novel adapted from *The Sign of the Cross* that would be published next year. Three more plays, besides his next Lyric production, were also in the works. In November he completed a "problem play" called *The Wishing Cup* about a young couple whose new wealth brings them only bitterness. Barrett planned to open it at the Comedy with another company. Nothing came of this idea, however, and he eventually sold the play to Charles Frohman for production in the United States. Another domestic play, *The Sledgehammer*, adapted from the Flemish original of Neston le Thiers, was completed early in 1897. It is a melodrama of murder, false accusation, wrong conviction, and tables turned on the criminals and had its debut with one of Barrett's own road companies in February at the Theatre Royal in Kilbern. And finally, there was another play about an inventor, this time Thomas Edison. Barrett had been introduced to Edison when last in Boston. Edison promised to loan him the use of some spectacular new invention to be used in the last act of the play. The year was too busy, however, and the play was never completed. Barrett also received invitations from others to perform. Shaw wanted him to play Sartorius in *Widower's Houses*.

Eighteen ninety-six, a year which ended fully as successfully as it began, proved to be a second watershed in Barrett's career. All debts were paid, a successful play was on the boards, profitable tours were out, and Barrett's position among the theatrical leadership of Great Britain was once more secure. There would be no more years of anonymity; everything he did from now on was observed and recorded by an interested press and read by an eager public. But there was another side of this outwardly successful situation. Barrett was fifty years old in 1896, and the arduous efforts of the last ten years had taken their toll on him. His remaining years would still contain a few surprises, and the intensity of his activities would never diminish, but after *The Sign of the Cross* Barrett's accomplishments would only be pale reflections of the past.

Among a certain circle of playgoers, Barrett's successful return to London this year prompted an unreasonable fear of renewed rivalry with Henry Irving, who was formally knighted in 1895 as the best representative of his profession. This time, however, at least one knowledgeable critic, Philip Amory, refused to withhold his views on the matter and chose to speak publicly of the scheming against Barrett that he had witnessed. Amory believed that Irving's eminence was strongly maintained by his carefully contrived relations with the press. An invitation to a Lyceum first night dinner, for example, was the mark of professional approval for dramatic critics, who too often responded by overlooking faults in Lyceum productions and by generally keeping down the competition. "It's as much as my place is worth," Amory wrote, "to criticize adversely any Lyceum production. And I should lose all chance of earning a living in my particular line of work if I called any living English actor greater than Irving." Amory further pointed out that the chief target of pro-Irving critics was Barrett. Then he revealed an illuminating insight into some possible reasons behind Barrett's first exile from London in 1886. Barrett seemed to have come to London in 1896 to stay, Amory said.

> *If* he stays—which it is to be hoped he will, in spite of the efforts made to get him out— you may depend upon it he will secure the leading position. That's what some people are afraid of. That's why they want to disgust him and drive him off. . . . [After all,] he's got everything in his favour: he's younger than Irving [who was 59 in 1896] and better looking, and knows how to mount his plays in a more magnificent and artistic style than Irving does. . . . When some eleven years ago Wilson Barrett played the finest Hamlet seen in the present day, one [press] ring . . . closed [on him] and hunted him down with a cruel persistency that well-nigh broke his heart and ruined him. Barrett was driven out of England, ruined, and there are several fellows among us who'd like to do it again, only he's got rather too firm a hold on the public this time for that kind of thing to be carried through without our being found out.

"The long and short of it is this," Amory concluded, "a great portion of the dramatic press is worked by unscrupulous methods, and plays into the hands of one or two men with a reckless disregard of the commonest fair-dealing and justice. This must not be allowed to go on."[18] Barrett, of course, had been through all this before. Though Amory could not have known it, from the start Barrett's stay in London would last just two years, possibly to avoid another distressing episode, but more probably because Barrett believed now that he could succeed in London only with a full-scale hit like *The Sign of the Cross.*

Meanwhile, a second religious-revival play entitled *The Daughters of Babylon* was produced at the Lyric, a Jewish sequel to *The Sign of the Cross.* Barrett's coauthor for the piece was his partner from *The Black Kitten*, Louis Napoleon Parker, and their new play was to treat the events of the Babylonian Captivity. The plot was a complex story about Lemuel's love for the woman betrothed to his brother and contained various arcane ceremonies and intricacies of Hebrew law. The scenario was, as usual, Barrett's; Parker supplied the dialogue and character drawing. Work had begun in July 1896, and by the time the play was complete in November, Barrett had done so much work on it that Parker offered him billing as sole author. Barrett declined. The scenery was finished in early December and was as elaborate as anything Barrett had ever produced. The preproduction costs were astronomical, nearly £10,000, but he was hopeful: "I have staked a fortune on *The Daughters*, but I think they will be good girls, and repay me."[19]

The Daughters of Babylon premiered at the Lyric on 6 February 1897. *The Jewish Chronicle* reported that the play was a faithful illustration of the justice and social customs of Hebrew law.[20] The scenery was excellent, "as good an idea as we are likely to get of Babylon, with its hanging gardens and its exhuberant life," said *The Athenaeum* critic.[21] There was also good music between the acts, including a sonata composed for the occasion by a distinguished concert violinist. And the whole, said George Bernard Shaw, was masterfully directed:

> Like all plays under Mr. Wilson Barrett's management, *The Daughters of Babylon* is excellently produced. . . . The cast, consisting of thirty three persons, all of them encouraged and worked up as if they were principals—a feature for which Mr. Wilson Barrett as manager can hardly have too much credit.[22]

Shaw's praise stopped short at the writing, which he felt to be an unskilled patchwork of Biblical phraseology.

Barrett didn't realize, however, that according to Amory the new play was doomed before it opened. "The word was passed among us to 'go' for *The Daughters of Babylon*," Amory wrote, "and we did it thoroughly. . . . It is quite an open secret that many of the dramatic critics were what we call 'packed' to run both [Barrett] and his play down."[23] The result was that critics from *The Era*, *The Sketch*, *The Daily Telegraph*, *The Stage*, and *The Theatrical World* condemned the play from first to last, while evidence of a conspiracy occurred when more than one of these critics condescendingly referred to the drama as a sort of "*Octoroon* set in ancient Assyria." As usual, William Archer led the attack, condemning the play's dialogue and Barrett's "staccato, peremptory style of acting." He liked the scenery but reserved his strongest criticism for the writing, complaining again that Barrett was not a modernist. Archer felt that the play proved that Barrett was sole author of all of Henry Arthur Jones's early plays; then, sarcastically alluding to the recent Barrett-Jones dispute over *The Silver King*, he pronounced that this new work acquitted Jones entirely of having written *The Silver King*. *The Daughters of Babylon*, Archer concluded, was nothing but "dolls and declamation."[24]

In the end, despite the theatrical enjoyment of the thing, the play lost nearly £1,400 during the twenty-nine weeks of its run. What was worse, a fire at Maples's Warehouse in Tottenham Court Road in February destroyed some important scenery belonging to the company along with some of Barrett's personal effects stored there. What enabled Barrett to keep the play running in the face of these losses was the increasing return from the large number of tours out in 1897. There were twenty companies playing Barrett plays, five of these belonging wholly to Barrett. The list included nine companies of *The Sign of the Cross* (north, south, William Greet's, one U.S. company temporarily playing in England, three of Ben Greet's, one midlands, and one U.S.), three of *The Silver King*, plus tours of *Ben My Chree*, *The Manxman*, *The Daughters of Babylon*, *The Golden Ladder*, and *The Sledgehammer*. Total receipts for 1897 amounted to £36,000, an average of £700 per week in royalties alone.[25] Furthermore, the novel of *The Sign of the Cross* had completely sold out its first printing of 5,000 copies; another edition of 20,000 was being prepared for England, 5,000 more for the United States.

Barrett continued his practice of reviving other plays at matinees, reintroducing *The Manxman* in April 1897 and *Othello* for one week at the end of May. This was the first time London audiences had seen Barrett in the latter role. Shaw thought he was too civilized and that his voice was not up to the musical demands of Shakespeare's verse. It is helpful to remember that Barrett's new school interpretation of Hamlet generated the same kind of comment from other reporters who were expecting a traditional declamatory style of acting in that role. Shaw may have misunderstood Barrett's interpretation of the Moor and the generally modern tone of the entire production, but he continued his praise of Barrett's directing talents. Barrett, Shaw said,

> produces the play very well. At the Lyceum everyone is bored to madness the moment Sir Henry Irving and Ellen Terry leave the stage; at the Lyric, as aforetime at the Princess's, the play goes briskly from beginning to end; and there are always three or four successes in smaller parts sparkling around Mr. Barrett's big part.[26]

Later, informal plans were discussed which would have led to a production of the play with Barrett and Johnston Forbes-Robertson alternating in the leading roles, but nothing came of this.

Things were going so well for Barrett financially that for the first time in his professional career he could afford to let the theatre rest and take a vacation. George R. Sims advised him that Germany would be a fine place to visit, especially a resort near Bad Pyrmont. Theatrical artists had been gathering there for years now, and the place had gained a reputation. Louis Parker made the arrangements, and Barrett took temporary leave of *The Daughters of Babylon* in August, traveling with his daughter Dorothy and the Heaths. The acting company was invited as well; they arrived and departed in groups of a dozen or so, staying for a few days, then returning to the play at the Lyric. Barrett apparently vacationed for about a month.

More serious matters injured Barrett's vanity, more properly his pride, during 1897. This was the Queen's Diamond Jubilee year, and according to custom she would honor certain citizens to celebrate the occasion. There was talk of honors for some of the leading actor-managers, specifically Barrett and Squire Bancroft, and in *The Referee* in April letters were published advancing Barrett's name. The public wanted Barrett to be the next theatrical knight because of the good work he had done for the stage as well as for his own merits. Unfortunately, opposing influences were brought to bear against him. Rumors were circulated that he had written the letters to *The Referee* himself. Barrett was further snubbed when he was not invited to an important dinner party at the Duke of Fife's; Wyndham, Toole, and Alexander were there along with Irving and Bancroft to meet the Prince of Wales. Amory wrote of this,

> There's a lot of back stair scheming going on to try to put a handle to the names of vastly inferior men, and to leave Barrett out, and give him no sort of public recognition whatever for the length of time he has been at work doing everything in his power for the improvement and refinement of the stage.[27]

Amory's appeal did no good, however, and Bancroft was the only actor knighted in 1897. Much to the discredit of the English theatrical profession of that time, Barrett's bid for knighthood was peremptorily dismissed and forgotten.

First Australian Tour

Over the past ten years Barrett's touring experience helped him to develop a policy that recognized traveling as an integral part of a modern actor-manager's activities. Australia, at first glance too far from England to be of any real value to Barrett's career, would actually become an important part of that policy. "After my almost incessant travels in America," he told a reporter, "Australia no longer seemed strange or far off to me." He continued,

> I had heard on all sides for years past of the magnificent way in which Australian pieces were staged. Not only from stars, but from countless stock actors, the same opinion reached me, thus preparing me to view with favour a country where the spectacular effects of my dramas would be fully appreciated. With this was coupled the desire to make a world-wide reputation, should I prove equal to the task. Then, too, the strain of appearing before the same audiences throughout an immense run, as at the Lyric, was very great. And Henry Irving's visits to America spring from the same cause—the absolute necessity which every artist feels for enlarging the scope of action so as to give himself and his regular audiences a rest.[28]

Barrett had actually received an invitation to travel to Australia back in 1895 from agents Thomas Williamson and George Musgrove. He had already worked with them regarding various royalty arrangements for earlier plays, and he trusted them. The success at the Lyric in 1895 temporarily made the tour impossible, but now that Barrett's lease was up, he decided to go. His newly regained prominence allowed him to secure good contractual terms. He wanted to use his own actors; it was agreed that he could bring along a company of twenty-three, to be supplemented by Australians if needed. The agents paid for the entire passenger and freight fares from England, amounting to £3,000, and further guaranteed Barrett a minimum profit for a sixteen-week tour, eight weeks each in Melbourne and Sydney.[29] Barrett would supply posters, band parts, his own fares and travel expenses within the country, costumes, scenery, and props together with eight productions. The agents arranged all bookings, room and board, company salaries and fares in Australia, transport of freight, chorus and supers, and £400 plus the services of scene painters to make the productions complete. The contract further stipulated that the agents were to receive the first £800 per week, and that Barrett would receive three-fifths of all above that. Preliminary to Barrett's arrival, the agents sent on a tour a stereoscopic display of scenes from various Barrett productions accompanied by an actress and a singer who presented readings and songs from selected plays. It was an effective publicity effort that assured the agents of provincial as well as metropolitan interest.

Barrett and the company arrived in Melbourne in early December 1897, opening with *Virginius* on the eleventh. The response was warm. "There were nine calls for the last two acts," he wrote home enthusiastically, "and even then the people would not leave the theatre—I had to speak to them. They are like Americans, too—accustomed to leaving without a call as a rule."[30] Later in December there was a very excited reception for *Claudian*. He had feared that the "anti-English feeling among the lower strata" might tend to hurt his welcome, but it did not. "The audience was very enthusiastic and what was better," he remarked, "as still as mice in the quiet scenes—a most unwarranted thing here for they are rather of the shifty, noisy, provincial [type]."[31] There were, however, problems with the scenery, some of which arrived severely damaged because of the trip across the world. "Musgrove has made a mess of the scenery business," he complained. "They had to paint for *Virginius* and *Ben My Chree* both—not, of course, nearly as well done as ours—and it has cost them five times the amount of the carriage of our own."[32] Moreover, the settings for *Hamlet*, his most popular play, had been delayed, and it was not certain when he could produce the show. Besides these difficulties, some important members of the Australian theatrical community were trying to persuade Barrett not to produce *The Sign of the Cross* there. It had been produced last year in Australia's major cities, and they felt Barrett's own production would spoil the impression of the original. He went ahead with the performances as planned.

By March all the troubles had been checked, and Barrett was extremely pleased at the efficient manner in which the tour was being conducted:

> All has been done for me in the theatre that I could wish for. Williamson is the best
> manager I have met—he knows the whole business—has the best staff I ever came cross—
> is liberal and unsparing and has produced plays for which I did not bring scenery with a
> completeness that is wonderful considering the few performances we can give of them. It
> has been delightful to be in the theatre so far as the people are concerned. They would
> work night and day for me and the quiet and order while I am about are remarkable.[33]

Barrett and his daughter Dorothy were escorted in Melbourne by his
nephew, Fred Wood, son of his mother's brother who had emigrated. In fact,
Barrett was treated royally by a long list of political and cultural dignitaries.
The weather, though, was miserable. Throughout the entire tour the country
was besieged with dry heat, severe dust storms, and brush fires which caused
many deaths among the populace. "Drought and pestilence, rabbits were
piled up against the fences over which they had tried to climb for water,"
wrote the young Lillah McCarthy—a newcomer to the business of touring
with Barrett. "As the train crossed the desert, dry locusts beat like hail
against the windows. I yearned to get away."[34] Throughout all this Barrett's
mood remained relaxed and easy, though uncharacteristically introspective.
Despite the good houses and social affairs, he spent a good deal of time
alone in his hotel room. Now that he had reached success again, he
discovered he had no one with whom to share it. In January he wrote home:

> It is pretty lonely here. If I do not get marreid soon I think I shall go cracked from
> melancholia. Frank [Barrett's son] says I am a misanthrope and no wonder. If you know
> of a gem in the way of a wife—that wants a-setting—let me know—of course I want
> everything that is beautiful, good, clever, etc.[35]

At any rate, Barrett's entire Melbourne professional engagement was
more than successful. He wrote:

> We finished in Melbourne March second to another packed house for Virginius and a
> wild scene of excitement. Three quarters of an hour from after the curtain fell the crowds
> outside the stage were so dense that I had to have two policemen to make a lane through
> them to enable me to get to my cab. Then we could not start for the people were all over
> the wheels, horse, and steps. When eventually I got through, they took cabs and followed
> to the hotel to cheer again.[36]

The reception for Barrett was equally good at Sydney, where Williamson
and Musgrove asked Barrett to consider extending the run another eight
weeks. Barrett had already scheduled a brief provincial tour for his return,
but he cabled home to cancel a few of the early dates and added ten more
days at Adelaide in south Australia.

Average receipts in Australia were over £1,700 per week, a total of
£14,300 profit for him.[37] Finances also continued to improve at home.
During 1898 there were nineteen troupes playing Barrett productions on

four continents. Besides Australia, his own organization sponsored five: two of *The Silver King* and three of *The Sign of the Cross*. Royaties from these tours alone amounted to £5,000.[38] Ben Greet had four companies out: three playing *The Sledgehammer* and one *The Sign of the Cross*. In all there were seven companies playing *The Sign of the Cross*, including one each in Brussels and South Africa. Barrett's healthy financial condition prompted a conciliatory attitude toward his profligate sons, "They are expensive luxuries, these sons of mine," he finally decided.[39] The Pearpoint affair was also settled. One last check of the books revealed that the ex-solicitor had bungled even worse than first thought, this time well over £8,000 worth. But it was over now, once and for all; Barrett was calm, or at least he said so to Frank Heath:

> This ends I hope a very strange and most painful episode in my life. It has come out fairly right—but it is hard to tell what Pearpoint really had of me—and what I really had of him. The worry and anxiety he caused me over money matters will remain with me for I am sure it affected my health, but there is still a sort of affection for him—why, I hardly know.[40]

Barrett's immediate personal plans concerned rest for himself and his company. Before leaving England he had promised Maud Jeffries three months at the end of the tour to visit her family. In May Barrett released her for the trip, then treated himself to a long, leisurely return home via Suez, Port Said, Naples, Berlin, and Paris. He brought with him to London some new company members. "I bring three Australian girls with me," he wrote, "two have decided talent—the third is a sister of one of these—travelling as a companion. The parents pay their expenses to England in order that they may begin with me. Both aspirants are under seventeen."[41] In truth, all three were sisters: Blanche, Maude, and Edyth Latimer. Barrett may have been deliberately misleading here, for in a short time Edyth Latimer would exercise considerable influence over Barrett's personal life. Furthermore, she may have been the immediate cause of Maud Jeffries's "vacation" and of a growing personal tension between Barrett and Jeffries which began about this time.

Barrett was also involved this year with another matter relating to a previous leading lady of his, Mary Eastlake. Eastlake's sister and brother-in-law, Colonel and Mrs. Charles Routledge, appear to have been blackmailing Barrett about some secret information regarding himself and Miss Eastlake. "I am quite aware that my wife [Eastlake's sister] has been writing to you," Routledge wrote in a very incriminating letter, "and I think it only right for you to hear what she has to say. If anything ever came out in public it might injure your reputation. Hoping you will take our meaning."[42] There is no indication what the secret was.

Barrett arrived home in July and was about to begin a new play when he was handed an injunction from Henry Arthur Jones. The event that triggered Jones's wrath this time was an obscure newspaper interview that Barrett had granted the *Sydney Morning Herald* in which Barrett claimed a share of the writing of *The Silver King*, though he was not officially listed in the program as part author. Jones sent a scathing letter to Barrett in which he called *The Sign of the Cross* "holy-mouth diarrhoea" and Barrett's acting "rant." He included an injunction stating his intention to sue for back royalties he earlier agreed to forego in Barrett's case because of *The Silver King*'s expensive mounting costs on tour.[43] Then, to make matters worse, it was discovered that someone had mistakenly placed Barrett's name along with that of Jones and Herman on the Stationer's Register. When Jones learned this, he refused to yield any share in the royalties whatsoever until he was returned all the fees for past "free" performances. Barrett was angry at this impolitic welcome back to England, especially from someone he had helped to make wealthy. It is not known exactly what he said to Jones; an incident of carping criticism regarding his interpretation of *Hamlet* in Australia generated a letter from Barrett to the press there that may give some idea of his increasingly indignant attitude to the unfair treatment he had been receiving from many quarters:

> There are men whose little lives are rendered unendurably wretched by the successes of their betters. Men whose undesirable and unhappy natures make them furious at the seemingly easy triumphs of those who flit by them in the race for fame and honour. Men whose malevolence is so overpowering that whenever they behold success—no matter how far it is removed from their own spheres of action—cannot resist the desire to belittle it. They are like little dirty boys, who seeing a white unsullied wall, are miserable until they have pelted it with filth. Such men as these are to be found in every sphere of society.[44]

Barrett decided to let Charles Wyndham and William Greet settle the affair with Jones. They concluded that though Barrett was formally incorrect in claiming part authorship for *The Silver King*, nevertheless all original royalty agreements should stand.[45]

This done, Barrett went back to work. When Jeffries returned from her visit home, he began a provincial tour lasting several months—the one he had postponed in order to spend more time in Australia. The main attraction of this tour was *The Manxman*. Barrett profited £10,700 from two tours beginning late in 1898 and extending to July 1899.[46] Another brief vacation in Germany followed.

Meanwhile, Irving's financial condition at the Lyceum had not been good, and Barrett heard from Squire Bancroft about Irving's distress. "I had a long talk with Bancroft yesterday," Barrett informed Frank Heath, "he is very shrewd indeed. Spoke kindly of H.I. but frankly said it was over—except for some now and then engagements in London, etc. A large sum was collected to stop the mouths of the smaller creditors."[47] The Lyceum was about to fold. In his twenty years there Irving had accumulated huge debts. His creditors were hounding him so severely that it was clear he would soon have to abandon the playhouse and resort to short-term engagements to satisfy them.[48] Matters were aggravated further in February when the Lyceum storage in Bear Lane, Southwark, burned to the ground, resulting in over £30,000 worth of damages. In order to begin eliminating his debts, Irving transferred the lease for the Lyceum, furniture, and fittings for £36,000 to a company headed by Comyns Carr and his two brothers, under an agreement in which Irving would act at the Lyceum only periodically. Bancroft was informal agent for the company and wrote to Barrett asking whether he would take over the theatre. Barrett agreed; he was promised two-thirds of the gross receipts, but at the time he did not anticipate the trouble he would have finding a good new script. It was not just that few writers would work with him, as had been the case in earlier years; now it was due to something else. He had never been received so warmly as he had in Australia, yet because of his melancholy mood he had not put pen to paper for several months. "I am sorry I have not written [any new plays]," he wrote to Reverend Heath, "I cannot write. . . . I seem to have some ideas—not many—but a few—but then I cannot get them on paper. I wish I could get one other big play. I suppose it will come one day."[49] Now, with Lyceum plans ahead, the problem grew acute.

The ideas he mentioned numbered four or five, and his work on them, together with his relationships with their coauthors, gives a good account of the kinds of difficulties he was facing. One theme, dealing with the reign of George III, was to be a collaboration with the American writer Elwyn Barron, whom Barrett met as a journalist with the *Chicago Inter-Ocean*. In their projected new work Barrett would play a chivalrous colonel named Esmond. Barron, essentially a novelist, was put off by Barrett's criticism of his dramatic efforts. "I must have hurt Barron's feelings by telling him of the lack of action," he wrote in April, "it is his fault and always has been—he fritters away a situation in dialogue and the quality of acting in dialogue he does not possess."[50] The play was never completed.

Other unfinished ideas followed. One was a play to be called *The Londoners*, written with Robert Hichens, who had helped to write *The Medicine Man* for Irving in 1898. Another was a play about Paolo and Francesca da Rimini, written by a friend of the writer Richard LeGallienne, Barrett's new personal secretary. LeGallienne had toured with Barrett in 1889, but illness forced him out. Now, broke and married, he was given the job of writing Barrett's biography, a task he undertook only periodically and for which he received large advances from Barrett, though he never finished more than a few chapters. The script by his friend had potential. Writing to LeGallienne in March, Barrett said, "There is much that is beautiful in the work. There is great tenderness and touching pathos." But, he continued, "the construction is not equal to the writing." Moreover, the play needed a smaller playhouse than the relatively large Lyceum; it required, said Barrett, "careful handling and a moderate size theatre—The Lyric or Haymarket." He wrote further,

> There are so many duologues that a large theatre would kill. There would seem to be a lack of action that would make the play slow. In a small place, nice inflections of voice and expansion of gesture would help to make them interesting. . . . It is certainly a fine piece for a thoughtful audience able to feel sympathy for two well intentioned but weak people, viz. Paolo and Francesca. The average man would ask "Why the devil Paolo did not go away—and why the something else his mother didn't get rid of him?" The latter played for all it is worth would gain the palm. This makes its success uncertain. All the same it is a fine effort—distinctly a play to be proud of—and I congratulate your friend on his achievement. I should like to know him. Thanks for the thoughtfulness."[51]

By June Barrett had completed another play with Louis Napoleon Parker entitled *The Outcast King.* He bought the play outright from Parker for £200 plus royalties, but it proved to be unsuited to his plans and was shelved. A play adapted from the novel *Quo Vadis* seemed to be one of his best hopes; Barrett had already written a full adaptation and begun rehearsals on it. Then he had discovered that a private version by Stanislaus Strange had been produced at the McVickers Theatre in Chicago and was about to open at the Adelphi in London. He sued and won, for earlier he had purchased the rights from the novel's author. When the play was produced in London and failed, he decided against taking a chance with his own version at this time. In desperation he turned back to George R. Sims. He had sought Sims for the task before the Australian tour, but an argument ensued and they separated. When he returned to Sims again in the summer of 1899, he discovered that Sims would still be of no help as he was broke and utterly depressed. Barrett generously gave him £100, but there was no hope of a new play there.

Much to Barrett's distress, another new play written with Hall Caine had already been disposed of. In 1897 Caine published his novel *The Christian* and proceeded to write his own stage version, which he sent to Barrett the next year. Caine, however, was never a good solo playwright; there were consequently many difficulties with the script. *The Christian* is the story of a Soho clergyman who fears that his childhood girlfriend has become a prostitute. In a long letter to Caine in September 1898 Barrett enumerated the problems in Caine's adaptation, some of which give valuable insight why Barrett was a good critic and adviser for fledgling playwrights.

The bird in the prologue is dangerous. A gull is wild and dirty, may spoil your heroine's entrance, and her dress as well. It *may* fly off the stage, *may* fly into the auditorium. If a dummy is used it will be ridiculous. . . .

The end of the prologue is very forced. Lord Storm's position is contemptible and lowers your hero's dignity and importance. When John Saxton broke his stick over his son's head at the end of the first act of *Nowadays*, the act was strictly in keeping with the character of the man—was led up to by preceding events, and again led up to strong situations later on. This in your Gloria does not happen. It is not prepared, and leads to nothing. It may end the act fairly well, but nothing comes of it. . . .

The picnic will go well—if not overdone. Take care that it does not degenerage into pantomime. It comes at an awkward time and may set the audience on a wrong tack with the play. I do not like it myself, but it may do well. . . .

It is an artistic error to repeat the same effects in the next act. The same people are again eating and drinking, shouting and singing, jingling glasses, etc., etc., etc. These repetitions are bad in every way—and in London there could be trouble. . . .

The dance in the second act stops the action of the play and will do so whether it is well or ill done. . . .

I am strongly of the opinion that the Archdeacon will cause trouble in England. Some audiences will look on him as "one of the villains of the piece" and hiss and hoot him accordingly. This will give grave offence to the church. You risk much and gain little by retaining this man's clerical character. Why not change it as I did [in *The Sign of the Cross*]? You have then a much freer hand—and give more freedom to the *actor*. . . .

Be careful of that crucifix at the end of Act III. Used in that way in Ireland it would stand a good chance of ruining the whole play—and I think most Catholics would object to it. If you instance the [attempted "rape"] scene in *The Sign of the Cross*, I would remind you that there the situations are reversed. In your play the woman is the would-be seducer. The man is in no danger (I presume) of being raped.[52]

Adapting plays from novels was no easy task. Barrett disliked it immensely for reasons already given, but his stake in Caine's career encouraged him to work assiduously on the new play for several months. "The task is not a congenial one," he said, "but it means money."[53] He even tried it out a few times in Australia to test its stageworthiness. He was hopeful enough about it to sign a production agreement. When work was interrupted by Barrett's fit of writing depression, however, Caine assumed that the play would never be produced. He therefore planned to produce it in London under Charles Frohman's guidance. Barrett filed suit when he found out. The version Caine wanted to use included a great deal of Barrett's work: in fact, everything about the play that was stageworthy. Predictably, Caine filed a countersuit alleging that he had never given Barrett permission to produce the play. A lengthy and costly arbitration followed that came to no conclusion. Barrett finally gave up on the whole idea just to be rid of the bother. Actually, as with *The Manxman*, Barrett's ideas about the play were different than Caine's anyway. Caine felt that had Barrett continued, he would have "turned the play completely around."[54]

After all these wasted efforts on Caine's play and the others, Barrett at last managed to secure a produceable play by relying on an old ally, his superstition. An idea came to him in a dream about a play which would be a psychological study of modern life and deal with the problems of drugs and the sexes. The title was *Man and His Makers*. Barrett wrote to his brother-in-law: "'It is in ourselves that we are thus and thus' (W.S.). . . . Man and His Makers: His God, His Ancestors, His Woman, Himself. Is not this very strong?"[55] The play was written on a contract basis with Louis Napoleon Parker and tells the story of a respectable lawyer, who has inherited an addiction to drugs. This was a modern theme and for Barrett marked another important adventure into "problem plays" like *The Black Kitten* and *The Wishing Cup*, plays which cloaked traditional melodramatic incidents in the framework of the well-made play. Moreover, *Man and His Makers* was another drama in which Barrett seemed to have a personal stake.

Unfortunately, delays prevented the new play from being completed in time for Barrett's Lyceum opening, and his premiere there had to be a revival. On 2 September *The Silver King* opened for a run of fifty-one performances, including matinees. Barrett's recent melancholia and inability to come up with a new play tempted him to look for a new leading lady again, perhaps seeking fresh inspiration. The actress he had in mind was Lena Ashwell, who made her London debut in 1891 and seemed to have a brilliant future ahead of her. She was signed to play Jane Faber in *Man and His Makers*, but due to some confusion over the contract she was unable to fulfill the complete agreement, and Jeffries remained. When *Man and His Makers* subsequently opened on 7 October, the reception was mixed. In trying to please both artistic camps, Barrett failed to please either one. Max Beerbohm pointed out that the blend of traditional melodrama with modernist intentions would never really succeed because "natural writing in any melodrama immediately shows up the impossibility of the situations."[56] During the run Lillah McCarthy finally persuaded Barrett to stop using the elevator shoes he had worn ever since 1880 (he was about 5'7" tall), but neither the quality of Barrett's acting nor his new shoes was enough to save the play. It closed after ten performances to losses of £1,000.[57] There was no other new play to take its place. The rest of Barrett's potentially promising Lyceum season contained more revivals, including *The Sign of the Cross*, *The Manxman*, *Othello*, and in mid-December, *Hamlet*. The engagement closed on 16 December 1899.

From a high point of nineteen plays touring in 1898, Barrett's organization dropped to thirteen in 1899. The initial impact of *The Sign of the Cross* was wearing thin, and there were now fewer requests for rights to his plays. Seven tours of *The Sign of the Cross* were out: four of Barrett's own plus one of Ben Greet's, and one each in the United States and South Africa. Other plays out were *The Silver King*, *The Sledgehammer*, *The Golden Ladder*, and *Ben My Chree*. In all, there were £38,500 in royalties in 1899.[58] Lyceum

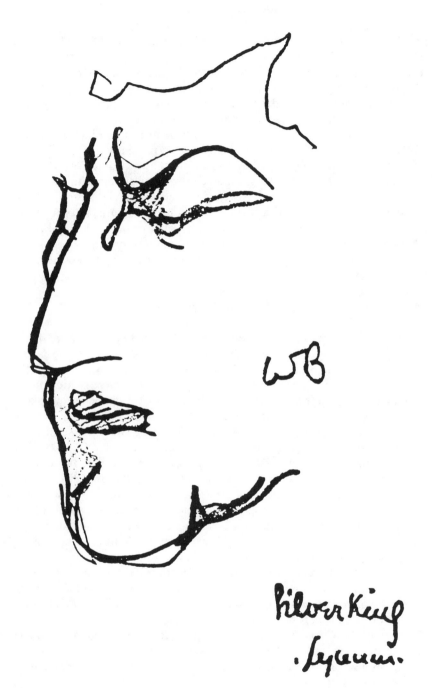

12. Sketch of Wilson Barrett by Gordon Craig.

profits, despite the failure of the new play, amounted to £3,900.[59] This meant that profits for the entire year were close to £53,100, not including money from the published versions of *The Sign of the Cross* and *The Daughters of Babylon* (this last written with Robert Hichens), as well as from *The Wilson Barrett Birthday Book*, a diary with quotations from Barrett's plays and photographs of him and various company members.

The end of 1899 marked the extent of the upswing in Barrett's career that began in 1895. The fame he sought was permanently his now, and his financial picture was bright enough to insure that he would never have to work again if he chose. The knighthood controversy left him with additional stature, for even though it was unsuccessful, the reception in Australia and at home in the provinces afterwards proved that he had secured a lasting place in the hearts of British playgoers no matter what certain influential critics believed. Moreover, his new adventure into modernist domestic melodrama seemed to have potential, if only the difficulties of putting new wine in old bottles could be solved.

Second Australian Tour and South Africa

In 1900 Barrett returned still again to his established pattern of provincial touring. Unfortunately, the overexposure due to the dozens of Barrett productions touring since 1896 had the effect of draining away much of the interest in his plays. He had expected to see provincial audiences attending in large numbers when they learned they would be seeing him in his own plays; he used a very large company of nearly 100 and a full complement of scenery. Expenses for this tour were an astonishing £880 per week, more than for a major London playhouse. The result was a loss of £8,900 for the tour. If it had not been for the £26,300 royalties from the other tours out this year, there would have been a financial disaster of the pre-1895 variety.

Barrett mounted his only new production of the year on 11 June when he opened *Quo Vadis* at the Lyceum in Edinburgh. He had been working on the play periodically since the previous summer when his plans for it were interrupted by the private production in the United States. Now, with the failure of that version in mind, he was having a difficult time developing a script of his own that would sufficiently differ from *The Sign of the Cross*. "I find it a hard nut to crack," he wrote to Frank Heath early in the year, "to avoid *The Sign* and yet not to weaken *Quo Vadis* is not easy."[60] When the play finally did open, it proved to be a dull script, not equal to the caliber of *The Sign of the Cross*, but more a series of tableaux. The leading character of Petronius was not the kind of role Barrett could play well. There was hidden strength in the character, but Petronius's banter and light-hearted cynicism were too much in the comic satire vein. Ben Greet liked the play, though, and Barrett gave him the rights for certain provincial towns. The

French actor Constant Coquelin, who earlier had tried to secure his own option on the play, also liked Barrett's version. He traveled to England to see the play and was generously awarded all French rights for a symbolic one shilling and one percent of the gross.[61]

Losses continued on the 1901 tour which commenced in January and was in the red £1,560 by June.[62] Large production expenses were again the cause. In August the picture brightened as Barrett began his second tour of Australia, this time to include an additional three months in the major towns of New Zealand. The contract for the first leg of the engagement stipulated that Barrett would receive £250 of the first £800, one-half of the next £200, and two-thirds of all receipts over £1,000 each week. By the end of the Australian part of the tour in December, Barrett had accumulated £12,900; the New Zealand adventure was not as good.[63] Barrett was nervous about touring in New Zealand to begin with, and the managers had to guarantee him a minimum of £3,500 to persuade him to do it. Later, Barrett's reluctance proved to be well founded, for in contrast to Australia, theatrical facilities in New Zealand were terrible. He complained bitterly about bad working conditions and wondered why the state had not stepped in to straighten things out the way they had done there with the schools and libraries. Profits for this leg, which ended in mid-March 1902, amounted to only £2,900, and the managers were required to pay £600 to make up the deficit against the minimum guarantee. The entire Australian tour then brought Barrett £16,420. Revenues from other plays on tour were £26,770, bringing total profits (less the losses from the 1901 provincial tour) to a still healthy £42,632.[64] But even though accounts were good, Barrett was not hopeful about the immediate future at home. "I fear that next season in England will be worse than this," he wrote in February. "The [Boer] War [1898–1902] seems no nearer conclusion, the increase in taxes, and other horrors will deter people from going to the theatres—only very strong attractions will draw at all."[65]

Furthermore, Barrett was becoming restless again. Despite the profits he had found no new "big play," and he was actually beginning to think about slowing down. What was worse, he lost the actress who had been such an inspiration to him during the last ten years. Maud Jeffries left the company before the foreign tour and joined Beerbohm Tree at the Haymarket, later becoming his wife. She hated the rigors of the last Australian adventure; it seems likely that the thought of a repeat, besides the presence of Edyth Latimer, prompted her to quit. But Lillah McCarthy, not Miss Latimer, was elevated to the post of leading lady in her place. McCarthy had joined the company in 1895, while Barrett was touring the provinces with *The Sign of the Cross* before its London debut. Latimer's influence persisted, however, and Barrett soon suggested that McCarthy consider touring with her own company to play Phaedra, Magda, and Lady

Macbeth. McCarthy won this battle; she remained his leading lady until the end of his career.

A change was coming over Barrett. His health was becoming a problem. His digestion was troublesome, and a persistent and painful sinus infection forced him to seek relief in frequent, almost daily, minor surgery that was often as painful as the malady itself. Morever, he was fifty-six in 1902, his hair was graying, and the stoutness that accompanied his age was making it harder to carry off his important heroic roles as convincingly as in the past. These difficulties notwithstanding, in 1902 Barrett was the only major English actor who could play heroic parts well. A critic for *The Westminster Review* observed the year before that "actors with a fine physique and ringing voice are becoming rarer and rarer; also actors who can conceive a part in a bold and vigorous spirit."[66] Modernist realistic plays demanded different talents from actors. As a result, there was "an absence of joyousness [and] strength" in the new generation of actors, the critic complained, and no "illumination of real passion." In light of these comments, Barrett in 1902 could count on some success because he held a monopoly in the field. But he also felt a moral responsibility to continue. Some of his friends recognized signs of exhaustion in him stemming from his superhuman schedule of activities. They begged him to think seriously of retiring, if only because of his health. He replied that too many people depended on him who had helped him in the past, including certain company members who were relatives of old friends and others whose income as members of Barrett's subscription list was their only means of support. Barrett decided to work on, still eccentrically dressed in his frock coat, flannel cricketing shirt open at the neck, and top hat. The advance of Daniel McCarthy, Lillah's brother, to the post of literary advisor, and of Percy Burton as business manager, may have helped to relieve some of the burden.

In May Barrett began a tour into the heart of South Africa. The contract was arranged during the previous August when the war was at its most ferocious. Fortunately, by May 1902 the hostilities were subsiding (a treaty was signed later in the month), and Barrett and his company did not have to face that dire prospect. The agent for the tour was Lascombe Searelle, a sometime playwright and theatrical manager in South Africa, and his agreemnt with Barrett stipulated that the star would receive one-half of the gross. Searelle also guaranteed all travel expenses plus a minimum of £200 per week. At first he wanted Barrett to come just with McCarthy. "It is simply a suicidal policy to take out expensive [London] people to support you," he wrote, when it was clear that Barrett could secure a good South Africa company for less than £110 per week.[67] His argument did not sway Barrett.

The country was excited about peace when Barrett arrived. Lillah McCarthy reported that "British soldiers [were] eager to adore us—any or all of us."[68] Numerous times on trains between towns, for example, soldiers recognized Barrett. One company of Lancashire men who had seen him perform in their hometowns called him "our Will" and joked that they greatly preferred seeing him at home rather than in South Africa. Audiences were equally receptive, and time after time Barrett was called upon to give an impromptu curtain speech, not the usual practice in South African theatres. He used the occasion to talk on political subjects, such as the use of foreign labor. Barrett often spoke on political topics now; his letters, too, contain frequent political references. From Sydney back in April he had written,

> I met the Attorney General the other night . . . and he repeated before others what he said four years ago, that "I made the best speech on federation that he had ever heard." This Premiere Barton also told me. Perhaps after all I have mistaken my vocation.[69]

In South Africa he was asked to stand for Parliament. This was evidence, perhaps, of renewed interest on Barrett's part in the possibility of a political career after retirement. As a matter of fact, he was desperately sick during the entire South African adventure. Once he even collapsed after a performance and had to be hospitalized against his will for several days. Doctors warned him of exhaustion, but he still felt that he needed a new hit before he could stop touring. He also recognized other pressures being brought to bear on him. From his bed in Johannesburg in July he wrote to Frank Heath, who was urging him to return home,

> The London business is awful, Greet tells me. I should have lost thousands [there] and to what end? They had made up their minds for [Charles]Wyndham's light comedies [at the Criterion] long ago. John Hare will be roaring mad—and he will come next, then Tree. The old lie [i.e., the scandal] clings round me and will for all my life block me. I don't much care. I have the people with me—that's something. I would rather like to retire for a few years, but fear that once I stop, I stop altogether.[70]

The South African tour ended on 23 August, but not before Barrett promised Searelle a return engagement. Profits were a sound £7,980 for thirteen weeks, while income from nine other Barrett productions this year was £32,740.[71] *The Sign of the Cross* and *The Silver King* remained his most popular plays.

Meanwhile, one possible new play was lost and two added. Interest in the script written with Elwyn Barron dealing with the reign of George III had revived again in Australia, only to be dropped because of Barron's double-dealing. It seems that a contract was signed for the play, but Barron took Barrett's money and advice and wrote his own play. By now all the unfair scheming Barrett had been victimized by throughout his life was taking its toll on his optimistic nature. "I hope I shall never be fool enough again to try to help anyone," he complained of Barron, "except to put my hand in my pocket and hand them so much money—gratitude is impossible—fair dealings almost as rare." He continued,

> Human nature is too fixed a quantity—I find it monotonous and depressing. I think you had better tell Aunt Emily [his brother Robert's wife] that there must be no looking to me for her keep and that of the girls, that [her] boys shall have another year's schooling and the child [his brother George's] will be educated, but that the time has come when they are able and must take care of themselves. I am not saving money and I do not see who of the lot I can turn to to keep me if anything happens to stop my work. I wish someone would leave me a fortune—I *ache* to stop work. What a glorious thing it would be to rest.[72]

Another play, entitled *The Never Never Land*, was having a better fate. It was a story dealing with Australia that Barrett had begun writing during his last trip, and he was excited about it. "I hope you will like my new piece *The Never Never Land*," he wrote in February, "the motive is entirely my own and has I think never been used. . . . The parts are all so good that it must play well. . . . The title is strange—but I like strange titles—they provoke comment."[73] The play was among the very first to deal with life "down under," the title being an Australian synonym for drought-ridden Northern Queensland. *The Never Never Land* was to be accompanied by a novel:

> I am writing a novel of *The Never Never Land*. I want it published at the same time I produce the drama in England, viz.—in September [1902]. McQueen [publishers] would, I suppose, take it. . . . I feel quite certain that the book will contain the best work I have done and the praise for the story interest of the play makes me hopeful of the success of the novel. Running side by side they should help each other.[74]

Later, after a successful copyright performance during his provincial tour in the fall of 1902, Barrett decided to include the play regularly in his provincial repertoire. The success he had with it thereafter prompted him to sell the serial rights to *The Daily Mirror*; he hoped to open the drama in London in 1904. Actually, he could have opened the play earlier, as early as April in South Africa, but the scenery was too heavy for the railways there.

Last Years and Personal Victories

By now Barrett had a thoroughly worked out system for writing, rehearsing, and producing new plays while on tour. Each theatre where his company worked became a dramatic workshop for the new play. It was not unusual that during the preparation of *The Never Never Land* still another new work was being readied. *The Christian King, or Alfred of Engleland* was written and its scenery built in Australia; it, too, could have traveled to South Africa but for its heavy settings. This piece deals with the life of Alfred, the king who created the English navy and who put into practice Christian principles of politics. *The Christian King* was political melodrama; coming deftly on the heels of England's war with native Africans and at a time of increasing problems with empire, it possessed sharp relevance. This was Barrett's immediate inspiration for the play, but there were other influences as well, including earlier versions of the same story of several different authors. The most important source for Barrett must have been Sheridan Knowles's drama *Alfred the Great, or The Patriot*, written for Barrett's mentor William Charles Macready. It seems plausible that Barrett would return to Macready for inspiration now when he was beginning to undergo another, though less calamitous, period of Macready-like artistic doldrums.

The Christian King premiered at the Princess's Theatre in Bristol on 6 November 1902. Several dozen of Bristol's unemployed soldiers recently returned from South Africa were used as extras—Barrett thought that their military discipline made them the best pick-up actors he had ever worked with—and after the four-hour performance Barrett made a curtain speech pleading for help for recent veterans. He spoke of what he saw in South Africa, once again raising signals that indicated he might be thinking of politics. He persistently denied rumors that he was considering running for Parliament (Leeds would have elected him in an instant), yet his curtain speeches were only a few of the times he did speak on politics now. And most of the time his subject was England's relations with her colonies.

The play itself received mixed reviews. The scenery was lovely, but there seemed to be too many static tableaux. Act V was actually billed as a series of historical tableaux. Moreover, the dialogue was diffuse, and the whole play needed compressing, which it received as the company moved on from Bristol to continue the tour. On 18 December Murray Carson, a former company member, and William Greet scheduled Barrett's company for ten performances of *The Christian King* at the Adelphi in London. It was advertised as a valedictory engagement. Barrett expected lots of criticism from certain members of the press and got it. The difficulties with the script had been ironed out by this time, however; anti-Barrett critics had to look hard for something substantial to attack. The found it, of all places, in the play's imagery. The fastidious critic for *The Times* wrote:

> [We refer to] the coarseness of the language and thought with which the [play's] morality is associated. King Alfred is always alluding to his "body," his courtiers call it a "lusty body," and say it is full "to the skin." Then we hear of a lady's "sweet body" and of another lady's "fair body." "Take my body," says this latter lady, as with a blow from her dagger she lays herself dead at some man's feet. Morality's saved, of course, but it seems to us that delicacy and refinement are irretrievably lost.[75]

A more perceptive observer might have seen that the physiological images in the script were attempts at an artistic illustration of the spiritual-physical conflict within Alfred's soul in the story. As it was, the condescending tone of such criticism only served to revive the old myth of Barrett's vanity about his appearance, an excellent argument in Victorian London, but one which begged the question. Journalists aside, the general public remained on Barrett's side and liked the play so much that its run was extended several days. The valedictory engagement concluded with some revivals by popular demand.

Nineteen hundred and two turned out to be another profitable year even though Barrett had no new big hit. Innovative publicity helped immensely. By holding attention-getting essay contests for school children on the subject of the life and times of Alfred, and by cutting expenses to the bone, Barrett managed to make £770 from June through the end of December. This brought total receipts for the year to £48,420, not including the money from novels and other nondramatic sources, meaning that Barrett's finances had remained more or less stable since 1896.[76] He had been consistently £40,000 to £50,000 in the black each year.

In February 1903, after another well deserved rest in Germany during the previous month, Barrett began his provincial tour for that year. The season did not begin auspiciously when Hall Caine inexplicably published a letter in the theatrical press denouncing Barrett for having written the "Phillip" version of *The Manxman* without Caine's approval! In a long and carefully documented letter Barrett refuted the allegation. As quickly as this problem disappeared, another rose to take its place. Barrett had promised *The Daily Mirror* that he would produce *The Never Never Land* in London in 1904 to coincide with the newspaper's serialization of the novel. Try as he would, however, he could not secure a proper playhouse. Letters to managers went unanswered, and this deliberate abuse displeased him. He knew that his own record of professional accomplishments was honorable because it had always been an important part of his artistic policy to treat his associates civilly no matter what the provocation, not an easy thing to do at a time when the theatrical profession was riddled with charlatans eager to share in the wealth created by the tremendous growth of the art. "I determined if I ever got into a big position," he wrote to Frank Heath, "no one should suffer in the same way by me. I kept to this determination. It has cost me thousands of pounds in secretaries, and etc., but I have done it."[77] Unable to secure in London the professional approval he sought for so long, Barrett was settling now for personal victories, such as the support of his public and the maintenance of his own dignity.

Plans for new plays this year included two comedies. The first was an adaptation of *David Copperfield* with Barrett to play Ham Peggotty in a drama that would concentrate on the episodes with Little Emily and Steerforth. The play was never completed, but another was. Originally to be called *Sock and Buskin*, this story was about wandering players during the

13. Wilson Barrett.

seventeenth century in England. The character Barrett would play was an entirely new direction for his acting. The story concerns the actor Terence Springbourne and his efforts to secure for his nephew the family estate which is presently in the hands of a scoundrel uncle. Terence is an Irish actor, jovial, outgoing, Bohemian, and charming, decidedly not in the historic-heroic mold of Alfred the Great. Barrett would use an Irish brogue, dance, sing, and play on a pipe with all the ease of a professional variety entertainer. The subplot of the play, about the first English actress, occurs in the story when the company loses its apprentice, and Ellula (Lillah McCarthy) dressed as a boy steps in to take his place.

Rehearsals began in May and the play, now entitled *In The Middle of June* after Tennyson's line, opened at the Theatre Royal in Middlesborough on 11 June and toured afterwards as part of the repertoire. Barrett was an immediate hit, but journalistic response to the play was mixed. Those who liked it thought it was reminiscent of Barrett's best, yet had all the delicacy of construction of a play by Pinero.[78] But to others the plots were occasionally perplexing, and at least one critic used the old argument that Barrett's plays were insufficiently modernist. Barrett wrote too much to please his audience, the reporter said, and not enough to express himself, consequently there was nothing in the new work "to enrich, or illuminate, or stimulate."[79] Actually, like all that Barrett did, the play was a pure expression of his temperament.

In The Middle of June remained on Barrett's tour agenda, but he abandoned the idea of taking *The Never Never Land* to London because he still was unable to find a playhouse. In September he assigned the production rights for both plays to manager John Hart, who would tour them in the autumn of 1904. Hart was in partnership with Harry Armitage, Barrett's business manager, another person who refused to believe that Barrett was slowing down his theatrical activities. Barrett wrote to his brother-in-law about it in September 1903: "It will help Armitage, who is a fine fellow and deserves advancement. He says, and I think he means it, that nothing will induce him to leave me."[80] Barrett, in fact, was gradually slowing down and had to convince Armitage to go out on his own; the tour with Hart was the inducement.

Barrett showed no outward signs of dwindling capacities when it came to his touring activities; his theatrical operation was as big as it ever was, and he swept down on towns with the same seriousness and energy he had shown throughout his career. This was the heyday of theatrical touring. There were 110 companies touring the provinces in 1903. The extent of Barrett's operations were so massive that they towered above everyone else's in size and sophistication. Generally a theatre company traveled on Sundays, though smaller troupes occasionally journeyed in midweek. Barrett did so himself in the United States when he played brief stands in small towns. By 1903 the railway was offering special discounts to theatrical troupes, thanks to the efforts of Barrett and the Actor's Association. After all, theatrical companies made up nearly seventy-five percent of rail traffic during the year. Actors in transit with their company paid three-fourths fare; companies received use of one freight car free for the first thirty passengers and one more for every additional twenty. Barrett's was the most elaborate touring organization, carrying more than 110 members. Next in line were George Alexander's with about half as many, then the musical comedy troupes of George Edwards and George Dance with about thirty performers in each.[81]

Everywhere on tour Barrett behaved like the well-loved and successful entrepreneur he was. At one town he donated a £50 painting to the art academy, then gave a lecture on the humanistic values of art collecting. At Bury in August, where cotton-spinners were out of work and hungry because the mills were stopped due to a drop in the market, he made a generous offer. He wrote in a telegram to the mayor:

> Have read with much pain account of great distress prevailing among cotton workers of Bury. In remembrance of kindly treatment I received during my visit three years ago I beg to offer to pay for 4000 2 lb loaves to be equally divided between the clergymen of all denominations for distribution by them to utmost deserving cases. I undertake to repeat this offer in one week's time on condition that two other gentlemen will be responsible to a like account.[82]

Barrett made the same offer at several other provincial towns suffering similar hardships. Earlier in the year he took a strong (and prophetic) stand against Andrew Carnegie's offer to build a free library adjacent to Shakespeare's home in Stratford-upon-Avon. The building on the site was about to collapse, but Barrett suggested that if Carnegie really wanted to help the city, he should restore the entire street to its original seventeenth-century condition instead of destroying the architectural integrity of the town with an ugly new building.[83] There was much determined discussion in the press for several weeks on the subject; some siding with Barrett, others with the town and Carnegie. In the end the Stratford town council simply ignored artistic considerations and accepted Carnegie's gift.

Barrett's career was almost peremptorily cut short in April during a run of *The Christian King* at Manchester. His physician prescribed aconite (an arsenic derivative) for him as a mild stimulant when he was tired, but the chemist mistakenly gave Barrett an overdose. At the hotel after the performance he collapsed. Doctors feared he was dead when they could detect no hearbeat or pulse. As a last hope one physician gave Barrett a massive injection of adrenalin. Miraculously, Barrett began to recover at about 3:00 A.M. and was much better by 10:30, though still very weak. He insisted on returning to the stage that night. The chemist voluntarily gave Barrett £50 in damages; Barrett gave the money to a local charity.[84] Ironically, Barrett was having frequent premonitions of death about this time. "If anything should happen to me," he wrote in March, "I have made a new will."[85]

The twenty-first birthday of *The Silver King* was celebrated by the company while they were playing at Cheltenham in June. Barrett remarked at a dinner party for the occasion that the play had been produced around the world over 30,000 times and that it had taken in nearly £6,000,000 in gross receipts. This was also a banner year for *The Sign of the Cross*. By the end of 1903 the play had been seen by over 15,000,000 people; 80,000 copies of the illustrated program, 35,000 photographs of the actors, and an astonishing 2,500,000 copies of the 6d. novel had been sold.[86] Earlier, Barrett completed the novel of *The Never Never Land* and sold it to Lippincott's in the United States, who published 20,000 copies.

Barrett needed fees this year to make up for the comparative lack of success on his own tours. There were nine companies out, including his own, and profits were a very low £6,640.[87] Barrett's close friend John Coleman had recently died broke and despondent despite a long and influential career. Barrett paid for the funeral. He was depressed. "I must go to Africa," he wrote in May,

> the net profit of the spring tours since '97 amounts to about £11 a week!!! The average profit in Africa was £236!!! It is useless going on here. The work is very hard—it hurts my reputation to be playing to bad houses and the monotony is not nice.[88]

In an earlier note to his sons he warned that they would be on their own soon if he could not act. He once again tried to arrange another tour for Lillah McCarthy, this time going as far as setting up a small syndicate to handle it. Apparently, marriage to Edyth Latimer was imminent. And he continued to urge Harry Armitage to leave and manage on his own as well, rewriting *East Lynne* for his use. "I am hurrying to rewrite *East Lynne*. My! But it wants it. It shows once more what acting and story will do, no matter what the dialogue is. . . . They play it in three weeks' time, there is two month's work in it."[89]

It appeared as if Barrett was gradually disbanding the company; everything seemed to be pointing to retirement. But in December 1903 Barrett wrote to Frank Heath,

> You should get on Saturday the first act of *Lucky Durham*—my new play. Let me know what you all think of it as soon as you can spare the time and where you think the story is tending. I am anxious to know how much the audience will have grasped by the end of the act.[90]

This new play, still developing through March 1904, turned out to be the next big success he was looking for and the end of his depression and thoughts about retiring. Following the same lines as *The Black Kitten, The Wishing Cup,* and *Man and His Makers,* the new drama was to be a modernist melodrama, a "problem play." The subject was a "natural child" and the idea was "the gross injustice done to women (conveniently dubbed by men as 'fallen') and the still greater unjustice meted out to the offspring of their unblessed partnerships with men of their own choice."[91] Barrett wanted this theme "emphasized in a manner that strikes deeply" because he wanted to generate enough response to the subject to change the law making it illegal for a father to give his "natural child" either his name or his inheritance.[92] In New Zealand he had spoken often about the subject to various politicians, and he incorporated much of their dialogue, especially that of Prime Minister Seddon, directly into the playscript. Social concern was not the only similarity this play had to a few of its predecessors; there was also a personal interest. He admitted that the subject had been a matter of deep concern to him "ever since he first got the idea twenty years ago."[93] That would have been 1884, shortly before the death of Miss Heath, who was an illegitimate child.

The play was complete in April 1904. Barrett was nervous about it and planned to keep working on it until the fall, at which time he hoped to take it to London. His colleagues liked it in spite of its risky subject and urged him to try for London as soon as possible. Barrett agreed, but when the company arrived in Liverpool and received a very warm welcome, he decided to open the drama there on 9 June in an extended run with other plays from his repertoire. Critics recognized that it was a "problem play" and that the theme was treated uniquely, but the plot was not original. There was also some opinion that the story needed condensing and that the emphasis on Durham's illegitimacy was too strong. On the whole, however, the play was a decided hit, "full of interest, enthralling . . . picturesque and amusing."[94] Barrett's acting received high praise. John Durham, said one critic, was portrayed excellently "in demeanor, in accent, and in quiet sincerity." The role, he continued, "was illuminated by many subtle touches" and the entire performance was "exceptionally smooth throughout."[95]

Before the opening Barrett was disturbed because he could not convince the theatre owners in London that the play was good enough to warrant his leasing a playhouse there. The tempo of events suddenly picked up when word of the success of the piece reached London and metropolitan playgoers came to Liverpool to see for themselves. Even *The Times* sent a correspondent. Barrett was nervously hopeful: "For the first time in the history of the [Adelphi] theatre *The Times* has wired that they will send a representative!! . . . All journalistic Liverpool is agog they tell me. . . . What does it mean? . . . Does it mean slaughter or help?"[96] Three days later theatre offers started coming in:

Just had the Savoy Theatre offered for ten weeks. Very tempting. I am tired but will think it over. Management here strongly advise London at once. So do my own people. . . . Stalls and circles were crowded and were most enthusiastic. There is no reasonable doubt that I have a fortune and that it will do a power of good. Men and women were quite carried out of themselves last night too. Made loud comments. "Quite right," "True," "Bravo," "Hear, Hear," and cried openly. Roars of laughter are constant. You have no idea how the comedy tells. I could have arranged for at least £5,000 in advance of fees for England, America, and Australia yesterday. All say I am great in "John."[97]

Charles Frohman, who originally refused the play, was among the managers who were now anxious to secure the rights for it. There was talk of another U.S. tour for Barrett with Frohman sponsoring him in *Lucky Durham* in New York. On 15 June Barrett signed a lease for the Comedy Theatre in London for eight weeks beginning in late August. He chose this house over the Savoy because better terms were offered; it was managed by Ben Greet and Frank Curzon, old friends of Barrett. *Lucky Durham* would have to be a success. Profits this year were a dismal £3,036 from eleven tours, though the novel version of the new play was about to be published and promised to help the picture somewhat.[98] Even so, opening night proceeds were to go to the cause of allowing the illegitimate children of actors to enter the Actors' Orphanage.

Barrett's relations with other London managers this season were also significant. When Charles Wyndham heard that Barrett was coming back to London again, he feared for his business and countered by accusing Barrett of copying *Lucky Durham* from an old play called *The Crisis*, an adaptation of James Albery's and Emile Augier's play *Les Fourchambault*. This older play was first produced in London in 1878 at the Haymarket with Mary Eastlake in the cast and was not a success. Wyndham bought the rights, but since he could not make a part in it for himself, he forgot it for twenty-five years. Now he thought of bringing it out again when he heard of Barrett's success with a similar theme. Barrett wanted to take no chance on damaging his potential with his own play, so he immediately put the dispute to outside arbitration. The results were completely in his favor.

Earlier, in April, Barrett had been embroiled in a dispute with another London manager, Herbert Beerbohm Tree, whose proposal for a Dramatic Academy was receiving wide coverage in the press. Irving, Alexander, and Wyndham, among others, praised the idea. Barrett, who at the Princess's anticipated Tree in the idea of a dramatic academy, was opposed to it. He wrote in a telegram to Tree which was published in *The Daily Telegraph*:

Do not approve of your scheme. Hundreds of actors now out of engagement will have their ranks swelled by those who can afford to pay your fee. What of those with ability who cannot pay your tuition? The stage does not want recruits merely, but wants talent. Money and talent do not always go together. My sympathies go with merit.[99]

Barrett preferred Irving's, Benson's, and his own traditional policy of practical training and pointed out that Tree's own daughter did not go to a dramatic school, but worked her way up through the ranks. "I think the best training," he said, "is that given by a good manager to the recruits of his own company. Let the manager choose them with discretion, pay them a living wage, and advance them according to their merits." Then, with typical Barrett eccentricity, he added: "I will pay fees for three scholars selected for their ability from the aspirants who cannot afford to pay for themselves." Barett was the only leading actor-manager to disapprove of the scheme. Tree called his opposition "a discordant note" and made much of it in the press. Henry Irving took a less extreme view of Barrett's opinions and even made a personal move at this time to smooth out their uneven relationship once and for all.

Suddenly, events turned bad. On Monday, 11 July, Barrett was hit by severe intestinal pains. He had frequently suffered from stomach trouble; in fact, he was ravaged with it during the South African tour. This time his doctor prescribed hospitalization. Barrett was taken from his rooms at the Hotel Cecil on Wednesday, 13 July, and was transferred to the Medical Nursing Home in Devonshire Place. At first the problem was thought to be a gastric ulcer; Barrett insisted on taking along his typewriter so he could continue to work. He was in good spirits. He planned to call on Mrs. Clement Scott whose husband, a close friend of Barrett for years, had recently died. But Barrett's condition was not so easily remedied. When his physician told him he would have to be "opened" on 20 July, he joked, "Ah, I was to have opened myself on Monday."[100]

The operation, four hours long, revealed that the real cause of the distress was cancer. Apparently recovering from surgery well by 1:00 A.M., at 5:00 the pain suddenly grew worse and a second, then a third operation were performed. A little while later, around 8:00 A.M., his heart failed because of the severe trauma of surgery, and he died. It was reported that he was conscious to the end, not in pain, and talking quietly with those present. His last request was for the continued care of his "pensioners." His daughter Dorothy and his brother-in-law, Frank Heath, were in attendance along with close friend Sir Frederick Armour and Dr. Thomas Barlow. Barrett died in the arms of a private nurse sent by the Duchess of Portland for his comfort. Percy Burton said that the day Barrett went to the hospital his painting of Macready, hung prominently over the mantel in his room at the hotel, had been mysteriously tipped askew, but though Burton visited Barrett several times during the last few days on business matters, he declined to relate the incident to the superstitious actor.[101]

On Sunday, 24 July, Barrett's body was taken from the funeral home in Cambridge Place to All Saints Church in Norfolk Square for the service,

SACRED
TO THE MEMORY OF
WILSON BARRETT,
WHO DIED JULY 22ND 1904.
ALSO OF **ELLEN ANNA,**
AND **KATHERINE MARGARET,**
DAUGHTERS OF THE ABOVE,
WHO DIED MAY 20TH 1852,
AND AUGUST 2ND 1894.
"AND THERE SHALL BE NO MORE DEATH, NEITHER SORROW, NOR
CRYING, NEITHER SHALL THERE BE ANY MORE PAIN." REV. XXI. 4.

14.   Wilson Barrett gravesite, Hampstead Cemetery.

after which the casket was carried in a procession with seventy-five coaches to Hampstead Cemetery. There Barrett was interred with his daughters and brother. Mourners lined the streets along the way, and hundreds of floral tributes marked the grave, including one from Henry Irving ("In Remembrance, with Deep Regrets"), who was not present because he was in remote Cornwall and had only heard the news that day. With the exception of £1,000 each to his sons, Barrett left his entire legacy of £30,867 to his daughter Dorothy. Newspapers from around the Empire and the United States carried obituary notices, the total of which covers sixty pages of a large theatrical pressbook, over 3,500 column-inches of type. As for *Lucky Durham*, it eventually reached London, but with a different company and with a different actor in the title role, it closed after a brief and unsuccessful run. A short time after the funeral there was a movement headed by Beerbohm Tree to raise a memorial to Barrett, but daughter Dorothy, remembering Tree's discourteous treatment of her father during the discussions about the dramatic academy, stopped it cold. Nothing more could be done.

Epilogue

The Man: His Style and Significance

Like any active person, artistic or otherwise, Barrett had patterns into which his thoughts and work were forever fitting. Perhaps his predominant character trait was a talent for displaying courage and dignity in the face of adversity. "He had an adventurous career," Squire Bancroft recalled, "sometimes high on the wave of success, at others deep down in the trough of the sea of failure, but always strictly honourable."[1] Boyle Lawrence called Barrett "a Christian in a theatrical *Pilgrim's Progress.*"[2] This trait of his endeared him deeply to the British public, who recognized in him also someone with abiding sympathy for their hearts. His apprenticeship among the provincial towns and cities of England and his later tours there made him familiar with the hopes, fears, and prejudices of ordinary people. The result was that Barrett grew to possess an uncanny insight into the spirit of his audience, a quality Chance Newton called his "constant benevolence and unfailing sympathy with the poor and distressed, the anxious and the baffled."[3] Percy Burton further observed that Barrett "wrote and played frankly for the masses."[4] He was a veritable weather vane of public taste. Sophisticated critics may have jeered at the occasional excesses this particular characteristic led him to, but there never was a time when his enemies did not envy their effects upon a crowd. Barrett's popularity in the clean, human, and wholesome school of plays annoyed modernist critics because it enabled him to ignore them. They were powerless in the face of his achievements, which to them were inexplicable. "Flappers worshipped him and he drew all fashionable London to his melodramas," J.B. Booth remembered, "and even if certain of the critics had hard things to say of him and his artistic ideals, in the days of his popularity and success he could afford to laugh at the 'highbrows.'"[5] Barrett's real critics were himself and his audiences; his popularity guided by his sensibility was for him the true mark of success.

Nor was there a trace of hypocrisy or what the Victorians called "cant" about him. Mrs. Clement Scott recalled that "he called things by their right name. . . . If anyone tried to do him an injury or an act of injustice, woe betide them, for he would not rest until he had brought the offender to his knees and sifted the matter to the bitter end."[6] Barrett was called by George R. Sims, "the straightest and best of good fellows";[7] this stemmed from his fearless and determined religious faith in mankind's implicit goodness. His motto was that of the pre-Raphaelite painters: Earnestness and Truth. A skeptical opinion of his fellow man would have conflicted with his sincere piety and genuine belief that life would lead to salvation. For Barrett virtue was its own reward, and that he believed this is shown by his continual inability to guard against attempts to take advantage of him.

Another important personal quality was his extraordinary will power and energy. The range of his activities and interests is awesome. Moreover, as much as he may have contemplated retirement, he persisted in working up to the very end. His associates often remarked about his "volcanic energy"; he was always and forever at work. Daily routine seldom varied; awake at 7:00 A.M.; breakfast punctually at 8:00 A.M.; then reading letters, newspapers, theatre news, and politics. Next, personal correspondence, then work on a role in his private studio, followed by lunch and business talk, more rehearsal or a brief walk, then (unless there was a matinee) a complete rest in pajamas and robe before the evening performance. Afterwards, a late supper in his room, then another three or four hours writing or reading Shakespeare, whose intricacies of meaning intrigued him. He composed his plays rapidly, looking at an idea dozens of ways before settling upon one way of using it, then writing it down in an easily recognizable "cramped, over-driven, impetuous" hand.[8]

But if he drove himself mercilessly and was independent-minded to a fault, nevertheless he was a benevolent and generous friend to those who needed help. There are countless incidents related about this dimension of him, so unusual in a person so important. "One of the most generous, large-hearted men I ever met," said Parker.[9] He had the reputation, "a very rare one, of never forgetting an old friend or comrade," John Coleman wrote in a survey of his life.[10] Barrett's business manager stated that he gave away nearly £20,000 to charities during the last seven years of Barrett's career alone.

One last attribute of his character deserves attention; that is, his vanity, a trait critics used most often to attack him. In an obituary recorded in *The Athenaeum*, for example, there were these harsh words of remembrance for him: "Possessing in the highest degree the weaknesses of his craft, he loved to exhibit himself in super-fine and sometimes inadequate array, and in doing so raised an obstacle against his acceptance as a serious artist."[11] Barrett was proud of his looks; after all, they were an important part of his success. He had the ability to move with assurance and grace in historic costume. In fact, he was the only actor of his time whose physique was attractive enough to be shown in this way. Newspaper critics failed to see that there was another side to this vanity, a side with a charming aspect that many people enjoyed in him. "There was something curiously simple, even boyish in Barrett's frank love of admiration," Booth wrote, "and particularly the admiration of women. He revelled in it, and attempted no concealment of his joy when he found it."[12] His vanity, like his relations with others, was open, straightforward, and honest.

History is concerned with more than character, however, and it is in Barrett's work, not in his original personality, that the sources of his sigificance must be found. His career was more productive than any of his contemporaries and his following was wide; yet, surprisingly, he seldom seemed to achieve the heights of accomplishment that would have secured a permanent and superior place for him in theatrical annals. Part of the reason was the excessive modernist rhetoric aimed at him, but there were also more complex motives, and a close reading of journalistic commentary is needed to sort fact from fiction in this regard.

As an actor, Barrett in many ways represented old school traditions, and many new school adherents used this as a weapon against him. One of the most glaring instances of this concerned his stage movements, especially in period costume. New school movement was self-consciously prosaic. Barrett loved classical painting and sculpture so much that he occasionally copied historical art too carefully in his acting and was accused of posing. On the other hand, when he was at his best he had the capacity to absorb the spirit of his models. Austin Brereton, the critic who wrote a biography of Irving, said that Barrett excelled at stage movement. "One of the most perfect actors the stage possesses," he wrote. "His repose is perfect. His attitudes are never exaggerated, his gestures are never out of place."[13]

Barrett's old school-type voice was another subject of contention. In certain roles and at selected times he used a stage voice of the kind old school actors thought appropriate to illustrate elevated sentiments. This quality was labeled variously as falsetto, head tones, or ringing vibrato. Furthermore, Barrett occasionally combined use of this stage voice with an interpretative technique that strongly emphasized key words, a practice especially disliked by William Archer. Others, however, thought Barrett's vocal technique was unsurpassed. Max Beerbohm described his voice as "intermittent thunder."[14] Playwright Charles Reade praised Barrett's "numberless changes of voice and expression—all true to nature."[15] "Mr. Barrett . . . is the most telling of all stage elocutionists," a reporter for *The Illustrated London News* wrote. "He can pronounce, he can emphasize, and every word is heard."[16]

In several important roles Barrett abandoned old school acting traditions in favor of new school realism. *The Silver King, Ben My Chree*, and *The Manxman*, for example, were praised by critics of all persuasions. Paradoxically, when Barrett applied these same acting techniques to Shakespeare, new school observers failed to recognize what he was doing and called his efforts too unconventional. As it turns out, Barrett was an unusual blend of new school and old school acting methods. When compared to the tradition he came out of, his acting style was innovative, a move toward realism guided by the needs of each genre of play in which he acted. "His great aim," concluded one observant critic, "was to act as truly as he could to life without exaggeration for the purpose of stage effects, and with an eye to the homeliness and humanity of the man he was representing."[17]

All this is not to overlook the most significant aspect of his acting style, his star quality. His good looks were "eminently those then fashionable—a somewhat classical, very muscular archangel."[18] Added to this was a forceful personality that infused lustre into every character he played. His gestures and his presence enthralled Lillah McCarthy, who recognized in Barrett what she called "the traditional grand manner."[19] His detractors believed that this was the only reason for his success, that he had no genuine talent. "Mr. Barrett's greatness is a greatness rather of personality than of dramatic invention," said Max Beerbohm. But having said that, Beerbohm went on to praise that personality and the astute manner in which Barrett utilized it. Barrett, he said, could "banish from our minds all doubts as to the probability of any situation into which the dramatist may throw him. . . . [There is] a light in his eyes that never was on sea or land."[20]

New school critics had a difficult time with Barrett because he was a curious amalgam of old and new school methods. His characteristic voice, graceful movements, and charismatic personality were elements of his style that placed him firmly in the old school camp. But his ensemble philosophy of acting, his attention to detail, and his coherent interpretations were decidedly new school inclinations. The paradox that this collection of elements created was apparently unsuited to new school critics whose attitude seems to have been "all or nothing." Old school critics and audiences were less dogmatic and welcomed Barrett as the excellent actor he was.

More to the point here is the quality of Barrett's imagination, an element of his style unfortunately which critics of neither persuasion often considered. Barrett's creative powers were based on two things: his forceful personal presence and his acute sense of dramatic coherence. Blessed with the first by nature, he was because of it unable to be a literal transcriber of the playscript, as new school dramatists would have wished. He changed his characters with great freedom and unconventionality, and for this reason he was called, like Edmund Kean, a Romantic (i.e., old school) actor. Sometimes (as with *Quo Vadis*, for a notable example) his personality failed to illuminate the role. And here his sense of dramatic construction saved him. For even when he did fail in a role, it did not mean that he gave the impression that he had no temperament, expressiveness, or inner resources for effects. On the contrary, he possessed all of them in great abundance. He produced tears and laughter in an audience, but not consistently the kind that came from his soul. He was not enough of a genius to do that. Audiences loved him, but more because his acting was emotionally logical and his technique was sure. He excelled at revealing the inner design of a role and in his best portrayals he added a deep truth that persuaded many he was a genius.

That Barrett was a superlative organizer of stage effects and crowds is beyond dispute. John Coleman testified that Barrett was the first to use the complete technology of pantomime in legitimate drama, and numberless critics observed that Barrett's stage management was unexcelled by anyone. Shaw was one of Barrett's most ardent admirers in this respect. This dimension of Barrett's work alone is enough to secure him an honorable place in theatre history, but he did much more. His contribution to the role of director lay in the extraordinary sensitivity he brought to bear in his treatment of actors, resulting in productions that were fully *acted* from the lead to the lowliest super. True, Barrett was the star and was not unaware of the limelight, but at the same time he was the only actor-manager "who refused to let the glare of his limelight blind his vision to what was necessary for the production of a company of players."[21] "Mr. Barrett is fonder of his plays than of himself," wrote Shaw, "and is conspicuous among our theatre chiefs for making the most of his company."[22] Barrett's fervent faith in the capacities of his actors resulted in the discovery and development of a score of talents who helped to make this period one of the high water marks of English acting.

Barrett never published in play form any drama he wrote himself. His decision not to do so indicates that though the was serious about his plays, he did not claim any literary merit for them. His dialogue was never more than characteristic; his ideas never extravagant or startlingly original. What was important to him was taut dramatic structure, and he demonstrated this fundmental principle in all his plays. "What ever else Barrett was," said critic Chance Newton, "he was a fine crescendo constructor of drama."[23] Barrett's playwriting innovations came about when he combined his melodramatic sensibility with his keen sense of dramaturgy, bringing about what William Archer admitted was a "modern and saner form of melodrama."[24] He "freed melodrama [from the] bombast that had marred it, and made it a true and moving representation of life."[25] In Barrett's hands melodrama matured into the genteel form which today underwrites the success of most of the television and film industry.

Moverover, a significant outcome of Barrett's playwriting collaborations was a steadfast policy of encouraging plays by English authors. Even William Archer conceded that

Mr. Wilson Barrett has assuredly deserved well of the English drama. But for his insights and enterprise these new popular playwrights might have spent years forcing themselves to the front, and might even have given up the battle in despair. This must always be remembered to Mr. Wilson Barrett's credit.[26]

"Few managers have done more for so many young authors," Clement Scott agreed. "Many of our most successful dramatists owe their start in life to him."[27] Barrett's steady record of producing the plays of new English writers remains one of the strongest pieces of evidence in his favor.

One of the most valuable dimensions of the artist is the uncanny way he reflects and embodies the spirit of his time. Barrett was no exception to this, and it remains one of the great ironies of his life that the spirit which bound him to his age also blinded modernist critics to his importance. Matthew Arnold and John Ruskin, two who personified traditional Victorian aesthetics, were both admirers of Barrett. Arnold feared that the industrial age was throwing culture to the beasts and that principled artists should fight to maintain standards. Barrett, for his part, feared the "matter-of-fact commercial spirit which is so prevalent [and] has a hardening, narrowing tendency—it obscures the larger views of human life."[28] He recognized the theatre to be an effective anodyne for this malaise. Ruskin saw art as the conscious moral guardian of beauty and good taste, giving art a status almost equal to that of religion. Barrett, too, believed that art should have a moral purpose, a belief that was exemplified in his respect for the materialist philosophy of Alexander Bain (1818-1903), the Scottish logician and educational reformer whose conservative philosophy exercised an influence on the Victorian popular mind. Barrett saw in Bain's ideas an extension of the thoughts of Ruskin and Arnold. "Dr. Bain . . . says 'Art is nature freed from the painful,'" Barrett wrote in 1894, and he concluded from this that "whatever is repulsive and revolting is essentially painful, and has therefore no place in any art, above all, perhaps, in the drama."[29] This key insight— that moral purpose may be the proper alternative to secularism in modern theatre aesthetics—infuses each moment of Barrett's work. In fact, it was this viewpoint of his that made his work unintelligible to so many of his critics. William Archer, leader of the modernists, would never have been able to deal with Barrett's final quotation above other than mockingly. There was no room for moral philosophy in the aesthetics of the new school adherents. And so, Barrett and his work were dismissed by them as "vain" and "melodramatic." According to the standards of some critics, Barrett was not merely bad, but a living repudiation of the fundamental premises by which they evaluated life and art. Under such circumstances, Barrett had to be written off as an embarassment—either that or admit the possibility that he had something important to say.

But even setting moral philosophy aside, had some of these critics had the advantage of historical perspective, they might have seen that there were few actor-managers who could match the range of Barrett's accomplishments. Of his contemporaries, John Martin-Harvey, Johnston Forbes-Robertson, and Charles Wyndham were knighted solely because of the quality of their acting; Henry Irving, Herbert Beerbohm Tree, and Charles Hawtrey mainly for their acting and directing skills; and Philip Ben Greet, Frank Benson, and George Alexander for their efforts in actor training. Untitled Wilson Barrett, however, was the complete actor-manager. What distinguishes him is the copresence of powers usually divorced in his colleagues, for he united as none of them did all the talents of actor, director, producer, critic, thinker, dramatist, and teacher. His work refuted criticisms leveled at many of the above named actor-managers in complaints of their want of knowledge, their purely financial interests, their exclusive reliance on successful authors and untalented actors, and their conventionality and dread of the new.

"For a large share of its advancement," Austin Brereton said, "the drama of today owes much to his well-directed efforts and I do not think that I am wrong in placing him at the head and front of the English stage, and assigning him a position amongst the leaders of the drama and the greatest of actors."[30] Whatever suspicions may be suggested by the air of rhetoric which seems to prevail in this statement, its substance is in accordance with historical fact.

Notes

HRC, an abbreviation cited frequently in the notes, refers to the Humanities Research Center at the University of Texas, which houses the collected papers of Wilson Barrett.

Introduction

1. John Rankin Towse, *Sixty Years of the Theatre* (New York: Funk and Wagnall's, 1916), p.426.

2. Sir George Arthur, *From Phelps to Geilgud* (New York: Benjamin Blom, 1971, orig. pub. 1936), p.21.

3. William Winter, *The Wallet of Time* (New York: Moffat and Yard, 1918), 2:420.

4. George Bernard Shaw, *Dramatic Opinions and Essays* (New York: Brentano's, 1916), 2:173.

5. Clement Scott, *The Drama of Yesterday and Today* (London: George Suckling, 1901), 2:384.

6. Austin Brereton, "Wilson Barrett," *The Theatre*, January 1883, p.33.

7. George Bernard Shaw, *Collected Letters*, ed. Dan H. Lawrence (New York: Dodd, Mead, 1965), 5:688.

8. J.B. Booth, *"Master" and Men* (London: T. Werner Lurie, 1927), p.244.

9. J.B. Booth, *Life, Laughter, and Brass Hats* (London: T. Werner Lurie, 1939), p.66.

10. H. Chance Newton, *Cues and Curtain Calls* (London: John Hane, 1927), p.155.

11. E.J. West, "From a Player's to a Playwright's Theatre," *Quarterly Journal of Speech* 28 (December 1942):432.

Chapter 1

1. Frank Wilson Barrett, *And Give Me Yesterday* (London: unpublished manuscript, 1966), p.6, HRC.

2. Ibid., p.7.

3. *The Era*, 11 October 1884.

4. *Louisville Journal*, 31 July 1904.

5. Barrett, *Yesterday*, p.7.

6.   Ibid.

7.   *Louisville Journal*, 31 July 1904.

8.   Ibid.

9.   Clement Scott, *Thirty Years at the Play* (London: Railway and General Automatic Library, 1891), pp.3-4.

10. *The Era*, 11 October 1884.

11. Ibid.

12. John Coleman, "Wilson Barrett and His Work," *Longman's* 7 (November 1885), p.64.

13. *Boston Transcript*, 22 July 1904.

14. Coleman, "Wilson Barrett," p.64.

15. Barrett, *Yesterday*, pp.7-8.

16. Mrs. Clement Scott, *Old Days in Bohemian London* (New York: Frederick Stokes, n.d.), p.130.

17. *The Era*, 11 October 1884.

18. Barrett, *Yesterday*, p.18.

19. Untitled newspaper article, n.d., HRC.

20. *The Era*, 11 October 1884.

21. Ibid.

22. *The Daily News*, 26 July 1904.

23. *The Era*, 11 October 1884.

24. M. Glen Wilson, "Charles Kean: Tragedian in Transition," *Quarterly Journal of Speech* 10 (February 1974), 45ff.

25. Coleman, "Wilson Barrett," p.66.

26. *The Era*, 11 October 1884.

27. Barrett, *Yesterday*, p.46.

28. Ibid.

29. *The Sunday Times*, 30 June 1867.

30. *Belfast Morning News*, 28 November 1868.

31. Drury Lane Playbills, 1868-1869, *passim*, British Museum and Guildhall Library.

32. Newton, *Cues*, p.101.

33. *Edinburgh Evening Courant*, 25 September 1869.

34. Coleman, "Wilson Barrett," p.67.

35. *The Era*, 28 August 1886.

36. Wilson Barrett Company Tour Accounts, 1870-1878, HRC.

37. Tour Accounts, 1870-1871, HRC.

38. Theatre Royal, Halifax, Accounts, 1871-1878, HRC.

39. Maurice Wilson Disher, *Melodrama: Plots That Thrilled* (New York: Macmillan, 1954), p.103.

40. *The Theatre*, November 1879, p.190.

41. Wilson Barrett to Frank Heath, March 1876, HRC.

42. Wilson Barrett-F.B. Chatterton Contract, 20 November 1876, HRC.

43. Joseph Knight, *Theatrical Notes* (New York: Benjamin Blom, 1972, orig. pub. 1893), p.156.

44. Barrett, *Yesterday*, p.57.

45. Tour Accounts, 1877, HRC.

46. Theatre Royal, Hull, Contract, 10 October 1877, HRC.

47. See Donald Roy, "Theatre Royal, Hull; or, The Vanishing Circuit," *Nineteenth Century British Theatre*, ed. Kenneth Richards and Peter Thompson (London: Methuen, 1971), pp.25–38.

48. Dutton Cook, *Nights at the Play* (London: Chatto and Windus, 1883), 2:185.

49. John Beaumont to Frank Wilson Barrett, 5 April 1963, HRC.

50. *Yorkshire Post*, 25 August 1894.

51. Errol Sherson, *London's Lost Theatres of the Nineteenth Century* (London: John Hane, 1925), p.122.

Chapter 2

1. Wilson Barrett to Mary Brunell Barrett, 14 May 1877, HRC.

2. Wilson Barrett-D.L. Claremont Contract, 15 August 1879, HRC.

3. *The Figaro*, August [?] 1879.

4. *Dramatic Notes*, December 1879, p.60.

5. *Saturday Review*, 27 September 1879, pp.376–77.

6. Marjorie Thompson, "Henry Arthur Jones and Wilson Barrett: Some Correspondence," *Theatre Notebook* 11 (October 1956), pp.42–43.

7. Ibid.

8. *The Theatre*, November 1879, p.232.

9. Doris Arthur Jones, *Taking the Curtain Call: The Life and Letters of Henry Arthur Jones* (New York: Macmillan, 1930), pp.30–31.

10. Cook, *Nights*, p.235.

11. *The Theatre*, January 1880, p.36.

12. Helena Modjeska to Wilson Barrett, 10 August 1880, HRC.

13. Helena Modjeska, *Memories and Impressions of Helena Modjeska* (New York: Macmillan, 1910), p.399.

14. *The Theatre*, January 1880, p.359.

15. *The Theatre*, February 1881, p.121.

16. Theatre Royal, Hull, and Grand Theatre, Leeds, Accounts, 1877–1880, HRC.

17. Wilson Barrett to Alfred Cuthbert, 10 February 1880, HRC.

18. Lease for The Priory, 22 October 1881, HRC.

19. Wilson Barrett to Mary Heath, 1881 [?], HRC.

20. *The Theatre*, January 1883, p.36.

21. Clement Scott, *The Drama of Yesterday and Today* (London: George Suckling, 1901, ex. illus. ed.), 6:305.

22. Modjeska, *Memories*, p.400.

23. Royal Court Theatre, Accounts, 1879–1880, HRC.

24. Sherson, *Lost Theatres*, p.2.

25. *The Era*, 28 August 1878, p.2.

26. *The Theatre*, August 1878, p.2.

27. Wilson, "Charles Kean," p.48.

28. *The Theatre*, August 1878, pp.3–4.

29. Arthur Goddard, *Players of the Period* (London: Dean and Son, 1891), 1:122.

30. *The Theatre*, July 1881, p.45.

31. Ibid., p.46.

32. Booth, *"Master" and Men*, pp.243–45.

33. George R. Sims-Wilson Barrett Contract for *Lights o' London*, n.d., HRC.

34. Cook, *Nights*, p.334.

35. *The Theatre*, January 1883, pp.34–35.

36. *Punch*, 24 September 1881, p.136.

37. Ibid.

38. *The Theatre*, October 1881, p.238.

39. *The Athenaeum*, 24 September 1881, pp.379–80.

40. *The Theatre*, October 1881, p.238.

41. *The Theatre*, January 1883, p.37.

42. *The Theatre*, October 1881, p.238.

43. Augustin Filon, *The English Stage*, trans. Frederick Whyte (New York: Kennicot, 1920, orig. pub. 1897), p.301.

44. Sherson, *Lost Theatres*, p.127.

45. Ibid., p.173.

46. *The Theatre*, October 1881, p.239.

47. Princess's Theatre Accounts, 1881, HRC.

48. George R. Sims, *My Life* (London: Nash, 1917), pp.129–30.

49. George Eliot, *The George Eliot Letters*, ed. Gordon S. Haight (New Haven, CT: Yale University Press, 1955), 4:107-17.

50. *The Theatre*, July 1882, p.39.

51. Ibid.

52. *Dramatic Notes*, 1882, p.29.

53. *The Theatre*, May 1882, p.310.

54. *The Theatre*, July 1882, p.40.

55. Sims, *Life*, p.131.

56. Henry Arthur Jones to Wilson Barrett, 1882 [?], HRC.

Chapter 3

1. Jones, *Curtain Call*, p.31.

2. Wilson Barrett to Henry Arthur Jones, 1882 [?], HRC.

3. *The Era*, 12 September 1885.

4. George M. Young, *Victorian England, Portrait of an Age* (London: Humphrey Mildord, 1936), *passim*.

5. Goddard, *Players*, p.130.

6. *Pall Mall Gazette*, 6 December 1882, p.4.

7. Bronson Howard to Wilson Barrett, 1882 [?], HRC.

8. Towse, *Sixty Years*, p.426.

9. *The Theatre*, December 1882, pp.357-61.

10. George R. Sims to Wilson Barrett, December 1882, HRC.

11. Brereton, "Wilson Barrett," p.47.

12. *Pall Mall Gazette*, 6 December 1882, p.4.

13. Jones, *Curtain Call*, p.63.

14. Charles Reade to Wilson Barrett, n.d., HRC.

15. Henry Arthur Jones to Wilson Barrett, 1883, HRC.

16. Bronson Howard to Wilson Barrett, 11 October 1882, HRC.

17. Scott, *Yesterday and Today*, 7:391.

18. E.J. West, "The London Stage, 1870-1890," *University of Colorado Studies* 2 (May 1943), p.436.

19. *The Theatre*, December 1882, p.360.

20. *The Theatre*, January 1883, p.37.

21. *The Times*, 23 July 1904.

22. Princess's Theatre Accounts, 1882-1883, HRC.

23. Jones, *Curtain Call*, p.40.

24. *Pall Mall Gazette*, 6 December 1882, p.4.

25. Tour Accounts, 1882–1883, HRC.

26. *Punch*, 24 March 1883, pp.136–37.

27. William Gorman Wills-Wilson Barrett Contract for *Claudian*, 14 July 1883, HRC.

28. Henry Herman to Wilson Barrett, (I), August 1883 [?], HRC.

29. Ibid.

30. Henry Herman to Wilson Barrett, (II), September 1883 [?], HRC.

31. Ibid.

32. See Dudley Harbroun, *The Conscious Stone: The Life of Edward William Godwin* (London: Latimer House, 1949), *passim*.

33. Ibid., p.106.

34. Metropolitan Board of Works Injunction, 1884, HRC.

35. *The Fortnightly Review*, 15 December 1884, pp.478–79.

36. Harbroun, *Conscious Stone*, p.120.

37. John Ruskin to Wilson Barrett, 16 February 1884, HRC.

38. Henry Herman, "The Stage as a School of Art and Archeology," *Magazine of Art* (1888), p.337.

39. *The Times*, 9 December 1883.

40. Harbroun, *Conscious Stone*, p.120.

41. H. Barton Baker, *History of the London Stage* (London: George Routledge, 1904), p.495.

42. Helen Faucit to Wilson Barrett, 1 September 1884, HRC.

43. *The Theatre*, January 1884, p.47.

44. Winter. *Wallet*, pp.414–16.

45. *The Theatre*, January 1884, p.48.

46. Winter, *Wallet*, p.418.

47. *The Theatre*, April 1884, p.219.

48. *The Illustrated London News*, 17 December 1883, p.574.

49. *The Fortnightly Review*, 15 December 1884, pp.478–79.

50. *The Illustrated London News*, 17 December 1883, p.574; *The Theatre*, January 1884, p.44.

51. Winter, *Wallet*, p.417.

52. Princess's Theatre Accounts, 1883–1884, HRC.

53. Tour Accounts, 1884, HRC.

54. Disher, *Melodrama*, p.101.

55. Lord Lytton to Wilson Barrett, 22 May 1884, HRC.

56. *The Theatre*, November 1884, p.286.

57. Henry Arthur Jones to Wilson Barrett, 28 March 1883, HRC.

58. *The Theatre*, November 1884, p.243.

59. Hesketh Pearson, *G.B.S.—A Full Length Portrait* (New York: Harper, 1942), p.138.

60. Readers wishing a more complete discussion of this production will find it in my essay "Wilson Barrett's *Hamlet*," *Theatre Journal* 31 (December 1979), pp.479–500.

61. *The Stage*, 24 October 1884.

62. *The Illustrated London News*, 25 October 1884.

63. *The Nation*, 6 November 1884.

64. Bronson Howard to Wilson Barrett, 25 October 1884, HRC.

65. *The Era*, 17 October 1884.

66. *The World*, 22 October 1884.

67. *Saturday Review*, 8 November 1884, p.595.

68. Charles H. Shattuck, *The Hamlet of Edwin Booth* (Urbana, IL: University of Illinois, 1969), p.xxiii.

69. Wilson Barrett, "Hamlet," *Lippincott's* 45 (April 1890), p.580.

70. *The Stage*, 24 October 1884.

71. *The Era*, 17 October 1884.

72. *Shakespeariana* 4 (1887), p.29.

73. *The Times*, 17 October 1884.

74. *The Daily Telegraph*, 17 October 1884.

75. George C. Odell, *Shakespeare from Betterton to Irving* (New York: Scribners, 1920), 2:381.

76. Princess's Accounts, 1883–1884, HRC.

77. Cited in newspaper reviews, *passim*.

78. Henry Arthur Jones-Samuel French Agreements, 1884 [?], HRC.

79. Lord Lytton to Wilson Barrett, 12 July 1884, HRC.

80. Lord Lytton to Wilson Barrett, 3 February 1885, HRC.

81. *Punch*, 1 March 1885, p.120.

82. Princess's Accounts, 1884–1885, HRC.

83. Ibid.

84. Henry Arthur Jones to Wilson Barrett, 1885, HRC.

85. Henry Arthur Jones-Wilson Barrett Contract for *Hoodman Blind*, 1885, HRC.

86. Wilson Barrett to Dorothy Barrett, 29 June 1885, HRC.

87. *The Athenaeum*, 29 August 1885.

88. *The Theatre*, September 1885, p.162.

89. *The Athenaeum*, 29 August 1885.

90. *The Theatre*, September 1885, p.162.

91. *The Ilustrated London News*, 22 August 1885, p.85.

92. *The Theatre*, September 1885, p.162.

93. *Truth*, September 1885, p.328.

94. *The Theatre*, September 1885, p.162.

95. Henry Arthur Jones to Wilson Barrett, 29 September 1888, HRC.

96. *The Era*, 5 September 1885.

97. Henry Arthur Jones to Wilson Barrett, 1885, HRC.

98. *The Theatre*, March 1885, p.155.

99. *The Athenaeum*, 27 February 1886, p.305.

100. *The Theatre*, May 1885.

101. *The Era*, 28 May 1885.

102. William Archer, *About the Theatre* (London: T. Fisher Unwin, 1886), p.76.

103. *The Theatre*, June 1886, pp.329–30.

104. *Saturday Review*, 8 May 1886, p.639.

105. *The Theatre*, June 1886, p.330.

106. William Archer to Wilson Barrett, 13 June 1886, HRC.

107. Letter of License, 1886, HRC.

108. Mortgages, 1885–1886, *passim*, HRC.

109. *New York Times*, 24 July 1886.

Chapter 4

1. Henry Abbey-Wilson Barrett Tour Contract, 1886, HRC.

2. *The Era*, 30 November 1886.

3. George C. Odell, *Annals of the New York Stage* (New York: Columbia University, 1942), 13:228–29.

4. T. Allston Brown, *A History of the New York Stage* (New York: Dodd, Mead, 1903), 2:317.

5. Odell, *Annals*, 13:228.

6. Newspaper article cited in Barrett, *Yesterday*, n.t., n.d., n.a., pp.146–48, HRC.

7. *New York Tribune*, 12 October 1886.

8. Dr. Wells [?]-Wilson Barrett Interview, 1886 [?], n.p., HRC.

9. Wilson Barrett to Caroline Heath, 15 February 1887, HRC.

10. *The World*, 27 March 1887.

11. Tour Accounts, 1886–1887, HRC.

12. Henry Arthur Jones to Wilson Barrett, 30 March 1887, HRC.

13. Henry Arthur Jones to Wilson Barrett, 26 March 1887, HRC.

14. Henry Arthur Jones to Wilson Barrett, 29 August 1887, HRC.

15. *The Theatre*, February 1888, p.86.

16. *Dramatic Notes*, December 1887, p.138.

17. *The Theatre*, February 1888, p.86.

18. Tour Accounts, 1887, HRC.

19. *The Weekly Dispatch*, 3 January 1896.

20. Tour Accounts, 1887, HRC.

21. Hall Caine, *My Story* (New York: D. Appleton, 1908), p.247.

22. Hall Caine to Wilson Barrett, 7 February 1888, HRC.

23. Hall Caine to Wilson Barrett, 21 July 1886, HRC.

24. Hall Caine to Wilson Barrett, 7 February 1888, HRC.

25. Ibid.

26. Ibid.

27. Hall Caine-Wilson Barrett Contract for *Ben My Chree*, 16 March 1888, HRC.

28. Ibid.

29. Hall Caine to Wilson Barrett, 2 April 1888, HRC.

30. Hall Caine to Wilson Barrett, 8 April 1888, HRC.

31. Ibid.

32. *Dramatic Notes*, May 1888, p.77.

33. Richard LeGallienne, *The Stage Life of Wilson Barrett* (London: incomplete manuscript, 1897), p.161, HRC.

34. Booth, *Brass Hats*, p.74.

35. *Dramatic Notes*, May 1888, p.78.

36. *The Theatre*, June 1888, p.313.

37. *Ben My Chree* Accounts, 1888, HRC.

38. Booth, *Brass Hats*, p.74.

39. Wilson Barrett to Henry Arthur Jones, 29 September 1888, HRC.

40. Wilson Barrett to Henry Arthur Jones, cited in Jones, *Curtain Call*, p.42.

41. Tour Accounts, 1888, HRC.

42. Barrett-Hawthorne Contract, 12 January 1889, HRC.

43. *The Theatre*, March 1889, p.215.

44. Goddard, *Players*, p.174.

45. *The Theatre*, March 1889, p.215.

46. *Dramatic Notes*, February 1889, p.24.

47. *The Theatre*, March 1889, p.215.

48. *Dramatic Notes*, February 1889, p.24.

49. Tour Accounts, 1889, HRC.

50. Theatre Royal, Hull, and Grand Theatre, Leeds, Accounts, 1889, HRC.

51. Royalty Accounts, 1889, HRC.

52. *New York Times*, 2 October 1889, 20 November, 27 November, resp.

53. Eugene Tompkins, *The History of the Boston Theatre* (New York: Houghton, Mifflin, 1908), p.367.

54. Isaac Marcosson and Daniel Frohman, *Charles Frohman: Manager and Man* (New York: Harper, 1916), p.121.

55. Wilson Barrett to Brainerd [?], 31 January 1890, HRC.

56. Wilson Barrett to Dorothy Barrett, 26 April 1890, HRC.

57. Wilson Barrett to Dorothy Barrett, 13 May 1890, HRC.

58. Ibid.

59. Wilson Barrett to Frank Heath, 17 June 1890, HRC.

60. Ibid.

61. Wilson Barrett to Frank Heath, June 1890, HRC.

62. Wilson Barrett to Frank Heath, 27 June 1890, HRC.

63. Wilson Barrett to Mulholland, 28 September 1890, HRC.

64. Wilson Barrett-Victor Widnell Contract for *The People's Idol*, 30 September 1889, HRC.

65. Raymond Mander and Joe Mitchinson, *The Lost Theatres of London* (London: Rupert Hart-Davis, 1968), p.285.

66. *The Theatre*, January 1891, p.44.

67. Ibid., pp.142–43.

68. Henry Arthur Jones to Wilson Barrett, 1887 [?], HRC.

69. *The Theatre*, May 1891, p.7.

70. Olympic Theatre Accounts, 1890–1891, HRC.

71. Theatre Royal, Hull, and Grand Theatre, Leeds, Accounts, 1890, HRC.

72. Tour Accounts, 1892, HRC.

73. *The Theatre*, December 1891, p.249.

74. *The Echo*, 23 November 1891.

75. *Lady's Pictorial*, 31 November 1891, p.794.

76. *The Theatre*, December 1891, pp.249–50.

77. Wilson Barrett "The Moral Influence of the Drama," (Dunedin, New Zealand: unpublished manuscript, 1902).

78. Sidney Grundy, "Marching to Our Doom," *The Theatre*, March 1896, p.132.

79. Booth, *"Master" and Men*, pp.238–39.

80. *Montreal Sun*, 16 January 1893.

81. M.B. Leavitt, *Fifty Years in Theatrical Management* (New York: Broadway, 1912), p.707.

82. Tour Accounts, 1892–1893, HRC.

83. *Baltimore Sun*, 12 December 1892.

84. *South Wales Daily News*, 30 August 1893.

85. *Washington Post*, 9 April 1894.

86. Globe Theatre Contract, November 1893, HRC.

87. Globe Theatre Accounts, 1893, HRC.

88. Odell, *Annals*, 15:620.

89. Tour Accounts, 1893–1894, HRC.

90. Ibid.

91. Austin Melford to Frank Wilson Barrett, 1963, HRC.

92. Lillah McCarthy, *Myself and My Friends* (London: Thornton Butterworth, 1933), pp.43–44.

93. Disher, *Melodrama*, p.119.

94. Ibid.

95. Hall Caine to Wilson Barrett, 2 May 1894, HRC.

96. Wilson Barrett to Hall Caine, 10 October 1894, HRC.

97. *Manxman* Agreement, 10 November 1894, HRC.

98. Scott, *Old Days*, p.133.

99. *Isle of Man Times*, 8 August 1894.

100. *Liverpool Express*, 3 November 1894.

101. *Yorkshire Evening Post*, 16 November 1894.

102. Barrett, *Yesterday*, p.192.

103. *Yorkshire Evening Post*, 25 August 1894.

Chapter 5

1. Newspaper interview, n.p., n.d., HRC.

2. Jerome K. Jerome, "A History of the Sign of the Cross," *Idler*, March 1896, pp.265–66.

3. Booth, *"Master" and Men*, pp.238–39.

4. Wilson Barrett to Frank Heath, 1 December 1894, HRC.

5. Newspaper interview, n.p., n.d., HRC.

6. Wilson Barrett to Frank Heath, 31 March 1895, HRC.

7. *St. Louis Republican*, 1 March 1895.

8. Wilson Barrett to Frank Heath, 31 March 1895, HRC.

9. Tour Accounts, 1894–1895, HRC.

10. *Idler*, August 1895, p.119.

11. Sherson, *Lost Theatres*, p.178.

12. Souvenir Program, *The Sign of the Cross*, HRC.

13. J.M. Barrie to Wilson Barrett, 5 January 1895, HRC.

14. Wilson Barrett to Frank Heath, 15 December 1895, HRC.

15. Lyric Theatre Accounts and Tour Accounts, 1895–1896, HRC.

16. *Saturday Review*, 5 December 1896, p.584.

17. *Theatrical World*, 1896, p.322.

18. Philip Amory, "Mr. and Mrs. John Bull Pretend," *The Comet*, May 1897, *passim*.

19. Scott, *Old Days*, p.135.

20. *Jewish Chronicle*, 12 February 1897.

21. *The Athenaeum*, 13 February 1897, p.233.

22. *Saturday Review*, 13 February 1897, pp.69–70.

23. Amory, "John Bull," p.38.

24. *Theatre World*, 1897, pp.30–32.

25. Tour Accounts, 1897, HRC.

26. *Saturday Review*, 29 May 1897, pp.603–5.

27. Amory, "John Bull," p.34.

28. Newspaper interview, Sydney, Australia, 1898 [?], HRC.

29. Australian Tour Contract, 1898, HRC.

30. Wilson Barrett to Polly Heath, 29 January 1898, HRC.

31. Wilson Barrett to Polly Heath, 19 December 1897, HRC.

32. Wilson Barrett to Polly Heath, 29 January 1898, HRC.

33. Wilson Barrett to Frank Heath, 2 March 1898, HRC.

34. McCarthy, *Myself*, p.47.

35. Wilson Barrett to Frank Heath, 23 January 1898, HRC.

36. Wilson Barrett to Frank Heath, 5 March 1898, HRC.

37. Tour Accounts, 1897–1898, HRC.

38. Royalty Accounts, 1897–1898, HRC.

39. Wilson Barrett to Frank Heath, 31 May 1898, HRC.

40. Wilson Barrett to Frank Heath, 24 April 1898, HRC.

41. Wilson Barrett to Frank Heath, 31 May 1898, HRC.

42. Charles Routledge to Wilson Barrett, 8 April 1899, HRC.

43. Jones, *Curtain Call*, pp.45–48.

44. *Sydney Daily Telegraph*, 17 May 1898.

45. Arbitration Agreement, 1898, HRC.

46. Tour Accounts, 1898–1899, HRC.

47. Wilson Barrett to Frank Heath, February 1899, HRC.

48. Squire Bancroft to Wilson Barrett, 8 February 1899, HRC.

49. Wilson Barrett to Frank Heath, 12 April 1898, HRC.

50. Ibid.

51. Wilson Barrett to Richard LeGallienne, 5 March 1899, HRC.

52. Hall Caine to Wilson Barrett 10 September 1898, HRC.

53. Wilson Barrett to Dorothy Barrett, June 1899, HRC.

54. Wilson Barrett to Frank Heath, 15 January 1900, HRC.

55. Wilson Barrett to Frank Heath, 1899 [?], HRC.

56. Max Beerbohm, *More Theatres* (New York: Taplinger, 1969, orig. pub. 1931), p.196.

57. Lyceum Accounts, 1899, HRC.

58. Tour Accounts, 1899, HRC.

59. Lyceum Accounts, 1899, HRC.

60. Wilson Barrett to Frank Heath, 1900 [?], HRC.

61. Coquelin-Barrett Contract for *Quo Vadis*, 1900, HRC.

62. Tour Accounts, 1901, HRC.

63. Tour Accounts, 1901–1902, HRC.

64. Ibid.

65. Wilson Barrett to Frank Heath, 21 February 1902, HRC.

66. *The Westminster Review*, 4 April 1901, p.442.

67. Lascombe Searelle to Wilson Barrett, 4 August 1901, HRC.

68. McCarthy, *Myself*, p.48.

69. Wilson Barrett to Frank Heath, 21 April 1902, HRC.

70. Wilson Barrett to Frank Heath, 3 July 1902, HRC.

71. Tour Accounts, 1902, HRC.

72. Wilson Barrett to Frank Heath, 17 September 1901, HRC.

73. Wilson Barrett to Frank Heath, 21 February 1902, HRC.

74. Wilson Barrett to Frank Heath, 2 March 1902, HRC.

75. *The Times*, 19 December 1902.

76. Tour Accounts, 1902, HRC.

77. Wilson Barrett to Frank Heath, 23 February 1903, HRC.

78. *Western Daily Mercury*, 14 August 1903.

79. *Manchester Courier*, 1 September 1903.

80. Wilson Barrett to Frank Heath, 22 September 1903, HRC.

81. *Liverpool Daily Express*, 28 December 1903.

82. *Bury Advertiser*, 12 August 1903.

83. *Birmingham Morning Post*, 3 February 1903.

84. *Manchester Dispatch*, 28 April 1903.

85. Wilson Barrett to Frank Heath, 4 March 1903, HRC.

86. *Middleborough Evening Gazette*, 6 June 1903.

87. Tour Accounts, 1903, HRC.

88. Wilson Barrett to Frank Heath, 14 May 1903, HRC.

89. Wilson Barrett to Frank Heath, 4 May 1903, HRC.

90. Wilson Barrett to Frank Heath, 3 December 1903, HRC.

91. *Referee*, 19 April 1904.

92. *Nottingham Express*, 10 January 1904.

93. *Referee*, 19 April 1904.

94. *Liverpool Daily Post*, 10 April 1904.

95. Wilson Barrett to Frank Heath, 8 June 1904, HRC.

96. Wilson Barrett to Frank Heath, 11 June 1904, HRC.

97. Curzon to Wilson Barrett, 15 June 1904, HRC.

98. Tour Accounts, 1904, HRC.

99. *Daily Telegraph*, 25 April 1904.

100. George R. Sims, *My Life* (London: Evelaigh Nash, 1927), p.131.

101. Ibid.

Epilogue

1. Squire Bancroft, *Empty Chairs* (New York: Stokes, 1925), p.194.

2. Lawrence Boyle, *Celebrities of the Stage* (London: George Newnes, 1900), p.32.

3. Newton, *Cues*, p.155.

4. Percy Burton, *Adventures Among the Immortals* (London: Hutchinson, 1938), p.52.

5. Booth, *"Master" and Men*, p.235.

6. Scott, *Old Days*, p.129.

7. George R. Sims, *Bohemian London* (London: Nash, 1917), p.130.

8. *Boston Sunday Globe*, 13 May 1894; Jerome, "*Sign of the Cross*," p.286.

9. Louis Napoleon Parker, *Several of My Lives* (London: Chapman and Hall, 1927), p.184.

10. Coleman, "Wilson Barrett," p.65.

11. *The Athenaeum*, 3 July 1904, p.156.

12. Booth, "*Master*" *and Men*, p.243.

13. Brereton, "Wilson Barrett," p.39–40.

14. Beerbohm, *More Theatres*, p.197.

15. Charles Reade to Wilson Barrett, 1884 [?], HRC.

16. *The Illustrated London News*, 22 August 1885, p.187.

17. *Nottingham Express*, 23 July 1904.

18. Disher, *Melodrama*, p.103.

19. McCarthy, *Myself*, p.42.

20. Beerbohm, *More Theatres*, p.197.

21. McCarthy, *Myself*, p.116.

22. George Bernard Shaw, *Our Theatre in the Nineties* (London: Constable, 1932), 3:119.

23. Newton, *Cues*, p.158.

24. William Archer, "A Plea for the Playwright," *Shakespeariana* 3 (1886), p.290.

25. Newton, *Cues*, p.161.

26. Archer, "A Plea for the Playwright," p.291.

27. Scott, *Yesterday and Today*, 6:384.

28. Wells interview, HRC.

29. *Liverpool Express*, 3 November 1894.

30. Brereton, "Wilson Barrett," p.41.

Selected Bibliography

Books

Allen, Shirley S. *Samuel Phelps and Sadler's Wells Theatre*. Middletown, CT: Wesleyan University Press, 1971.

Archer, William. *About the Theatre*. London: T. Fisher Unwin, 1886.

_____. *English Dramatists of Today*. London: S. Low, Marston, Searle, and Rivington, 1882.

_____. *Henry Irving: Actor and Manager*. London: Field and Turner, n.d.

_____. *Masks or Faces?* London: Longman's, Green, 1888.

_____. *The Old Drama and the New*. Boston: Small, Maynard and Co., 1923.

_____. *The Theatrical World, 1893-1896*. 4 vols. London: Walter Scott, 1897.

Armstrong, Cecil Ferard. *A Century of Great Actors*. New York: Arno, 1977; orig. pub. 1912.

Arnold, Matthew. *Culture and Anarchy*. Cambridge: Cambridge University Press, 1946.

Arthur, Sir George. *From Phelps to Gielgud*. New York: Benjamin Blom, 1972; orig. pub. 1936.

Ausubel, Herman. *The Later Victorians, A Short History*. New York: D. Van Nostrand, 1955.

Avery, Gillman. *The Victorian People*. New York: Holt, Rinehart, and Winston, 1970.

Baker, H. Barton. *A History of the London Stage and Its Famous Players*. London: George Routledge, 1904.

Baker, Michael. *The Rise of the Victorian Actor*. London: Corn and Littlefield, 1978.

Bancroft, Squire. *Empty Chairs*. New York: Frederick Stokes, 1925.

Bancroft, Squire, and Bancroft, Marie. *The Bancrofts' Recollections of Sixty Years*. New York: E.P. Dutton, 1909.

_____. *Mr. and Mrs. Bancroft On and Off the Stage*. 2 vols. London: Richard Bentley, 1888.

Barrett, Frank Wilson. *And Give me Yesterday*. Manuscript. London, 1966. Humanities Research Center, University of Texas.

Barrett, Wilson. *The Dog Star and Other Stories*. Leeds: Barr and Co., 1893.

Beerbohm, Max. *Around Theatres*. New York: Alfred A. Knopf, 1930.

_____. *More Theatres*. New York: Taplinger, 1969; orig. pub. 1931.

Benson, Sir Frank. *My Memories*. London: n.p., 1930.

Bernheim, Alfred L. *The Business of the Theatre*. New York: Actor's Equity Association, 1932.

Bingham, Madeleine. *Henry Irving: The Greatest Victorian Actor*. New York: Stein and Day, 1978.

Booth, J.B. *Life, Laughter, and Brass Hats*. London: T. Werner Lurie, 1939.

_____. *"Master" and Men*. London: T. Werner Lurie, 1927.

_____. *Sporting Times*. London: T. Werner Lurie, 1938.

Booth, Michael R. *English Melodrama*. London: Herbert Jenkins, 1965.

Boucicault, Dion. *The Art of Acting*. New York: Columbia University Press, 1926.

Boyle, Lawrence. *Celebrities of the Stage*. London: George Newnes, 1900.

Brown, T. Allston. *A History of the New York Stage*. 3 vols. New York: Dodd, Mead, 1903.

Burton, Percy. *Adventures Among the Immortals*. London: Hutchinson, 1938.

Caine, Hall. *My Story*. New York: D. Appleton, 1908.

Cheltnam, Charles, ed. *The Dramatic Yearbook and Stage Directory, 1891*. London: Trischler, 1892.

Cole, John William. *The Life and Times of Charles Kean*. 2 vols. London: Richard Bentley, 1859.

Cole, Toby, and Chinoy, Helen Krich. *Actors on Acting*. New York: Crown, 1920.

Coleman, John. *Fifty Years of an Actor's Life*. New York: James Pott, 1904.

———. *Players and Playwrights I Have Known*. 2 vols. London: Chatto and Windus, 1888.

Collier, Constance. *Harlinquinade: The Story of My Life*. London: John Hane, 1929.

Cook, Dutton. *A Book of the Play*. London: S. Low, Marston, Searle, and Rivington, 1876.

———. *Hours With the Players*. London: Chatto and Windus, 1883.

———. *Nights at the Play*. 2 vols. London: Chatto and Windus, 1883.

———. *On the Stage*. London: S. Low, Marston, Searle, and Rivington, 1883.

Coquelin, Constance. *Art and the Actor*. New York: Columbia University Press, 1915.

Coquelin, Constance; Irving, Henry; and Boucicault, Dion. *The Art of Acting*. New York: Columbia University Press, 1926.

Craig, Gordon. *Henry Irving*. New York: Longman's, Green, 1930.

Daly, Joseph F. *The Life of Augustin Daly*. New York: Macmillan, 1917.

Darton, F.Q. *Vincent Crummles: His Theatre and His Times*. London: Darton, 1926.

Deurr, Edwin. *The Length and Depth of Acting*. New York: Holt, Rinehart, and Winston, 1962.

Dibdin, James C. *Annals of the Edinburgh Stage*. Edinburgh: Richard Cameron, 1888.

Dickinson, Thomas. *The Contemporary Drama of England*. Boston: Little, Brown, 1917.

Disher, Maurice Wilson. *Melodrama: Plots that Thrilled*. New York: Macmillan, 1954.

Donaldson, Francis. *The Actor-Managers*. Chicago: Henry Regnery, 1970.

Donohue, Joseph. *The Theatrical Manager in England and America*. Princeton: Princeton University Press, 1971.

Downer, Alan S. *The Eminent Tragedian: William Charles Macready*. Cambridge: Harvard University Press, 1966.

Dukore, Bernard F. *Bernard Shaw, Director*. Seattle: University of Washington Press, 1971.

Eliot, George. *The Letters of George Eliot*. 4 vols. Edited by Gordon S. Haight. New Haven: Yale University Press, 1955.

Ervine, St. John. *The Theatre in My Time*. London: Rich and Cowan, 1933.

Filon, Augustin. *The English Stage, Being an Account of the Victorian Drama*. Translated by Frederick Whyte. London: n.p., 1897.

Fitzgerald, Percy. *The Art of Acting*. London: Swan Sonnenschein, 1892.

———. *The World Behind the Scenes*. New York: Benjamin Blom, 1972; orig. pub. 1881.

Foote, G.W. *The Sign of the Cross: A Candid Criticism*. London: Forder, 1896.

Forbes-Robertson, Sir Johnston. *A Player Under Three Reigns*. Boston: Little, Brown, 1925.

Friedell, Egon. *A Cultural History of the Modern Age*. 3 vols. New York: Alfred A. Knopf, 1932.

Frohman, Daniel. *Memories of a Manager*. New York: Doubleday, Page, 1911.

Goddard, Arthur. *Players of the Period*. 2 vols. London: Dean and Son, 1891.

Hamilton, Clayton. *Studies in Stagecraft*. New York: Holt and Co., 1914.

———. *The Theory of the Theatre*. New York: Holt and Co., 1910.

Hammerton, John. *The Actor's Art*. London: n.p., 1897.

Harbroun, Dudley. *The Conscious Stone: The Life of Edward William Godwin*. London: Latimer House, 1949.

Heilman, Robert B. *Iceman, Arsonist, and Troubled Agent*. Seattle: University of Washington Press, 1973.

_____. *Tragedy and Melodrama*. Seattle University of Washington Press, 1968.

Howard, Diana. *London Theatres and Music Halls, 1850–1950*. London: Library Association, 1970.

Irving, Lawrence. *Henry Irving: The Actor and His World*. New York: Macmillan, 1952.

Jerome, Jerome K. *Stage Land*. Leipzig: Heinemann and Balessitier, 1891.

Jones, Doris Arthur. *Taking the Curtain Call: The Life and Letters of Henry Arthur Jones*. New York: Macmillan, 1930.

Jones, Henry Arthur. *The Renascence of the English Drama*. London: Macmillan, 1895.

Knight, Joseph. *Theatrical Notes*. New York: Benjamin Blom, 1972; orig. pub. 1893.

Leavitt, M.B. *Fifty Years in Theatrical Management*. New York: Broadway Publishing, 1912.

LeGallienne, Richard. *The Stage Life of Wilson Barrett*. Incomplete manuscript. London, 1897. Humanities Research Center, University of Texas.

Lewes, George Henry. *On Actors and the Art of Acting*. New York: Grove Press, 1957.

Macqueen-Pope, W. *Ghosts and Greasepaint*. London: W. Robert Hale, 1953.

_____. *Shirtfronts and Sables*. London: W. Robert Hale, 1953.

Mander, Raymond, and Mitchinson, Joe. *The Lost Theatres of London*. London: Rupert Hart-Davis, 1968.

Marcosson, Isaac F., and Frohman, Daniel. *Charles Frohman: Manager and Man*. New York: Harper, 1916.

Martin-Harvey, John. *The Autobiography of Sir John Martin-Harvey*. London: Sampson, Low, Marston, n.d.

McCarthy, Lillah. *Myself and My Friends*. London: Thornton Butterworth, 1933.

Miller, Anna Irene. *The Independent Theatre in Europe*. New York: Ray Long and Richard R. Smith, 1931.

Modjeska, Helena. *Memories and Impressions of Helena Modjeska*. New York: Macmillan, 1910.

Newton, H. "Chance." *Crime and the Drama*. London: S. Paul, 1927.

_____. *Cues and Curtain Calls*. London: John Hane, 1927.

Nicoll, Alardyce. *A History of Late-Nineteenth Century Drama*. 2 vols. Cambridge: Cambridge University Press, 1962.

_____. *English Drama, 1900–1930*. Cambridge: Cambridge University Press, 1973.

Odell, George C. *Annals of the New York Stage*. 15 vols. New York: Columbia University Press, 1942.

_____. *Shakespeare from Betterton to Irving*. 2 vols. New York: Scribners, 1920.

Parker, Louis Napoleon. *Several of My Lives*. London: Chapman and Hall, 1927.

Pearson, Hesketh. *Beerbohm-Tree: His Life and Laughter*. London: Methuen, 1956.

_____. *G.B.S.: A Full-Length Portrait*. New York: Harper, 1952.

_____. *The Last Actor-Managers*. New York: Harper, 1950.

Plummer, Gail. *The Business of Show Business*. New York: Harper, 1961.

R.M.S. *Letters of an Unsuccessful Actor*. Boston: Small, Maynard, n.d.

Rahill, Frank. *The World of Melodrama*. University Park, PA: Pennsylvania State University Press, 1967.

Rowell, George. *The Victorian Theatre*. London: Oxford University Press, 1956.

_____. *Victorian Dramatic Criticism: A Survey*. London: Methuen, 1971.

Ruskin, John. *The Art Teaching of John Ruskin*. Edited by W.G. Collingwood. New York: Putnam, 1891.

Scott, Clement. *Some Notable Hamlets*. New York: Benjamin Blom, 1969; orig. pub. 1900.

_____. *The Drama of Yesterday and Today*. 7 vols. London: George Suckling, 1901.

_____. *The Old Drama and the New*. London: George Suckling, 1901.

_____. *Thirty Years at the Play*. London: Railway and General Automatic Library, 1891.

Scott, Mrs. Clement. *Old Days in Bohemian London*. New York: Frederick Stokes, n.d.

Shattuck, Charles H. *The Hamlet of Edwin Booth*. Urbana, IL: University of Illinois Press, 1969.

Shaw, George Bernard. *Collected Letters*. Edited by Dan H. Lawrence. New York: Dodd, Mead, 1965.

———. *Dramatic Opinions and Essays*. New York: Brentano's, 1917.

———. *Our Theatre in the Nineties*. 3 vols. London: Constable, 1932.

———. *Shaw's Dramatic Criticism*. Edited by John F. Matthews. New York: Hill and Wang, 1959.

Sherson, Erroll. *London's Lost Theatres of the Nineteenth Century*. London: John Hane, 1925.

Short, Ernest. *Sixty Years of Theatre*. London: Eyre and Spottiswoode, 1952.

Sims, George R. *Bohemian London*. London: Evelaigh Nash, 1917.

———. *Glances Back*. London: Jarrolds, 1917.

———. *My Life*. London: Evelaigh Nash, 1917.

Southern, Richard. *The Victorian Theatre: A Pictorial Survey*. New York: Theatre Arts, 1970.

Sprague, Arthur Colby. *Shakespeare and the Actors*. Cambridge: Harvard University Press, 1944.

Stavisky, Aron Y. *Shakespeare and the Victorians*. Norman, OK: Oklahoma University Press, 1969.

Stirling, Edward. *Old Drury Lane*. London: Chatto and Windus, 1881.

Terry, Ellen. *The Story of My Life*. New York: Doubleday, Page, 1909.

Tompkins, Eugene. *The History of the Boston Theatre*. New York: Houghton, Mifflin, 1908.

Towse, John Rankin. *Sixty Years of the Theatre*. New York: Funk and Wagnall's, 1916.

Vardac, A. Nicholas. *From Stage to Screen: Theatrical Method from Garrick to Griffith*. New York: Benjamin Blom, 1968; orig. pub. 1949.

Walsh, Townsend. *The Career of Dion Boucicault*. New York: Benjamin Blom, 1967; orig. pub. 1915.

Watson, Ernest Bradley. *Sheridan to Robertson, A Study of the Nineteenth-Century Stage*. Cambridge: Harvard University Press, 1926.

Weales, Gerald. *Religion in Modern English Drama*. Philadelphia, PA: University of Pennsylvania Press, 1961.

Wilson, A.E. *The Lyceum*. London: Dennis Yates, 1952.

Wilson, Garff B. *A History of American Acting*. Bloomington, IN: University of Indiana Press, 1966.

Wingfield-Stratford, Esme. *The Victorian Sunset*. London: George Routledge, 1932.

Winter, William. *Shadows of the Stage*. Second Series. New York: Macmillan, 1893.

———. *Shakespeare on the Stage*. New York: Moffat and Yard, 1911.

———. *The Wallet of Time*. 2 vols. New York: Moffat and Yard, 1918.

Wood, Anthony. *Nineteenth-Century Britain*. New York: David McKay, 1960.

Young, George M. *Victorian England: Portrait of an Age*. London: Oxford University Press, 1936.

Articles

———. "Alone in London." *Truth*, 12 November 1885, p.756.

———. "Dramatic Author vs. Actor-Manager." *Saturday Review*, 9 August 1890, pp.168–70.

———. "English and French Stage Art." *Theatre*, August 1879, p.3.

———. "Miss Heath." *Theatre*, November 1879, pp.189–90.

———. "Our Stage: Its Present and Its Probable Future." *Theatre*, August 1878, pp.1–7.

———. "The Dutch Players at the Imperial Theatre." *Punch* 68 (1880):285.

———. "The First Stage and the Last." *Punch* 86 (1884):226.

———. "The Provinces as a Dramatic School," *Saturday Review*, 13 October 1888, pp.433–34.

————. "What Playwrights Earn." *Idler* 8 (1895):285-87.

Adams, W. Davenport. "'Stock' v. 'Star' Companies." *Theatre*, November 1878, pp.277-81.

Amory, Philip. "Mr. and Mrs. John Bull Pretend." *The Comet*, May 1897, pp.30-43.

Archer, William. "A Plea for the Playwright." *Shakespeariana* 3 (1886):289-301.

————. "Scene Painter and Actor." *Magazine of Art*, 1883, pp.314-16.

————. "What Does the Public Want?" *Theatre*, June 1885, pp.269-75.

Arnold, Matthew. "*Hamlet* Once More." *Pall Mall Gazette*, 23 October 1884, p.4.

Aveling, Edward. "*Hamlet* at the Princess's." *To-Day*, November 1884, pp.516-37.

Barrett, Wilson. "Dobbie." In *Theatre Annual*, edited by Clement Scott, pp.48-51. London: Carson and Comerford, 1888.

————. "Wilson Barrett Analyses *Hamlet*." *Lippincott's* 45 (1890):pp.580-88.

————. "Harlequin's Last Leap." In *Theatre Annual*, edited by Clement Scott, pp.3-10. London: Carson and Comerford, 1886.

————. "On Hamlet's Age." *Shakespeariana* 3 (1886):584-86.

————. "Mora: A Fairy Tale." In *Behind the Scenes*, pp.28-30. London: Gilbert and Dalziel, 1891.

————. "Mr. Wilson Barrett on the Character of Hamlet." *The Scotsman*, 9 December 1887, p.5.

————. "The Dog Actor." In *Theatre Annual*, edited by Clement Scott, pp.10-14. London: Carson and Comerford, 1884.

————. "The Moral Influence of the Drama." Unpublished manuscript. Dunedin, New Zealand: 1902, HRC.

————. "The Spider's Whistle." *Theatre* 22:17.

Bean. A.W. "Artistic Stage Interiors." *Theatre*, July 1891, pp.16-20.

Beck, Philip. "Realism." *Theatre*, September 1883, pp.127-31.

Bettany, Lewis. "Criticism and the Renascent Drama." *Theatre*, June 1892, pp.277-83.

Brand, Wilhelm. "The Meiningen Players and Their Visit to London." *Theatre*, June 1881, pp.328-32.

Brereton, Austin. "Wilson Barrett." *Theatre*, January 1883, pp.33-41.

Brokaw, John. "Wilson Barrett's Papers: A Theatrical Legacy." *Library Chronicle*, University of Texas, Austin, pp.7-10.

Carr, J. Comyns. "English Actors: Yesterday and Today." *Fortnightly Review* 39 (1883):222.

Carroll, L. "The Stage and the Spirit of Reverence." *Theatre*, 1888.

Coleman, John. "Wilson Barrett and His Work." *Longman's Magazine* 7 (1885):63-82.

Craig, Edward M. "E.W. Godwin and the Theatre." *Theatre Notebook* 31 (1977):30-33.

Crawford, Oswald. "A Rejoinder." *Fortnightly Review* 46 (1890):931-36.

————. "The London Stage." *Fortnightly Review* 46 (1890):499-516.

Downer, Alan S. "Players and Painted Stage: Nineteenth-Century Acting." *PMLA* 61 (1946).

Favorini, Attilio. "The Old School of Acting and the English Provinces." *QJS* 58:199-208.

Fitzgerald, Percy. "Players of Our Day." *Gentleman's Magazine* 233 (1872):312.

Granville-Barker, Harley. "Exit Planche—Enter Gilbert." *London Mercury* 25:457-66.

Grundy, Sidney. "Marching to Our Doom." *Theatre*, March 1896, pp.131-37.

Harris, Augustus. "Spectacle." *Magazine of Art*, 1889, pp.109-13.

Herman, Henry. "The Stage as a School of Art and Archeology." *Magazine of Art*, 1888, pp.332-37.

Irving, Henry. "Actor-Managers." *Fortnightly Review* 46 (1890):1052-53.

Jerome, Jerome K. "A History of *The Sign of the Cross*." *Idler*, March 1896, pp.262-76.

Jones Henry Arthur. "The Actor-Manager." *Fortnightly Review* 46 (1890):1-16.

Labouchere, Henry. "The American Actors." *Truth* 17 (1884):174.

Laidlaw, F. Alan. "Drama on the Downward Grade." *Westminister Review* 153 (1900):318-19.

————. "Morbid Actors." *Westminister Review* 155 (1901):439.

_____. "The New School of Acting." *Gentleman's Magazine* 240 (1876):471–75.

Marius, M. "A Few Words From the Unseen." *Theatre*, May 1889, pp.260–61.

O'Grady, M. "Wilson Barrett." *Canadian Magazine* 11:238.

Porter, Charlotte. "Mr. Wilson Barrett's *Hamlet*." *Shakespeariana* 4 (1887):29–40.

Reece, Robert. "Stage Management." *Theatre*, November 1879, pp.207–10.

Rose, Edward. "Our Visitors." *Theatre*, June 1879, pp.313–14.

Roy, Donald. "Theatre Royal, Hull; or, The Vanishing Circuit." In *Nineteenth Century British Theatre*, edited by Kenneth Richards and Peter Thompson, pp.25–38. London: Methuen, 1971.

Russel, Edward R. "Mr. Irving's Work." *Fortnightly Review* 40 (1884):408–9.

Scott, Clement. "The Progress of the Player." *Theatre*, July 1897, pp.1–4.

Stoker, Bram. "Actor-Managers." *Fortnightly Review* 46 (1890):1040–51.

Stottlar, James F. "A Victorian Stage Adapter at Work: W.G. Wills 'Rehabilitates' the Classics." *Victorian Studies* 16:421–32.

Taylor, L., and Williams, K. "The Actor and His World." *New Society* 27 (1930).

Telbin, William. "Stage Scenery." *Magazine of Art*, 1889, pp.92–97.

Thomas, James. "Wilson Barrett's *Hamlet*." *Theatre Journal* 31 (1979):479–500.

Thompson, Marjorie. "Henry Arthur Jones and Wilson Barrett: Some Correspondence." *Theatre Notebook* 11 (1956).

Tree, H. Beerbohm. "The London Stage: A Reply." *Fortnightly Review* 46 (1890):922–36.

Van Laun, Henri. "Down Among the Dutchmen." *Theatre*, July 1880, pp.28–35.

Vicinus, Martha. "The Study of Victorian Popular Culture." *Victorian Studies* 18 (1975): 473–83.

Wedmore, Frederick. "The Theatrical Revival." *Nineteenth Century* 13 (1883):225.

West E.J. "From a Player's to a Playwright's Theatre." *QJS* 28 (1942):430–50.

_____. "The London Stage, 1870–1890: A Study of the Conflict of the Old and New Schools of Acting." *University of Colorado Studies* 2 (1943):31–84.

_____. "The Victorian Voice on the Stage: Samuel Phelps, 'Faultless Elocutionist.'" *QJS* 31 (1945):29–34.

Wilde Oscar. "Shakespeare and Stage Costume." *Nineteenth Century* 17 (1885):817–18.

Wilson, H. Schutz. "Die Meininger." *Theatre*, August 1881, pp.102–5.

Wilson, M. Glen. "Charles Kean: Tragedian in Transition." *QJS* 60 (1974):45–57.

_____. "The Career of Charles Kean: A Financial Report." In *Nineteenth-Century British Theatre*, edited by Kenneth Richards and Peter Thompson, pp.39–51. London: Methuen, 1971.

Wingfield, Lewis. "Costume Designing." *Magazine of Art*, 1888, pp.403–9.

Wyndham, Charles. "Actor-Managers." *Fortnightly Review*, June 1890, pp.1054–58.

Plays and Novels

Barrett, Wilson. *Lucky Durham*. Manuscript. The Lord Chamberlain's Plays, British Library Department of Manuscripts, 1904.

_____. *Nowadays, A Tale of the Turf*. Manuscript. The Lord Chamberlain's Plays, British Library Department of Manuscripts, 1889.

_____. *Pharaoh*. Manuscript. The Lord Chamberlain's Plays, British Library Department of Manuscripts, 1892.

_____. *Quo Vadis*, adapted from the novel by Henry Sienkiewicz. Manuscript. Humanities Research Center, University of Texas, 1900.

_____. *The Never-Never Land* [novel]. London: Methuen, 1904.

_____. *The Sign of the Cross* [novel]. Philadelphia: Lippincotts, 1896.

Barrett, Wilson, and Caine, Hall. *The Good Old Times*. Manuscript. The Lord Chamberlain's Plays, British Library Department of Manuscripts, 1889.

Barrett, Wilson, and Parker, Louis Napoleon. *Man and His Makers.* Manuscript. The Lord Chamberlain's Plays, British Library Department of Manuscripts, 1898.

————. *The Daughters of Babylon* [novel]. London: Macqueen, 1899.

Barrett, Wilson, and Sims, George R. *The Golden Ladder.* Manuscript. The Lord Chamberlain's Plays, British Library Department of Manuscripts, 1887.

Barrett, Wilson, and Widnel, Victor. *The People's Idol.* Manuscript. The Lord Chamberlain's Plays, British Library Department of Manuscripts, 1890.

Bulwer-Lytton, Lord. *Junius, or The Household Gods.* Manuscript. The Lord Chamberlain's Plays, British Library Department of Manuscripts, 1885.

Caine, Hall. *Ben My Chree.* Manuscript. The Lord Chamberlain's Plays, British Library Department of Manuscripts, 1888.

————. *The Manxman.* Manuscript. Humanities Research Center, University of Texas, 1894.

Grundy, Sidney, and Barrett, Wilson. *Clito.* Manuscript. The Lord Chamberlain's Plays, British Library Department of Manuscripts, 1886.

Jones, Henry Arthur, and Barrett Wilson. *Hoodman Blind.* Manuscript. The Lord Chamberlain's Plays, British Library Department of Manuscripts, 1885.

————. *The Lord Harry.* Manuscript. The Lord Chamberlain's Plays, British Library Department of Manuscripts, 1886.

Jones, Henry Arthur, and Herman, Henry. *The Silver King.* London: Samuel French, 1907.

Shakespeare, William. *Hamlet,* as adapted for the stage by Wilson Barrett. London: Brogue, 1884.

Sims, George R. *Lights o' London.* Manuscript. The Lord Chamberlain's Plays, British Library Department of Manuscripts, 1881.

————. *The Romany Rye.* Manuscript. The Lord Chamberlain's Plays, British Library Department of Manuscripts, 1882.

Wills, William Gorman. *Juana.* Manuscript. The Lord Chamberlain's Plays, British Museum Department of Manuscripts, 1881.

Wills, William Gorman, and Herman, Henry. *Claudian.* Manuscript. The Lord Chamberlain's Plays, British Museum Department of Manuscripts, 1883.

Miscellaneous Materials

Barrett, Wilson. Business Records (1871–1904). Humanities Research Center, University of Texas.

————. Letters (1875–1904). Humanities Research Center, University of Texas.

————. Manuscripts, Photographs, Programs, Playbills, Contracts and Agreements (1871–1904). Humanities Research Center, University of Texas.

Index